Work and life on Raroia

PLATE I The northern part of Raroia atoll seen from the air. Only the area with vegetation and a few sand dunes is permanently above the high water mark. (Photograph by the Pacific Science Board 1952 Expedition to Raroia.)

BENGT DANIELSSON

Work and life on Raroia

An acculturation study

from the Tuamotu group

French Oceania

London GEORGE ALLEN AND UNWIN

FIRST PUBLISHED IN GREAT BRITAIN 1956

PRINTED IN GREAT BRITAIN BY

NOVELLO & COMPANY LTD

LONDON W.I.

What is that canoe that hither sails,
Overarched by the rainbow,
Encompassed about by white terns?
The land of Raroia is encircled.
This is Raroia, land of soft breezes,
From which sounds the lament of Marere-nui.
Softly sound the rustling coconut leaves.

Oh, how my land
Inspires love!

Ancient Raroian song, translated by Peter Buck

Contents

CONTENTS

TABLES

FIGURES

MAPS

Illustrations

Acknowledgements

My first thanks are due to my numerous friends on Raroia, who kindly consented to subject themselves to the ordeal of being treated as scientific research material and with good humour answered all the trying questions an anthropologist can ask. They did, however, even more than this. They also adopted me as one of their own and made me feel completely at home on Raroia.

Turning now to the US, where I spent most of the time between my expeditions, I am especially indebted to Dr. George A. Lundberg for his friendly advice and the personal interest he has always shown in my work, both during my time as research fellow at the University of Washington 1947—48 and later. An equally great obligation is felt towards Dr. Kenneth P. Emory, who did his utmost to make my stay in Honolulu 1952—53 as associate anthropologist at the Bernice P. Bishop Museum not only profitable but also extremely agreeable. Grateful thanks are also given the Director of the Museum, Dr. Alexander Spoehr, the Librarian, Miss Margaret Titcomb, and the entire staff. Much kindness was also shown me by Dr. Leonard Mason, Dr. Samuel H. Riesenberg, and Dr. Samuel Elbert of the University of Hawaii.

To Dr. George P. Murdock, Dr. Harold J. Coolidge, Mrs. Leonore Smith, and Miss Ernestine Akers I wish to express my sincere appreciation for the generous help and encouragement I received in connection with my participation in the Pacific Science Board Expedition to the Tuamotus in 1952. Grateful acknowledgements are also due to the US Office of Naval Research, whose allocation of funds to the National Academy of Sciences by contract N7onr-291 (04) NR 388-001 made this project possible. My thanks naturally also go to the other members of our research team, especially to Dr. Norman D. Newell of Columbia

University and Dr. Maxwell Doty of the University of Hawaii, from whom I learned much. From the Wenner-Gren Foundation, New York, I was happy to receive in 1953 a pre-doctoral fellowhip which enabled me to return to French Oceania once more and finally to find time to complete this study.

In French Oceania, I am particularly indebted to Governor René Petitbon, who has always taken a personal interest in my work, to the Président of the *Société des Etudes Océaniennes,* Mr. Henri Jacquier, who has helped me in various ways, to Miss Aurore Natua, who as my assistant during the Pacific Science Board Expedition in 1952 rendered me invaluable services, and to Mr. Frank J. Stimson, who has generously given me advice in the field of Polynesian linguistics. In the French metropol Father Patrick O'Reilly, secretary of the *Société des Océanistes,* has helped me in various other ways and inspired me through his contagious enthusiasm for Polynesian studies.

Of all persons in my native Sweden who have stimulated me in my work or helped me in various other ways I especially wish to mention my first academic teachers in sociology and anthropology, Dr. Torgny T. Segerstedt, Dr. Sture Lagercrantz and Dr. Bertil Lundman of the University of Upsala and Dr. K. G. Izikowitz of the University of Gothenburg. In addition Dr. Lagercrantz has helped me see the study through the press and Dr. Lundman has helped me with the computation of the anthropometric data. For the translation of chapters I—III, XII and numerous quotations in French, Dutch and German into English I am indebted to Mrs. Marianne Nordfors, M. A., Upsala, and for a checking of the remaining chapters, which I wrote directly in English, I wish to thank Mr. James McConnaughey, Tahiti, and Mrs. Margaret Chalker, B. A., Upsala. When reaching the final stage of this study affectionate thoughts go naturally also to my wife Marie-Thérèse, who not only was a cheerful companion and co-worker during my field-work on Raroia 1949—51, but who has also helped me with numerous suggestions and with the preparation of the manuscript.

Last but not least a special acknowledgment to my friend Thor Heyerdahl, on board whose splendid sailing raft I first reached Raroia in 1947, and my most sincere thanks to Mr. David Lindström, Stockholm, who has kindly assured the publication of the study.

To all these persons I say: Mauruuru!

Introduction

Anthropologists working in Polynesia or on published material from that area have hitherto been interested almost exclusively in the "pure" or pre-European culture. To quote Keesing (1953 b, p. 3) "materials relating ... to the contemporary modes of life of these peoples, were interesting to most of the scholars concerned mainly as needing to be sifted out and discarded when necessary in the interests of reconstructing the genuinely old". The efforts of these anthropologists were of course fully justified, as it was of the greatest importance to "salvage" as much as possible of the old native culture before it vanished entirely. Their difficult and arduous task has now in the main been completed, however. Peter Buck (1945, p. 123), who himself contributed so brilliantly to Polynesian anthropology, has summed up the results of these historical-minded students: "The field survey on Polynesia has been practically completed. ... Bishop Museum publications of the field studies have practically covered every phase of anthropology in history, legends, material culture, social organization, religion, and physical anthropology. Though the information may be thin in parts, such weaknesses are not due to the authors but to the fact that the native informants could not supply what they did not have. The information supplied by present-day informants was supplemented by earlier information contained in old native manuscripts, and the published literature was carefully combed for additional information. Thus, the data on each island group has been brought up-to-date and will save students the tiresome task of searching through other works which may not be available to them."

The situation is more or less the same in many other regions of the world, and for want of wholly untouched primitive societies an increasing number of anthropologists have begun to consider also the partly

13

westernized and modified native cultures as fully legitimate objects for study. Especially the changes themselves and their causes, i. e. the formerly too frequently neglected *dynamic* aspects of culture, have recently attracted much attention. As is well known, social change is an aspect which many sociologists have investigated, but their studies have been almost entirely limited to changes *within* one culture. However, changes can also be produced by the *influence* of one culture on another, and it is for this process that the term "acculturation" has been coined. The latest American Social Science Research Council Seminar (Seminar, p. 974) has defined "acculturation" as being "culture change that is initiated by the conjunction of two or more autonomous cultural systems", and it is in this sense the word is used in the present study.

In his excellent survey of the literature on "Acculturation in Polynesia" Keesing, himself one of the pioneers, remarks (1947, p. 33), "Most acculturation studies in Polynesia to date have dealt in a generalized way with a whole island group or people. The modern situation, however, represents a great number of differing experiments in which each island, population element, district, community, kin group, household, and individual has tended to respond in special ways to the varying local conditions of contact. So far, very few studies have been made sampling this rich texture of detail—investigations of actual communities, biographical records, and so on—which will give precise understanding of acculturation processes, and test the generalizations made in the pioneer studies." To be specific only *three* field studies of Polynesian communities exist: Ernest and Pearl Beaglehole's *Pangai: Village in Tonga, Some Modern Maoris* by the same authors and Hawthorn's *The Maori.* Even if we include two studies in preparation, Douglas Oliver's from the Society Islands and George Shehan's from the Marquesas Islands, we must admit that the number is miserably small. It is therefore hardly an exaggeration to say, as I did in a recent paper (Danielsson, 1954 a, p. 31), that we actually know more about Polynesian culture as it was two hundred years ago than about present conditions.

The aim of the present study is therefore to contribute to a better knowledge of the work and life of the natives in an altogether too little known Polynesian group, and to reach a deeper understanding of what caused the changes that have occured in post-contact times. The study was originally conceived in 1947, when I visited Raroia for the first time.

Though I only spent a fortnight on the atoll on that occasion, it was enough to arouse my interest in the acculturation processes in the Tuamotus and to convince me of the advantages of undertaking a study of this aspect of the culture on Raroia, where (a) the population was small enough to be studied in its entirety and not just by means of sampling and (b) I could be sure of whole-hearted cooperation with the islanders. My project was eventually realized when I returned to Raroia in November, 1949. The total time spent on the island was eighteen months (until April, 1951), and the period covered by my study is the whole year of 1950.[1] During a previous stay of six months in Tahiti I had learnt enough of the Tuamotuan dialect to be able to converse tolerably well with the Raroians in their own language from the very beginning. This was the more necessary, as only one person knew French.

A year later I was fortunate enough to be able to return to Raroia, this time as anthropologist of the Pacific Science Board team. The stay lasted from 19th June to 7th September 1952. In accordance with the research program pursued by this organization (Danielsson, 1953 c, pp. 139—141) I devoted most of the time to a detailed study of the ecological relationship and to checking my previous data. Some rough outlines were prepared even while I was still in the field, but practical duties and the collaboration with other team members on various studies made it impossible for me to write up the material on the spot, although I had originally planned to do so in order to achieve maximum accuracy.

The six months immediately following this third visit were devoted to library research in the Bernice P. Bishop Museum, Honolulu, with the principal aim of gaining a deeper insight into the pre-European culture and the history of the Tuamotu group. A shorter version of chapters IV to XI of the present study was completed in 1953—54 in Tahiti, where I was also able to recheck many details with Raroian friends visiting me. Later these parts of the study appeared in an issue of the mimeographed series *Atoll Research Bulletin* (Danielsson, 1954 b). The study received its final form during the winter 1954—55, when it was presented as a thesis for the doctor's degree at the University of Upsala, Sweden.

In spite of the relatively long periods I have spent on Raroia, I did not find time to make a complete investigation of *all* the aspects of the

[1] For an informal account, see Danielsson, 1953 a.

culture. (Whether *any* investigator could succeed with such a scheme is doubtful.) I, at any rate, deliberately chose to limit my investigations to the social and economic conditions. The only exceptions are some data on physical anthropology, various word lists and occasional references to political organization, church practices and other information necessary for illuminating certain interrelationships and processes. The study is principally descriptive, i.e. I have been more concerned with gathering new primary material than with trying to verify any pet theory. But convinced by the writings of a sociologist like George A. Lundberg and an anthropologist like George P. Murdock that progress in the social sciences depends on the construction of laws of probability, verifiable in the same way as other scientific laws, I have gathered quantitative data to the greatest possible extent in order to facilitate future manipulations in the event such would prove fruitful.

If it must necessarily be labelled, the study may presumably be called "functional", but it must be pointed out that at least in one important respect I have not been able to follow Malinowski's research rules. Actuated by the unscientific character of certain historical reconstructions Malinowski went as far as to deny the value of *all* historical research for anthropological investigations.[1] In his posthumous work *The Dynamics of Culture Change* which deals with acculturation in Africa he says, for example (pp. 29–31): "To trust to the memories of old men or to current accounts of what used to be would, for the purposes of reconstruction, be futile. To the student of culture change what really matters is not the objectively true past, scientifically reconstructed and all-important to the antiquarian, but the psychological reality of today ... We are thus faced with this position: at times reconstruction is quite impossible; when it is possible it produces results of second-class quality as compared with up-to-date field work. To compare such results with modern conditions is hardly ever legitimate. The ethnographer working on the reconstructed past would have to appear before the practical man

---

[1] It must be acknowledged here that the diffusionists have as a rule shown a much greater understanding than the functionalists for the *dynamic* aspect of society, which is the focus of all acculturation studies. That it should be so is only natural, since diffusion is but acculturation in the past, while acculturation is diffusion still going on. I am of the opinion that at the present stage of development in anthropology it is most fruitful to be eclectic, and I think that the scientific value of an anthropological study depends on *how* it is made, be it diffusionistic or functional.

with, at the best, 'damaged goods' in the line of practical advice and theoretical insight... If we were to take one institution after another; if we were to survey the various aspects — economic, legal, educational or political—we should find everywhere that part at least of the 'zero conditions' of the historical past, as it existed before the advent of Europeans, is dead and buried, and as such irrelevant."

None of Malinowski's principal disciples have accepted his intransigeant views on this subject. Both Piddington and Firth have for instance made historical reconstructions of Polynesian cultures, and Firth even plans to publish *The History and Traditions of Tikopia* (see Burrows, 1947, p. 77). All other leading students of acculturation have also stressed the easily understandable importance of knowing what a culture was like *before* it changed, in order to find out *how* it has changed. Herskovits has fittingly expressed the general opinion when he says (1938, pp. 24—25) that "by means of a judicious employment of questions answered by a number of informants, and by balancing such material against reports of those who had contact with the tribe in the days of its cultural vigor and the findings of colleagues who have worked with related tribes, it is entirely possible to obtain workable descriptions of the antecedent patternings of cultures that today are only fragmentary —accounts which, moreover, can even attain the living quality of a field study of a tribe that at present has a relatively stable existence. The reconstruction thus obtained is the point of departure for a study of the effects of the impact on the culture under analysis of a foreign body of tradition whose results are at hand through observation of the contemporary mode of life."

Wagner (1936, p. 317) has still better outlined the place of history in a research program for studies of acculturation: "First it is necessary to obtain as concise a picture as possible of native culture prior to the contact. Secondly the nature of the various contact agencies must be determined. The third problem will be the functional analysis of the present stage of the cultural process that is resulting from the contact. A knowledge of this contact process as a whole ... can only be gained by following all three approaches. An analysis dealing merely with the phase of the process in evidence at the time of investigation, which disregarded the basis from which it started and the variety of causes that set it in motion and still keep it going, would be suspended in the air." Convinced of the necessity of fixing the "zero level" of change, even if this is as difficult and unsatisfactory as in the present case, I have in Chapter II tried to reconstruct the Tuamotuan culture such as it was at the moment of the first intensive contact with foreign cultures.

As in most other acculturation studies it is also here assumed that our own Western culture is known, which is of course far from being correct, since Western culture is by no means homogeneous. But the detailed information about the agents of change, or persons with intracultural roles, found in Chapter III in my opinion makes such a description of the culture they belonged to unnecessary here. Though completely unaware of the fact when planning my research, I have moreover made the gratifying discovery in a recent issue of the *American Anthropologist* that I have in two specific cases conformed to the recommendations of the latest symposium of American specialists on acculturation (Seminar, p. 979) who write: "A comprehensive study of acculturation must include an assessment of those noncultural and nonsocial phenomena that provide the contact setting and establish certain limits of cultural adaptation. The most important of these are the ecological context and the demographic characteristics of the respective peoples."[1] The ecological setting has been described in Chapter I and the demographic characteristics in Chapter IV.

Some other considerations have also determined the scope of the study. As Beals (p. 634) rightly points out in his excellent summary of

[1] I have a definite feeling that I would agree with most of what is said in this article, but unfortunately the greater part of it is incomprehensible. Sample quotations: "The patterns of these conjunctive relations may be conceptualized as intercultural role networks that not only establish the framework of contact but also provide the channels through which the content of one cultural system must be communicated and transmitted to the other" (p. 980). "The architecture of the intercultural role network also provides communication and transmission lines between the two contacting cultures, and it organizes the acculturative flow between the two. It is at once a profile of contacting cultures and a communication system contributing to their modification" (p. 982). "As in analyzing autonomous systems, one must deal with dysfunction in an intercultural system. In communication terms this means a discrepancy between the intentions of a sender and the meaning of the message to a receiver. The fact of internal misinterpretation of intentions suggests the hypothesis that the chances for discrepant communication rise with the degree of intercultural difference. The apperceptive mass, to mention only an obvious factor, is very differently constituted for communicators reared in diverse traditions" (p. 983). The apperceptive author of this thesis, very differently constituted and reared in diverse traditions, is at any rate unable to make sense of this.

our present knowledge of the acculturation process, future research should aim at comparability. (How little standardized even basic research methods are in anthropology was most clearly shown by the numerous gaps discovered when preparing the Yale Cross-Cultural Survey, see Murdock, 1949, pp. VII—X.) In order to achieve comparability in the Pacific area the Pacific Science Board has established certain guiding principles according to which (Handbook, 1953, p. 109) acculturation research should:

(a) Focus on the present rather than the aboriginal past
(b) Elucidate processes involved rather than static patterns
(c) Operate with a set of problems suitable for comparative
    investigations

The type of data which it was judged essential to gather for a study of this type were grouped by Mason (Handbook, p. 111) under the following headings:

1. population inventory
2. economic activities
3. land tenure
4. social and political organization
5. movement of peoples

I have adhered as rigidly as possibly to this general outline in order to achieve the goal which I believe is of utmost importance, viz. to provide a common basis for comparisons. It is also my conviction that only through this standardization of methods will it be possible, ultimately, to transcend the short-time *practical* value of the studies and make contributions to the more important *theoretical* task of discerning and formulating basic social laws.

It should also be noted that though preceding in time the so-called Tri-Institutional research program on acculturation in the Pacific, initiated in 1953 jointly by Yale University, Bishop Museum and University of Hawaii, my outline conforms fairly well to the recommendations made by the executive committee (Spoehr, 1954, pp. 26—28). Of the three fields of special interest to the South Pacific Commission it covers two, viz. Economic and Social Development (Keesing, 1953 b), and even partly follows the program for coral atoll research of immediate practical value outlined in Project No E. 6 of the Commission.

Thus, while my *selection* of data has been determined by the considerations detailed above, the *presentation* has been guided by their place in the functional context. Both the population inventory and the data on inter- and intra-island movements are for instance grouped together in the same chapter. Two specific chapters are devoted to surplus production and subsistence activities, whereas discussions of social implications of the economic organization are interspersed throughout the text. Land tenure is linked with inheritance practices and legal problems, and so on.[1] Wherever necessary for the elucidation of the situation, historical material has been included. The curious situation on Raroia, where the economy is neither primitive nor modern but somewhere in between, has made it impossible to use the conventional classification of the material under the heads of Production, Distribution, Exchange and Consumption, and in this case also the functional context has, therefore, determined the presentation of the material.

Another thing must finally also be pointed out. We students of acculturation usually think that we are investigating the *dynamic* aspect of society. Actually, we are hardly ever able to observe the changes *themselves* with our own eyes, but only the *results* or end products. Whereupon we try by means of historical research to clarify the processes that have preceded them. The zero level chosen for measuring the amount of change that has occurred is in the majority of cases, as in

---

[1] On the other hand, this point must not be over-stressed, as Izikowitz (p. 318) rightly cautions: "It is a wellknown thing that when analysing and describing a community, one can as a matter of fact take any one of the many aspects as a starting point. The more points of view there are, the better the picture of reality is likely to be. In sociology one often comes across a common mode of expression which says that 'everything is interrelated.' If we should set out from a principle like this, one aspect only ought to really suffice, for then we could include all the details in the social activity into a single starting point. If we set out from culture or from community life as an entirety, it is indeed very possible that everything depends upon everything else, that is to say, all parts and categories within community life, but it is not necessarily true that every part is immediately dependant on every other part in a culture, nor that one part of a culture must necessarily cohere with another. For example, sometimes religion and art are coupled into one category, sometimes they are independent of each other, sometimes the economic life can affect important and large sections of community life, but it happens quite as often that with economy as a starting point, one finds that everything does not cohere with it. Thus it is not always the case that such a thing as certain esthetic manifestations like music must necessarily cohere with economy, not even religion."

this study, the native culture as it was at the time of the initial contact with one or more alien cultures. But since it has become increasingly difficult to reconstruct this zero level, safer and more reliable results would perhaps be obtained by using the first thorough description of the culture as the starting point and then, returning after a long interval, by means of the *same* methods determine what changes have taken place. Such a re-study of a previously well described society, is at present being made in Polynesia on Tikopia, first visited by Firth 25 years ago. I hope to have the chance of re-visiting Raroia for a similar stock-taking some time in the future, when a suitable interval has elapsed. Successive descriptions of this kind, if they could be obtained, may be compared to the separate frames on a film strip which looked at one by one are still-pictures, but seen in a connected series give us an impression of life and movement.

A note on the Tuamotuan dialect

In the diacritical system devised by the students of the various Polynesian dialects it has been found necessary to indicate the following characteristics of the speech:

1. Loss of a vowel
2. Loss of a consonant
3. Vowel quantity
4. The glottal catch

The loss of a vowel or consonant is usually indicated with an apostrophe ('), the glottal catch with a hamzah or inverted comma (') and the vowel quantity with a macron (‾) or a micron (ˇ). Many other diacritical marks have been used (see e.g. Stimson, 1928, pp. 318–325), but those above are in my opinion the minimum number required.

As no loss of vowels or consonants, found in other Polynesian languages, has occured in the Tuamotuan dialect and no glottal catch exists, the only speech pecularity to show is the quantity of the vowels. This has unfortunately seldom been done, either in the case of the Tuamotuan or any other Polynesian dialect, which is the more surprising, as vowel quantity in Polynesia is phonemic. In order to give the various word lists I have put together maximum usefulness I have therefore undertaken the rather difficult task of showing vowel quantity in all words except personal and geographical names. Only one diacritical mark has, however, been judged necessary, viz. the macron (‾), indicating that the vowel is long. All other vowels are thus short. Stress has not been shown, since it is non-phonemic and easily predictable; it falls on the last long vowel, or, when all vowels are short, on the penultimate syllable.

As for the spelling of Tuamotuan words it should only be noted that the letter g stands for the sound η in accordance with the natives' own usage and the spelling adopted by the missionaries and the Bernice P. Bishop Museum. Unfortunately ng is used for this sound by the French authorities in the official spelling of the names of the atolls, and I have therefore in this case followed their practice against all logic.

CHAPTER I · **Environment and natural resources**

The Tuamotu group, which is a part of French Oceania (Etablissements Français de l'Oceanie), lies immediately east of Tahiti. It is made up of 78 atolls scattered over the huge area between 135 to 149 degrees west and 14 to 23 degrees south. The distance from Tahiti to the nearest atoll is 130 nautical miles and to the most distant atoll to the east 800 nautical miles. According to a survey of Raroia made in 1950 by the French Service Hydrographique de la Marine, the atoll lies between 15° 55′ and 16° 15′ south latitude and 142° 18′ and 142° 32′ west longitude. It is elliptical with the long dimension toward the northeast.

With the exception of the raised phosphate island of Makatea all the Tuamotuan atolls are low with a maximum elevation rarely exceeding 6 metres. Three of the atolls are more than 60 kilometres in length, thirty are less than 10 kilometres in diameter, and the rest are of all sizes in between. Most of the atolls in the western part of the group have passes deep enough for trading schooners; most of the atolls in the eastern half of the group lack passes.

1. Main characteristics of the climate

The Tuamotu group lies within the belt of eastern trade winds and enjoys a mild and dry climate. The temperature varies very little between night and day, and the sea water is only slightly cooler than the air. There are two clearly distinguishable seasons, one relatively rainy period with predominantly northeasterly winds lasting from November to April, and one relatively dry period with predominantly southeasterly

23

winds from May to October. I recorded meteorological data on Raroia for the whole year of 1950 with instruments kindly supplied by the Service Météorologique in Tahiti. These are published elsewhere (Danielsson, 1951, pp. 192—199, 236—243) and therefore only the main characteristics of the climate are given here in Table I.

The tidal fluctuations are moderate, normally only about half a metre and at the spring-tide rarely attaining more than one metre. Strong currents exist both in the lagoon and in the sea around Raroia. The ocean current usually travels towards the southwest at rates ranging from five to twenty-five miles a day, but it may during the rainy season occasionally set to the eastward at rates from one-half to two knots. Another noteworthy feature is the southwestern swell which continuously pounds the southern part of the atoll. The lack of islets or sand dunes in this section of the atoll is according to Newell (1954 a, p. 10) due to this exceptionally vigorous surf.

2. Cyclones of hurricane force

During the rainy season, from November to April, devastating cyclones occur at long intervals, and considering the profound effects they have sometimes had on the islanders' life I have summarized all the available data on cyclones in the Tuamotus. Visher (pp. 40—41) and Giovannelli (pp. 250—265) have published lists of Tuamotuan cyclones and I have been able to add very little new material. The list of cyclones of hurricane force (for definition see Visher, pp. 7—11), which usually are the only ones causing damage and casualties and therefore alone are of interest to us here, is as follows:

Cyclone of 1824 or 1825

This is the first recorded cyclone in the Tuamotus, and Ellis (III, pp. 306—307) gives us this account of it: "Anaa, when visited by Mr. Crook, in January, 1825, presented a scene of ruin and desolation, occasioned by a violent tempest, which had been accompanied by an impetuous inundation of the sea. Hundreds of large trees, torn up by the roots, lay strewn in wild confusion on the shore: a number of dwellings, and fourteen places of worship, were levelled to the ground. The calamity had been as sudden as it was severe: the falling of the trees, and the rising of the sea over those entangled among their trunks, and the ruins of their houses, had occasioned the loss of many lives."

Moerenhout (I, p. 365) states that the cyclone occurred in 1822, but this is certainly a mistake. In this case Ellis must be considered more trustworthy as he was still in Tahiti at that time without mentioning any cyclone, whereas Moerenhout did not arrive in the Pacific until 1829. No traditions about this cyclone are preserved on Raroia.

Cyclone of 2nd September, 1877

The atolls most severely hit were Manihi, Kaukura, Fakarava, Anaa and Nihiru (Giovannelli, pp. 256–257), but the intervening atolls must have suffered almost as much. Many stories are still told on Raroia about this cyclone, but as one can easily understand it is frequently mixed up with the following one.

Cyclone of 5th to 8th February, 1878

The *Messager de Tahiti* for March 1878 contains some information, but by luck I discovered a good account of this cyclone in the May 1878 issue of the missionary paper *The Friend,* published in Honolulu. In a letter dated 22nd March, 1878, the correspondent of this paper, the Rev. James L. Green writes (p. 2):

"On the 7th and 8th of February we were visited by a cyclone, which is, happily, an unusual occurence in our ports. We did not feel its full force in Tahiti; in Papeete we were in a perfect calm, with heat intense ... But it was at the Low Islands of the Puamotu Archipelago that

TABLE I: *Summary of meteorological data*

Observation	Jan.	Feb.	March	April	May	June	July	Aug.	Sept.	Oct.	Nov.	Dec.	Year 1950
n minimum temperature	23.8	23.8	24.3	24.1	23.4	23.1	21.6	22.3	22.9	23.1	23.6	23.7	23.3
n maximum temperature	30.4	30.3	32.0	32.0	29.4	28.5	28.0	29.1	31.6	30.4	32.4	30.2	30.4
fall in millimetres	352	142	72	67	282	48	14	32	16	18	44	94	1181
ber of days with rain	23	16	11	10	11	6	8	11	5	8	11	12	132
n wind velocity (Beaufort)	1.7	2.6	1.9	1.0	3.1	3.7	2.9	1.3	2.2	3.1	1.6	2.8	2.3
ber of clear days	9	17	22	23	14	23	15	14	24	22	17	15	215
ber of calm days	4	1	4	12	2	0	2	5	1	0	6	0	37

the severity of the cyclone was felt. Altogether, I believe ten white men were drowned, and at the island of Kaukura 117 natives were swept away. Several schooners were wrecked and some large cutter boats too were lost. Men who only a few hours before had a comfortable home were now, as it were, in a moment rendered houseless and homeless and dollar less.

At Anaa, the principal Island of the group, the distress was very great. It is reported that the sea rose, as it were, suddenly, and as a huge bank breaking with terribly destructive force on the land, sweeping everything before it ... It turns out, that the Islands of Anaa, Rairoa and Kaukura were the greatest sufferers, and it is reported that the loss in one place, a district alone, is estimated at 120,000 dollars, and that 112,000 cocoanut trees were destroyed."

It must be noted in passing that Cuzent (p. 62) evidently refers to this cyclone when describing its devastations on Anaa. But owing to a misprint the year given is 1858, and this explains why so many sources erroneously mention a non-existent cyclone that year.

Several persons perished on Raroia and the whole village of Tetou was destroyed according to old inhabitants, many of whom have personal recollections.

Cyclone of 14th to 15th January, 1903

There are several detailed descriptions of this cyclone, of which I here quote only Giovannelli's summary: "Its path is similar to that followed by the cyclone of February 1878, but situated about 200 miles east of the latter. The central Tuamotuan atolls have been especially badly hit by the storm; the greatest destruction was observed at Hikueru (village destroyed), at Makemo, Ravahere, Takume, Rairoa [should be Raroia] and Napuka. The death of 517 natives was deplored: the majority perished as a result of the sudden invasion of the low-lying islands by the sea. At Hikueru houses and inhabitants were carried away in the course of half an hour, by waves coming from the ocean (Dr. Brunati). The island was razed to the ground in the night between the 14th and 15th."[1]

[1] "Sa trajectoire est analogue à celle suivie par le cyclone de février 1878, mais elle se situe à 200 milles environ à l'Est de celle-ci. Les Tuamotu du centre ont été particulièrement ravagées par la tempête; les principaux dégâts ont été observés à

A French commander who visited Raroia immediately afterwards wrote: "This island has been destroyed, ravaged. It is unrecognizable. The destruction is comparable with that on Hikueru. Three quarters of the coconut palms are broken and lying on the ground mixed up with the wrecks of houses of schooners and of cutters, some of which have been thrown 200 yards inland." (Gibbings, p. 228.) I have elsewhere published a detailed account of what happened on Raroia. (Danielsson, 1953 a, pp. 131—136.)

Cyclone of 7th to 8th February, 1906

The western atolls were most severely hit and more than 150 natives perished, mostly drowned by the ocean swells. (Giovanelli, p. 260.) There is a general agreement that this cyclone was less violent than the previous one, and at any rate it was but feebly felt on Raroia. (Danielsson, 1953 a, p. 136.)

In addition to the cyclones, tidal waves occasionally reach the Tuamotus and the damage is frequently great owing to the slight elevation of the atolls above the sea level. The last tidal wave that flooded Raroia occurred on April 1, 1946.

The cyclones and tidal waves have changed the physical shape of Raroia several times, and old natives can describe in detail how for instance during the cyclone of 1903 whole islets disappeared in certain places whereas in other places completely new islets were formed. Newell notes (1954 a, p. 11): "Topographic forms of the islands, including conspicuous flow-lines in the coarse coral rubble, generally at right angles to the atoll rim strongly suggest that the land has been inundated many times, indeed built up in places, by translation waves that swept across the atoll rim to the lagoon." The possible effects of the cyclones on the island economy and their role in the general acculturation process will be discussed in later chapters.

Hikueru (village détruit), à Makemo, Ravahere, Takume, Rairoa et Napuka. On eut à déplorer la mort de 517 indigènes: la plupart ont péri par suite de l'envahissement brusque des îles basses par la mer. A Hikueru, dans l'espace d'une demi-heure, maisons et habitants ont été enlevés par les lames venant de la haute mer (Dr Brunati). L'île a été rasée dans la nuit du 14 au 15." (Giovanelli, p. 258.)

3. Physical features

Raroia is, according to the geologist of the 1952 Pacific Science Board team (Newell, 1954 a, p. 8) "in most respects typical of the group." The general characteristics of the atoll are (Newell, 1954 b, pp. 13—15):

Length	44	km
Breadth	14	km
Circumference at outer reef edge	90	km
Area of atoll (including lagoon)	400	km²
Area of lagoon	340	km²
Area of atoll rim	60	km²
Land area (35 % of rim)	21	km²
Average breadth of atoll rim	0.6	km
Maximum height of land	6	m
Maximum depth of lagoon	55	m
Visibility of 8″ secchi disk		
Ocean	34	m
Lagoon	28	m

"The rim of Raroia atoll is narrowest, averaging 500 to 700 meters wide, along the northwest side where there are relatively few channels and the greatest extent of vegetated island upland. Much of the surface here rises from one and a half meters to three meters above normal high water level. On the other hand the broadest sector of the rim, 800 to 1,250 meters wide, is at the south end of the atoll ... There is only one ship pass through the leeward rim ... The Raroia pass is narrow (700 m) and shallow (five and one-half to eight meters) and choked by vigorous coral growth which may eventually block the pass ... Elsewhere there are approximately 260 shallow channels across the rim ... There are roughly 280 islets around the atoll, of which only 60, including most of the larger and higher land areas, are on the leeward (northwest) side of the atoll ... In addition to the shallow channels or spillways between islets, there are some 160 deep, angular clefts or notches (incomplete channels) in the lagoon shore similar to the channels except that they do not extend across the island to the seaward side." (Newell, 1954 b, pp. 14—15.)

In the lagoon there are finally about 2,000 patch reefs, which are serious hindrances to navigation.

4. Native topographical terms

A description of the atoll environment is incomplete without some indications of the inhabitants' own knowledge and control of it, and an account of the topographical features from the natives' point of view is therefore presented here. A quick glance at the subsequent lists will show that the native terminology is extremely comprehensive and appropriate. In some cases it even seems that the native has a term wanting in the modern scientist's vocabulary which could profitably be borrowed. Let us for instance take the Tuamotuan and pan-Polynesian word *motu*, which means a part of the reef with vegetation, surrounded by water *or* dry arid beach rock. The English word "islet" is frequently used for translating *motu*, but it does not carry *all* the important connotations of the latter, i.e., that it may be separated by dry arid beach rock as well as by water, and that it always has some vegetation. Other Tuamotuan terms, which do not have any English counterparts, are: *tahuna, hōā, kapuku* and *tai,* which are all defined in the lists.

This detailed and exact terminology reflects a very close adaptation and utilization of the natural resources, as it was created during the endless search for food which naturally demanded a thorough knowledge of every part of the land, the reef and the lagoon. Another example of how the terminology has obviously grown out of an immediate need is the classification of the different types of coral patches in the lagoon. There are thousands of coral patches of all sizes and shapes, and the existence of precise and accurate terms for them greatly facilitates navigation.

An equally utilitarian attitude is shown in the use of place names. None of the five major islets on Raroia has, for instance, a name which applies to the whole of it, but different parts and features of them, which are of importance to the natives, are all named. Many names for various parts of the lagoon and the reef exist too, which from a Western point of view seem illogical and unnecessary at first glance, but which on closer examination are found to correspond admirably to certain native needs.

The following lists are by no means complete, and are deliberately limited to the terms most frequently in use. They could easily be supplemented through asking older men, who still remember archaic words no longer known to the younger generations. This disappearance of many terms is in itself very illuminating and constitutes a sort of measure of the changes which have already taken place. The former close dependence on the natural resources has to a large extent ceased to exist with the rise of the copra trade and the introduction of a money economy; and in the same way as the names of ancient cult-places have now to a large extent been forgotten owing to the natives' conversion to a new faith, probably most of the topographical terms will also eventually be lost during the continued acculturation process.

To begin with the main features four different parts of the atoll are distinguished and named. The northeastern part is called *gake,* the southeastern *kereteki,* the southwestern *raro* and the northern *tokerau* (see end map). These are not specific names, but general terms, which curiously enough represent two completely different principles of orientation. The words *tokerau* and *raro* are compass and wind directions, the former meaning "northeast" and the latter "below the wind." The

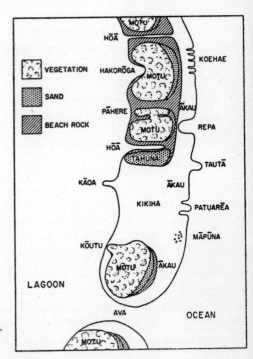

FIG. I. *Terms for land and reef features*

words *gake* and *kereteki* on the other hand indicate the relative position of these parts of the atoll in relation to the principal human settlement. When one stands in the main village facing the lagoon, *kereteki* is the part of the atoll farthest away to the right, whereas *gake* is the part farthest away to the left.

This double frame of reference is used all over the Tuamotus, and the underlying principle is still better recognized on other atolls of different shapes and patterns of settlement than Raroia, where due to the general NNE—SSW direction of the atoll, *gake* and *tokerau* to some extent overlap. The only explanation for this curious terminology seems to be that it was originally created in an island where it perfectly fitted the geography and human ecology, and then later carried as a part of the general culture to new islands.

The compass directions, of which a great number are distinguished by the natives, are not as a rule used for indicating the parts of the atoll, but only for determining the wind direction.

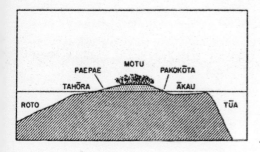

Fig. II. *Terms for land and reef features*

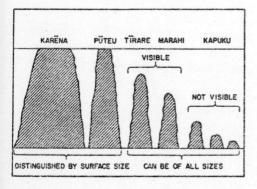

Fig. III. *Terms for coral patches*

A typical Polynesian way of indicating the relationship between two islands or points is with reference to the prevailing trade wind, which all the year round blows in the same principal direction, from the east. The island or place situated farthest towards the east and therefore windward, is said to be *ruga*, above, the other *raro*, or below. When the natives for instance say that Takume is situated "above" Raroia, this does not mean, as a non-Polynesian observer may suppose, that Takume is the northernmost atoll, but instead that it is situated slightly closer to the trade wind than Raroia. The name Raroia, or Raro-ia, itself means simply "(the land which) *is below* (Takume)."

Common terms expressing directions are *i ūta*, towards land, *i tūa*, *i tai*, towards the sea, and *i hōpaki*, towards the lagoon. A person trav- elling in a canoe is of course always moving *i ūta*, towards land, whether he is coming from the ocean or the lagoon side. A person walking from the lagoon beach towards the outer reef is also moving *i ūta*, until he reaches the centre of the islet, and then *i tūa* or *i tai*—the first term being used if he actually continues out into the sea swimming or by canoe, the second term if he stops before he reaches the edge of the reef. A person walking across the islet in the opposite direction is moving *i ūta* the first half of the distance, and then *i hōpaki*, towards the lagoon. The same terms are also used for indicating the relative position of lands and natural objects.

Land and reef features (see Figures I and II)

fenūa	atoll, islet or land
motu	part of the reef with vegetation, surrounded by water or arid dry rock. Literal meaning "broken off".
pāhere	small part of a *motu*, united with the main part only through a narrow strip of land
tahuna	sand dune without vegetation. Literal meaning "hidden".
piriatau	indurated sand forming the foundation of a *motu*
pakokōta	the uncovered platform of limestone conglomerate
papa	extremely flat coral platform on the lagoon side
ākau	outer reef flat, covered by water at high tide
hiti ākau	edge of the outer reef flat
tahōra	reef on the lagoon side close to the shore
papae	edge of the reef on the lagoon side
kōutu	land promontory

kikiha	wide stretch of the reef between two *motu*, covered by water at high tide
ava	pass, deep and wide channel in the reef circle
hōā	shallow channel beginning on the lagoon side, separating completely or partially two *motu*
tairua	closed *hōā*
poehoga	inner part of a closed *hōā*
kāoa	reef spur on the lagoon side
tautā	reef spur on the sea side
koehāe	surge channel on the outer reef
repa	open gap in the outer reef flat where the sea reaches the shore
puta	opening in the lagoon reef
māpūna	blow holes on the outer reef
patuarēa	spur on the sea side slightly higher than the surrounding reef
paepae	upper part of the lagoon beach
paraha	the part of the sandy lagoon beach intermittently wet by the swash

Features of the sea and the lagoon

roto, tairoto	lagoon
tai	the sea from the beach to the edge of the reef
tūa	the sea beyond the edge of the reef
moana	deep, blue water, either in ocean or lagoon
au	current
reva	depth
rokaroka	abyssal depth
kare	wave
garu	breaker
miti	salt water

Coral patches (see Figure III)

pūrari	isolated patch
tohitīka	patch rising up from the bottom in the form of a cylinder or slightly marked cone
pātahōra	mushroom-formed patch
magarua	U-shaped when seen from above
karēna	patch which reaches the surface, big size
pūteu, teu	patch which reaches the surface, but of smaller size
tīrare	patch not reaching the surface, but still visible
marahi	still visible, but lower than *tīrare*
kapuku	patches on the bottom, not visible from the surface
vata	open stretch of water

Miscellaneous terms

ahu	sand bank on the bottom
puratea	same, but of smaller size
patetea	same, but of still smaller size
kōnao	coral stone
gaere	sand

5. Natural resources

All the islets on Raroia are made up of sand and gravel with very little or no humus at all (see e.g. profiles in Newell, 1954 b, fig. 8, and descriptions in Doty-Morrison, pp. 18—20). No water other than the ground water exists, and due to the slight elevation of the atoll above sea level it has, of course, a high salinity, ranging in the open wells in the village from 13.9 to 16.6 ‰ and in some test pits dug across the plot Homohomo from 3.7 to 9.0 ‰. (Newell 1954 b, p. 17.) Doty (p. 28) ingeniously points out that the fresh water lens is indicated by the *Guettarda speciosa* tree *(kahāia)*.

That under these conditions any vegetation at all can thrive on Raroia is surprising at first sight, but Newell (1954 a, p. 6), summarizing current theories, gives the following explanation: "It may be considered as probable that the fertility of newly exposed accumulations of coral gravel and sand is to a large extent a result of the activities of nitrogen-fixing algae and bacteria having a range of osmotic tolerance such as characterizes the flora of the littoral zone. Some of these very likely are normal inhabitants of the sea. Sea birds, which rest on rocks and gravel bars, precede the terrestrial vegetation and enrich the ground with fertilizer gathered over a wide radius of open sea."

The number of wild plants and trees of pre-European introduction on Raroia is only just over thirty (I have published a complete list in Doty, pp. 13—14). The following can be considered as food plants: *Cocos nucifera (hakāri), Pandanus distinctus (fara, tima), Colocasia esculenta (fakēa), Tacca leontopetaloides (pia), Portulaca johnii (pokēa)* and *Lepidium bidentatum (nau, horahora)*. Useful for their wood are: *Calophyllum inophyllum (atī), Cordia subcordata (tōu), Messerschmidia argentea (geogeo), Pemphis acidula (mikimiki), Pisonia grandis (gatae)* and *Guettarda speciosa (kahāia)*. Of the remaining plants native medicines of one sort or another can be prepared and, as is well known, leaves, roots, husk and other parts of the coconut palm are also useful for various purposes.

Of wild land animals of pre-European introduction there is only one mammal, the Polynesian rat, *Rattus exulans*. Of birds there are 19 resident and migratory species (see Danielsson, 1954 b, pp. 100—101 and Morrison, 1954 b), but only a few species are sufficiently numerous to constitute an appreciable food-supply.

The poor land fauna is, however, to a large extent compensated for by the rich sea fauna. Both the lagoon and the surrounding sea teem with fish and the crustacea and molluscs are numerous. The ichtyologist of our Pacific Science Board team collected over 400 different species of fish on Raroia in three months (Harry 1953, p. 44) and considers that he could have collected over one hundred more if he had received the equipment tied up in Los Angeles by a strike. (Harry, 1952, p. 22.) The most common families of food fishes are *serranidae* (sea basses), *scaridae* (parrot fishes), *mullidae* (goat fishes), *carangidae* (jacks), *balistidae* (trigger fishes) and *acanthuridae* (surgeon fishes). Lobsters and many edible crabs exist, too, and about the molluscs, the zoologist, Dr. Morrison, says: "When the classification and determination of all the forms collected at Raroia are completed, the total number of species is likely to pass six hundred." (Morrison 1954 a, p. 1.) Only half a dozen species of molluscs are used for food, however.

CHAPTER II · **Aboriginal culture**

No comprehensive description by a contemporary eye-witness similar to those we have from other island groups in Polynesia has ever been published about native life and customs in the Tuamotus. The information we do have is scattered through the accounts of sea captains, traders, missionaries and administrators and usually restricted to such aspects of the culture as were easiest to observe or were of special interest to the visitors, i.e. material culture and religion. The disappearance of the voluminous notes made during their life-long sojourns by Father Fierens and Father Audran, the only persons with an intimate knowledge of the islands who might have written more comprehensive descriptions, is therefore to be sincerely regretted.

The number of topical studies by professional anthropologists is only about half a dozen. Stimson has published studies on religion, translated many legends and compiled an impressive dictionary. Emory has written on archaeology, religious ceremonies and material culture. (The last-mentioned study is still in manuscript form.) Burrows has analysed native music and Seurat has published a minor paper on fishing methods. No studies have, however, yet been published on those aspects of the culture that principally interest us here, namely the pre-European economic system and social organization. Fortunately the presence of the learned native scholar, Te Iho, on Raroia during my visits helped me to supply most of the background. In addition I have, of course, gathered whatever information I could find in the existing literature.

1. Principal informant

A few words about Te Iho are warranted. He was born shortly before the first Catholic missionary began his work on Raroia in 1869. Although the majority of the Raroians were soon afterwards converted, old religious beliefs and practices survived for a couple of generations at least, and changes in the economic system and social organization were slow and sporadic during the remainder of the 19th century. In his youth Te Iho was thus a direct participant in the ancient culture and had all its beliefs and customs explained to him by his father and grandfather, who were staunch supporters of "the old order". Of even greater significance here is the fact that Te Iho belonged to the most distinguished family on the island, and already as a child he was educated to become a native historian *(tahŭga)*. In this way he acquired a profound knowledge of the ancient culture.

Dr. K. P. Emory, who visited Raroia from the 16th to the 20th September 1929, writes (1932, p. 45): "At Raroia ... we stopped nearly a week, as much to interrogate the famous sage, Teihotepogi, as to measure the natives and prepare the yacht ... A man of exceptional energy, Teihotepogi has drilled the young people in the classical Tuamotuan songs, but these have been recast in the form of the Tahitian *himene,* and the young people sing them with little awareness of their meaning. As Teihotepogi could be sent for to come to Tahiti at any time, there was no need of prolonging our stay. This promising source still remains unworked."

In spite of his advanced age Te Iho was still extremely vigorous and possessed a very clear mind when I met him for the first time in 1947. Many happy hours were spent with him in 1949—51 and 1952, and a firm friendship developed. With the aid of a tape recorder I finally succeeded in collecting the greater part of the unbelievably numerous traditions, genealogies and sacred chants that Te Iho knew by heart. Other material was copied from such manuscripts as have been preserved. This wealth of information is to be published later in a separate study dealing exclusively with the traditional history, and I shall here limit myself to excerpts from Te Iho's account of the economic and social conditions as they were immediately before the great transformations occurred on the atoll at the end of the last century.[1]

It may here be fitting to quote again Dr. K. P. Emory (1932, p. 40) who in 1931, immediately after his return from the comprehensive Bishop Museum survey of the Tuamotus, expressed his opinion about the possibilities of reconstructing the ancient culture in these words:

"The dangers to navigation in these waters, the hostility of the natives, and the more alluring commercial prospects of the 'high islands' and the richer harvest they held for the missionaries so held up the advance of Western civilization to the Tuamotus that there are natives today, in the eastern part of the region, who reached adolescence before missionary or trader had effected any important change in their ancient mode of living ... The rising generation will be as completely Europeanized as the present-day Tahitian. But as long as natives of such far islands as Fagatau, Vahitahi and Reao, born in the '70's and '80's are still alive, it will be possible to hear ancient chants exactly as they were handed down from generation to generation in the past, and to learn how their ancestors lived."

To transmit faithfully genealogies, chants and detailed information about historical events is a wide-spread Polynesian practice, and Stimson (1933, p. 3) has very aptly summed up the prevalent attitude towards the ancient lore: "Throughout Polynesia it is a custom amounting almost to a law that the ancient *fagu* handed down from the ancestors must under no circumstances be tampered with or altered. The custom has of course been broken, but a sage who is publicly convicted of its infringement becomes permanently discredited." About the preservation of genealogies Peter Buck (1938, p. 22) has this to say: "Even the commoner could trace his lineage and family connections for generations with a certainty which a family of position in western society might envy. The chiefs and priests could trace their ancestry back to the gods. The experts took pride in reciting lineages before public gatherings, and the audience admired such demonstrations of classical knowledge."

A better informant than Te Iho could therefore hardly be found.

---

[1] The most important accounts and conversations—all in the native dialect—were recorded, and copies of the tapes are deposited in the Bernice P. Bishop Museum, Honolulu.

2. Names and ancient divisions

No other group in Polynesia has been given so many different names as the Tuamotus, and as there still seems to be a general confusion about the correct appellation a few words of explanation are warranted.

Hale writes (p. 6) after a visit to the group with Wilkes' exploring expedition, that "the native name ... is Pakumotu, or in Tahitian Paumotu" and continues that *paku* means "cloud" and that the whole name can therefore be translated by "Cloud of islands". Moerenhout (I, p. 158) calls the group Pomoutou, or "Islands of the night" without trying to explain why this strange name should have been bestowed. Finally, Carrington (Robertson, Appendix, p. 279) thinks that the group was "originally named by the Polynesians 'Poumotu'. 'Pou' means stone[1], but it also means 'stone pillar', and that is what the Polynesians intended, describing the islands as stone pillars arising from the depth of the ocean." Each one of these interpretations has found numerous supporters.

The answer to all this is that from the middle of the last century the official and widely used name has been Tuamotu, which probably means "Far-away islands". Earlier the islands were frequently called Paumotu, "Conquered or finished islands" — a very appropriate name after the devastating wars at the beginning of the 19th century. (See next chapter.) *Pau* is a completely different word from *pa'u*, the correctly spelled Tahitian form of the Tuamotuan word *paku*. The change from Paumotu to Tuamotu was officially made by the native Assembly at a meeting in 1851 at the request of the Tuamotuan delegates, who found the word Paumotu humiliating (Cuzent, p. 50), but it is still often heard to-day, especially in Tahiti.

Whether any name for the group as a whole was used in pre-European times is not clear, but the various parts of the archipelago had at any rate separate names, to which references are often made in the chants and traditions. Old natives on Raroia and elsewhere still remember these ancient divisions, indicated on the sketch map below made after Te Iho's directions.

These divisions seem to have been geographical and linguistic rather

---

[1] This statement is not correct. *Pou* simply means "pillar" or "log".

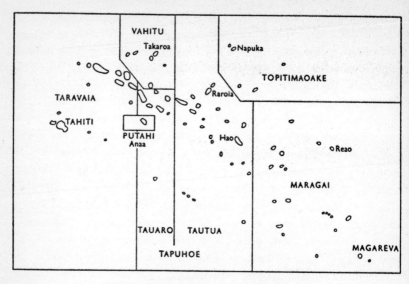

MAP A. *Ancient divisions of the Tuamotu group*

than political units, as all available information indicates that each atoll (or atoll pair like Takume-Raroia, Napuka-Tepoto, Takaroa-Takapoto, Hao-Amanu) was completely independent and often even at war with other atolls in the same division. It is interesting to note that the tentative cultural areas worked out on the basis of the rich material collected during the 1929–30 Bishop Museum survey by Emory (1932, pp. 40–50) coincide roughly with these traditional divisions. The only significant difference is that Putahi (Anaa) and the Tapuhoe divisions form one sub-area on Emory's map, but this is certainly due to the fact that the natives of Anaa at the beginning of the last century subjugated most of the atolls in this part of the group and imposed their language and customs. These cultural differences were, however, at any rate very small, and the main traits were definitely shared by all the Tuamotuan atolls.

3. Socio-political organization

This is what Te Iho had to tell:

"Takume and Raroia were discovered by a mighty chief by name

Taneariki, who arrived from Hiva Nui[1] thirty generations ago. He found the land good and built his home on the northern tip of Takume, which he called Tepukamaru. Gradually his children and followers spread out over the two atolls and divided them up among themselves. Taneariki's grandson Varoa was the first ruler over the two islands, and I descend myself from him. This is my genealogy[2]:

28. VAROA I TE PO (t) — Apoapo (v)
    Teakiukiu
    Gatata

27. Teakiukiu (t) — Teanau (v)
    Tahitohenua
    Garueharatini
    Tetapotu o te ragi

26. Tahitohenua (t) — Haniao (v)
    Varoa Tapu
    Mareikura
    Taivarokia

25. VAROA TAPU (t) — Mohomauaina (v)
    Pahukeone
    Tumakivao
    Tagaroahuritini

24. Pahukeone (t) — Teroromuhuariki (v)
    Tekuratagiorooro
    Papatuki

[1] This was probably one of the islands in the Marquesas group. Whereas all evidence shows that the western atolls were originally settled by Tahitian refugees, the northeastern atolls seem to have been populated from the Marquesas and some of the southeastern atolls from Mangareva.

[2] A great number of genealogies are preserved, and some of them trace the owner's descent all the way back to the gods or to persons who supposedly lived 70 to 80 generations ago in the mythical homeland Havaiki. Others begin more modestly with ancestors who lived in Hiva Nui at a later period. Te Iho's genealogy actually begins 74 generations ago, but the first part of it is left out here. Names in block letters indicate rulers over both atolls. A small (t) means *tāne*, man, and a small (v) means *vahīne*, woman.

23. Tekuratagiorooro (t) — Marere i te ata (v)
    Pupumaire
    Hinahorokaha
    Paea
    Fariua

22. Pupumaire (t) — Togi (v)
    Tagaroamakaihau

21. Tagaroamakaihau (t) — Turuturukiheragi (v)
    Varoa Kaipani
    Tehina
    Manuiaheiariki

20. VAROA KAIPANI (t) — Nukuterauta (v)
    Tepumatehoata
    Terorokapua
    Ituragi

19. Tepumatehoata (v) — Tiaveariki (t)
    Tehiga
    Teraveroariki

18. Tehiga (t) — Tufakirei (v)
    Varoa Nui
    Maruake

17. VAROA NUI (t) — Ponoatua (v)
    Karotaia
    Tetauru
    Tuarairua

16. Karotaia (t) — Tepiu (v)
    Marohaniao
    Nohouma
    Terikipuaragi

15. Marohaniao (v) — Tokotoko (t)
    Varoa Tikaroa

14. VAROA TIKAROA (t) — Tetaotariki (v)
    Tuhoe

13. Tuhoe (t) — Terapureariki (v)
    Kaoko

12. KAOKO (t) — Taitua o Keha (v)
   Tanerarofaki
   Tematahuira
   Teataivavao
11. Tanerarofaki (t) — Tumaiteahu (v)
   Temere
   Tokotoko
   Tekuratuao
10. Temere (t) — Tehina (v)
   Tekava
9. Tekava (v) — Tematahira (t)
   Temere
   Puia
   Taia
   Huarei
   Turu
8. Temere (t) — Tohuora (v)
   Tohutika
   Tehina
7. Tohutika (t) — Teuru (v)
   Tetahoa
   Tufakapuia
6. Tetahoa (t) — Marohua (v)
   Tepage
   Temaru
   Mahinui
5. Tepage (t) — Tufareipoko (v)
   Rarofaki
4. Rarofaki (t) — Tuhipo (v)
   Te Iho

In former times as now the people of Takume and Raroia formed one nation *(nūnāga)*, but contrary to present custom each island was then divided into districts *(matakeinaga)* with clearly defined border lines [map B]. The land was common property of the whole group living there, but the trees were owned by the various households *(utua-fare)* and sometimes even by particular individuals. There were no large

43

villages, but the houses were spread out fairly evenly around the lagoon. The inhabitants often moved around in their district in order to secure the largest possible amount of food, and some persons who had acquired double rights often alternated between two districts. They acquired double rights through the marriage of their father or mother to persons from another district. In each household there were more men and women than now and the biggest chiefs had several wives.

The founder of each district was a well-known man, a relative or follower of Taneariki, and all his descendants as a group were called

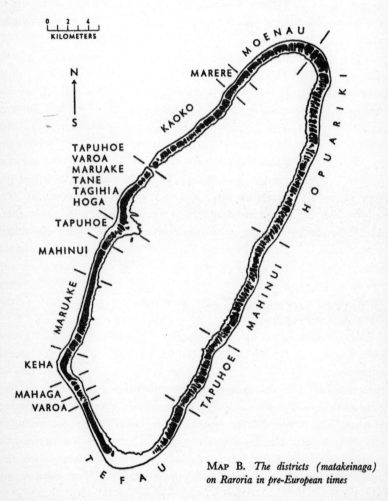

MAP B. *The districts (matakeinaga) on Raroria in pre-European times*

44

gāti. Some of the *gāti* later on broke up into smaller *gāti.* Each *gāti* took its name from the founder, and the foremost was *gāti* Varoa, so called after Taneariki's grandchild. Tradition has it that all the inhabitants on Takume and Raroia acknowledged the principal members of this *gāti* as their overlords *(ariki nūi)* down to Kaoko, who lived 12 generations ago. Kaoko brought his wife from another atoll, and that a hostile one, so the Raroian people did not want his son to reign but lived from then on without any overlords. When important decisions were to be made all the household heads in the district assembled. The person of highest descent, or chief, naturally decided, but everyone took a part in the deliberations. If a woman was of especially high birth she might be allowed to participate in the meetings.

Some men were more skilled than the rest and were called *tahūga.* There were several kinds of these. Some were canoe-builders, others manufactured tools, while a third group acted as physicians. The most respected, however, were those who knew the ancient traditions. Already as a child I was taught to become a *tahūga* and had to learn to recite the traditions by heart. Sometimes competitions took place between the learned men of Takume and Raroia, to see who knew the greatest number of traditions, genealogies and chants. Specialists also drilled the young men and women in songs and dances for the great festivals.

Men who distinguished themselves in war and used to lead the others were called *kaito.* They often made long voyages in their twin-hulled canoes *(vaka fauite)* in order to avenge injuries or just because they could not stand a settled life. Their weapons were wooden spears *(kōmore),* clubs *(paragi)* and stone slings *(maka).* The enemies they killed were often eaten. If possible they were taken home alive and eaten on the cult-place *(marae).*

Each household head had his own cult-place, where he prayed to the gods. No women or unincised youths were allowed to enter the sacred enclosure. At the cult-place of the highest ranking person or chief in each district the whole population gathered on important occasions. The chief could lead the ceremonies himself, but often a relative to him acted as priest. The principal gods were Tagaroa, Tane, Tu and Rogo, and it was very important to use the right ceremonies and prayers *(pūre)* to obtain their help. Fingernails and locks of hair were taken from the dead and kept in small boxes, which were now and then displayed at

45

certain celebrations. Certain men had the power of sorcery *(mūki)* and could cast evil spells on others. Dead souls *(tupapaku)* could also harm the living."

Looking for confirmations of Te Iho's statements from other sources, Montiton has this piece of information about the habitation pattern in his account of the native religion: "In their savage state our Paumotus lived scattered along the shores of their islands, though grouped according to families. The chief or the most influencial member established or consecrated his authority by the construction of a marae, a fact which at the same time made him the sole priest. Since time immemorial the property right had arisen among them by the occupation and cultivation of the land. Each coconut tree was owned by the person who had planted it or inherited it from his ancestors. The dunes and pandanus thickets as well as the corresponding adjoining parts of the inner lagoon were owned by those Indians who had first lived or built a hut there."[1]

From the neighbouring atoll Fangatau Father Audran reports (1919, p. 232) that "in the remote past the island was divided into three distinct districts peopled by three families known under the names of (1) Gati-Tane at Gake; (2) Gati-Mahinui at Raro and at Kereteki; (3) Gati-Tekopu (this family probably emigrated to Hao). These three tribes were almost always at enmity and often at war amongst themselves. If by any mischance a member of the Gati-Tane living at Te Matahoa ventured to enter the territory of another tribe, he would certainly be seized and immediately sent to the ovens; such, too, would be the fate of any member of another tribe venturing to enter his district. A trespasser was a prisoner of war."

Emory bases the following conclusions (1947, p. 7) on the study of a great number of manuscript books: "A tribe held an island or a

---

[1] "A l'état sauvage, nos Paumotous vivaient disséminés sur les bords de leurs iles, groupés cependant par famille. Le chef ou le membre le plus influent établissait ou consacrait son autorité par la construction d'un maraé, fait, qui en même temps, l'instituait prêtre unique. De temps immémorial, le droit de propriété s'était introduit chez eux par l'occupation et la culture du territoire. Chaque pied de cocotier avait pour maître celui qui l'avait planté ou hérité de ses ancêtres. Les landes et les bruyères de pandanus, ainsi que les portions limitrophes correspondantes de la lagune intérieure, avaient pour propriétaires les Indiens qui, les premiers, y avaient séjourné ou élevé une hutte." (Montiton, 1874, p. 502.)

certain portion of an island in common but in the title of its chief, who could say, 'I turn my back in one direction, I turn my back in the opposite direction, all that I see belongs to me' (chant of the chief of Napuka). But the tribal lands, such as those at Takaroa and Takapoto, were frequently divided into districts with fixed boundaries. Each district was the property of a kindred *(gati)* within the tribe, whose living representatives and whose land were both termed *matakeinaga*. The five *matakeinaga* divisions of Takapoto Island bore the names of five brothers, among whom the island had been evenly divided by their father, the first settler." The numerous sketch maps in Emory's study (1934) of Tuamotuan stone structures moreover very clearly indicate that practically all the atolls were divided up in districts *(matakeinaga)* in the same way.

Emory also (1947, p. 56) discusses "why a Tuamotuan calls himself a member of a certain kindred *(gati)* and speaks of a certain marae as being his. Names are considered the private property of a kindred, and if one examines Tuamotuan genealogies, he will find that some of the children had names from the mother's ancestors, others, names from the father's ancestors. The first-born, if a son, was usually given the name of one of his father's kindred. Hence, he belonged to the kindred on his father's side, and one of their maraes was his marae when he came of age. He had a right to sit on the other maraes of the kindred, or on any marae of any kindred, if he could trace blood relationship to it through either his father or mother. But the position he occupied on the others might be inferior." This well confirms Te Iho's account of persons with "double rights".

There are few references to the composition of the families, but Fierens has this to say about plural wives: "What made his [the native's] fate even more deplorable was polygamy, which had become a custom of the country. Some men had four, five, and even ten wives. We had much difficulty in eradicating this abuse."[1] With the help of the numerous genealogies I have collected on Raroia I have computed the number of wives of each overlord (see Te Iho's genealogy, pp. 41–43) and the figures are as follows:

[1] "Ce qui rendait son sort encore plus déplorable, c'est la polygamie, passée dans les mœurs du pays: quelques hommes avaient quatre, cinq et même dix femmes. Nous avons eu beaucoup de peine à déraciner cet abus." (Fierens, 1879, p. 438.)

Varoa i te po	2
Varoa Tapu	1
Varoa Kaipani	2
Varoa Nui	3
Varoa Tikaroa	5
Kaoko	3

The Raroian (and Tuamotuan) kinship terminology closely followed the general Polynesian pattern and was strongly classificatory (see Danielsson, 1953 b). The two main criteria according to which persons were grouped were generation and sex. In spite of their thorough genealogical knowledge the Raroians had special terms only for two generations above one's own, the word for grandparent, *tupuna*, being used for all preceding ancestors. For the generations below one's own they had, however, separate terms for as many as four generations (*tama, mokopuna, hina, hinarere*), whereas most of the other Polynesian tribes only had differentiated two (children and grandchildren).

The same term was used for all individuals belonging to the same generation both of lineal and collateral descent, e. g. *mākui* (parent, aunt, uncle), *tupuna* (grandparents and their siblings), *mokopuna* (grandchild, sibling's and cousin's grandchild). A notable exception was the use of the term *pōtiki* for siblings and cousin's child, thus distinguishing him from one's own child, called *tama, tamariki* or *tamaiti*.

Seniority was carefully indicated between individuals of the same generation, different terms being used for elder and younger siblings, *tuakana* and *teīna*. First cousins were regarded as siblings and the same terms used. In this case, however, seniority was not determined by the cousin's own age but followed the seniority rule of their parents. The stress on sex differences is shown by the use of distinct terms for a man's and a woman's brother. Another peculiarity is that emphasis many times was placed not simply on the sex of the person spoken to or of, but on the identity or difference of sex between him and the person addressing him. A sister of a woman was thus called *tuakana* or *teīna* (depending on whether she was older or younger), but a sister of a man was called *tūahine*.

Of specialists (*tahūga*) other than historians we know very little. To the prowesses of the warrior chiefs (*kaito*) we have, however, some testimonials. Audran (1917, pp. 53—62, 1930, pp. 561—562) has given a vivid account of the great Moeava's exploits, and the "illustrious sailors" the same author lists (1923, pp. 19—20) are of course just such roving warriors. Finally, Bodin relates an episode, which clearly reveals the viking spirit that animated a true *kaito*. "About forty years ago [i.e. around 1890] a 'Vaka' appeared in the south-western pass at Makemo. It contained a single man, who had come from Reao 450 miles away. He jumped ashore, carried his vessel to the sand and immediately attacked the few natives who were on that side of the island, very far from the village. Obliged to defend themselves, they said, four of them succeeded in drowning their aggressor in the lagoon after a long and arduous struggle."[1]

About the warriors' cannibalistic habits we learn from Fierens that "in some islands these cannibalistic peoples had made around their maraes wreaths of skulls and bones of human victims sacrificed principally in their wars."[2] Emory (1947, pp. 93—94) has gathered additional evidence. References to weapons are made among others by Byron (p. 95), George Forster (II, p. 42) and Montiton (1874, p. 498).

That the natives were skilled sailors and navigators is abundantly proved by the numerous references in the early accounts to native vessels encountered in the open sea often very far away from the home atoll of the crew. I shall here only quote Moerenhout, as he at the same time gives a good description of the special craft used in the group. He affirms that the natives of the Tuamotu archipelago "are known since time immemorial to be the hardiest sailors in the neighbourhood, using their large canoes, which often measure over 100 feet and are built after a design that makes them look much like our vessels, for they make a keel, an interior framework, the ribs of which determine the shape of the vessel, and which resting on the keel are covered with planking. It is in these canoes they cruise around these waters covering a distance of

---

[1] "C'est à Makemo, il y a une quarantaine d'années qu'une "Vaka" apparut à la passe du Sud-Ouest. Elle contenait un seul homme venu de Reao à 450 milles. Il sauta à terre, porta son embarcation sur le sable et attaqua aussitôt les quelques indigènes qui étaient de ce côté de l'ile, fort éloigné du village. Obligés de se défendre, dirent ils, ils parvinrent à quatre, après un long et pénible combat à noyer leur agresseur dans le lagon." (Bodin, 1932, pp. 7—8.)

[2] "Dans quelques îles ces peuples anthropophages avaient fait autour de leur maraès des couronnes composées des crânes et des ossements de victimes humaines, immolées principalement dans les guerres." (Fierens, 1872, p. 130.)

several degrees; but since they are too narrow in proportion to their length and height, they bind two together. In this way, by means of the platform in the middle they obtain a width of at least a third of the length. They are pointed at both ends, and they [the natives] do not veer them around to change direction, but turn the sail and the rudder."[1]

As the religion is the most thoroughly studied and described aspect of the native culture (see e.g. Montiton, 1874, Stimson, 1933, Emory, 1939, 1940, 1947) and the subject also to a large degree falls outside the scope of this study I shall limit myself to some cursory notes and remarks. The principal cult-places on Raroia are still remembered to-day, and though few remains were left old men pointed out 42 different *marae* sites in various parts of the atoll (Danielsson, 1952, p. 222). Their scattered distribution confirms Te Iho's statement that the whole atoll rim was inhabited in ancient times.

About the priest and his prestige Audran (1919, p. 234) says: "In the Tuamotu Group the chief officiating priest, who conducted, so to speak, divine worship, and represented the archpriest in our cathedrals, was known as the *kaunuku*. He was a great personage and very holy. Further, he enjoyed the highest privileges. He was exempt from ordinary work and from that forced labour at times so troublesome, such as cooking and the preparation of the turtle, for which the common people were liable. The smoke from the ovens was not to come near him or to touch him. Throughout the whole island there was but one authority (that of the king) superior to his, while at times his influence was as powerful as even that of the king."

Father Fierens says that the women "were forbidden to approach the altars. The men ate part of the fruit offered as a sacrifice; the women

---

[1] Les indigènes de l'archipel Tuamotu "passent, de temps immémorial, pour les plus hardis navigateurs des environs, au moyen de leur grandes pirogues, qui, souvent, ont plus de cent pieds, et sont construites sur un plan qui les fait beaucoup ressembler à nos vaisseaux; car ils y font une quille, une charpente intérieure, dont les membrures déterminent la forme du bâtiment, et qui, portant sur la quille, reçoivent les planches du bordage. C'est avec ces pirogues qu'ils parcourent ces mers à plusieurs degrés aux environs; mais comme elles sont trop étroites pour leur longueur et pour leur hauteur, ils en attachent deux ensemble; et alors, au moyen de la plate-forme du milieu, ils obtiennent en largeur au moins le tiers de leur longueur. Elles sont affilées aux deux extrémités, et ils ne les font point virer pour changer de direction; mais ils tournent la voile et le gouvernail." (Moerenhout, I, pp. 158—159.)

were not allowed to partake."[1] In accordance with the other special privileges conferred upon certain female rulers it is, however, not so surprising that they also occasionally were allowed to have their own *marae*. The Raroian traditions speak for instance of the mighty female chief Maruia of Takume who performed religious ceremonies herself, and Emory (1947, p. 57) concludes his investigations: "When the *ariki*, or head of a group, was a woman, she must have been allowed upon the marae on certain occasions. References to an *ariki vahine* upon a marae are not uncommon."

Shapiro (1930, p. 141) writes: "In the old days, admission to the *marae* ... was forbidden to the unincised, who were also not permitted to partake of the sacred feasts. The explanation given was that the unincised had not received *mana* or sacredness and, therefore, could not with impunity approach structures or partake of food endowed with *mana*."

The existence of an ancestor cult is confirmed by many writers, of whom I have chosen to quote Father Fierens: "They made the hair of their ancestors the object of a superstitious cult: these locks enshrined in little boxes and put on stone altars, became a sort of divinity. To these fetishes they attributed the abundance of a fish or turtle catch; also before eating their catch they put it on the marae."[2] Some magical practices and beliefs in ancestor spirits are described by Hervé (pp. 49 —56).

Finally, the important place of music and dance in the Tuamotuan culture is worth mentioning. Lucett (I, pp. 243—244) has left us the following description of a reception on Hao, a common scene which has many counterparts in the accounts from other Polynesian groups: "All the women residing at the spot where I landed assembled and greeted me with a dance. They stood in a row, and sang in concert to a singularly wild chant; keeping time with the hands and feet, and accompanying

---

[1] Il leur "était défendu d'approcher des autels. Les hommes mangeaient une partie des fruits offerts en sacrifice, les femmes ne pouvaient y participer". (Fierens, 1872, p. 130.)

[2] "Ils rendaient un culte superstitieux à la chevelure de leurs ancêtres: ces cheveux, renfermés dans de petites boites et déposés sur des autels en pierres, devenaient une sorte de divinité. C'est à ces fétiches qu'ils attribuaient l'abondance de la pêche, soit du poisson, soit de la tortue; aussi, avant de manger leur capture, ils la déposaient sur le *maraë*." (Fierens, 1879, p. 437.)

the song with extraordinary lascivious movements of the body, impossible to be conceived by Europeans. Their songs are all of a gross and sensual character." Father Montiton informs us that "they are crazy about music. Squatting in a circle or negligently stretched out here and there in their huts, the women on one side and the men on the other, they spend whole days in choral singing."[1] Buck, who owing to his profound knowledge of the Polynesian language was certainly better qualified than most other scholars to judge the aesthetic value of their music, thinks (1938, p. 186) that the Tuamotuans "developed a particular feeling for poetry and an ability to express themselves in beautiful words. Living on coral islands and watching the constant movement of the waves, they set their thoughts to the music of the surf beating against the outer reef."

4. Economy and material culture

First Te Iho's account:

"In former times life was much harder and it was much more difficult to get enough to eat. It is true that both the lagoon and the sea teemed with fish, but when the weather was bad or it blew too hard no fishing could take place and the lack was immediately felt by everyone. Besides, families were larger, so the men had to spend the greater part of the day fishing. The women collected tridacna *(pahŭa)* and other sorts of oysters *(tio)*. In order to open these, which also was the women's task, they used a stick *(pĭtoi)*. The shells were thrown away and you can still see large white heaps of them here and there on the beaches.

There was no salt and the only way of preserving the fish was to smoke it or dry it in the sun. Mussels were repeatedly baked and could in this way keep a very long time. Live fish were kept a few days in large stone enclosures, which the men made on a reef spur on the lagoon side *(kāoa)* near their homes. In such an enclosure certain kinds of fish could be kept alive for four or five days.

When large schools of fish came into the shallows, all those who lived in the neighbourhood hurriedly made a garland of palm leaves *(rena)*

---

[1] "Ils sont fous de musique. Accroupis en cercle ou négligemment étendus par-ci, par-là, dans leurs cases, les femmes d'un côté et les hommes de l'autre, ils passent les journées entières à chanter en chœur." (Montiton, 1855, p. 450.)

and everybody helped to haul in the catch, which was later shared equally among the whole team. Sometimes a group of men went off net fishing in a suitable bay, and when they returned the women straight-away made a fire and everybody sat down to eat, even if it was in the middle of the night. Often, however, we were content to eat the fish raw, because in the olden days we were always hungry on Raroia and eager to fill up our stomachs. When a man returned from a fishing trip he gave shares to his relatives, to the chief and to the priest.

Formerly there were many more pandanus trees than coconut palms, and both young and old kept chewing pandanus nuts almost all the time. Only a few species of nuts could be eaten raw, but people knew where the best trees stood and there were often quarrels about who owned them. The soft flesh in the lower part *(kohēro)* of the drupes *(tuke)* was scraped off by the women, who made it into a paste *(kāpenu)* and baked it. The paste could then be made into many different dishes. Inside the hard drupes were small nuts *(pagōa)* which were gathered after the drupes had been crushed with a cylindrical stone *(gote)*. In my childhood I used to hear the pounding of these stones all day long, just as the rattle of the tapa clubs was formerly always heard in Tahiti. The coconuts were drunk, of course, and the flesh grated and used for different dishes or sauces, just as now.

There were no bread-fruits as in Tahiti, but every family grew *taro (fakēa)*. It was quite hard work to make *taro* plantations, for one was forced to dig deep ditches *(māite)*, so that the plants could get as much water as possible. My ancestors dug with mussel-shell spades, and it took a long time to dig a whole ditch. Six months had to pass before the *taro* roots could be harvested, but they were never as big as in Tahiti. Most of them were very tiny, but at least they made a change in the menu. Purslane *(pokēa)* was never cultivated but grew wild. The roots were scraped like *taro* roots and baked in the earth oven.

Since the ground consisted of sand and stone everywhere it was difficult to make an earth oven and it was therefore as a rule necessary to construct a frame of palm logs. There were no really good stones either, so a few chiefs had brought back stones from Tahiti [undoubtedly basalt stones]. If there was anything to eat an earth oven was prepared once a day, otherwise not at all. Usually we had to make do with the brackish water in the wells, but when it rained properly rainwater was

53

collected. This was done by making convergent [V-shaped] cuts into the bark of coconut palms and holding wooden bowls *(pāroe)* underneath.

In my parents' time there were neither pigs nor fowls; those only began to be imported in my youth. Dogs were, however, kept by my forefathers long before, but I cannot say exactly when they came or who had brought them to the island. The dogs were eaten, of course. Sea birds and eggs were appreciated then as now, but the greatest delicacy was naturally turtle meat. Then as now everybody was fond of this delicacy, and during the season [June to September], all men, women and children were constantly on the look-out for turtles. The women were not allowed to eat turtle, however, for it was a sacred animal. This was also the case with some big fish such as tuna and bonito. Like turtles these fish were always eaten on the cult-place *(marae)*.

My ancestors were poor people. Their houses were not as fine as those we have now. The largest, called *fare rape* were oblong with straight corners [rectangular] but often without walls. Sometimes there was a veranda along the front, where one could sit and talk and rest. The smaller were called *fare puao* and were so low that you could not stand upright in them. Actually they only consisted of a small, oval roof, and a man could carry it around and put it up where it happened to be coolest and breeziest for the moment. Finally there were small shelters called *fare karuru*, that we put up provisionally when we did not spend more than a few nights at a place. The best type of wood for the frame of a house was *gatae* [Pisonia grandis], but this was scarce, so most people had to be content with pandanus or coconut palm wood. The roofs were made of pandanus leaves *(ueā)*, palm fronds *(gāofe)* or ferns *(kikīpa)*. Pandanus leaves kept longest.

The floor consisted of small coral stones on top of which one put a plaited mat of coconut palm leaves *(pakerere)*. Apart from a support for the back *(hirināki)* and a head rest *(urūga)* there was no furniture. As blankets we used fine pandanus mats *(peue)*. The bottom one was called *vauvau*, the top one *ropiropi*. The mens' clothes, consisting of a belt *(maro)*, and at times a cloak *(kahu)* to hang around the shoulders, were also made of pandanus. The women had a girdle *(hūme popoki)* or a loin cloth *(karēu)*. Both men and women were tattooed *(nanako)*.

Tools were made of mother-of-pearl shell, turtle carapace, wood, bone or stone. As no suitable stones for making adzes *(toki)* existed on Raroia, stones or ready-made adzes [of basalt undoubtedly] were often fetched from Tahiti.[1] In exchange we gave mother-of-pearl shells, which the Tahitians needed for making tuna and bonito hooks. Small adzes could, however, be made of tridacna *(pahūa)* shell. Mother-of-pearl shell and turtle carapace were excellent for fish hooks, but bone was best for prickers *(mākei)*. Instead of knives they had pieces of mother-of-pearl shell *(kuku)*, or a sharp-edged mussel called *kororā*. Fire was made by rubbing a stick *(aurima)* against the central groove of a split branch."

Turning now to other sources of information we find several good accounts of the former subsistence economy. Lucett (I, p. 242) describes conditions on Hao in 1842 in this way: "The natives live principally on fish and the fruit of the pandanus, which here grows abundantly, and is by them called fārā. The fruit is a collection of cones, which they separate. Very little of it is edible, but each cone contains three or four white kernels of the bigness of a plum-stone kernel; and after the small portion of esculent matter has been gnawed from the inner end of the cone, the natives may be seen, for hours at a stretch, pounding away at them to extract the kernels. I imagine they contain a deal of nourishment, as the people, far from being a puny race, are stout and robust, and fārā is the only vegetable production they have as daily food. I found breaking the cones hard labour, as it jars every muscle in your body. Use, and the absence of more easily acquired food, has reconciled the natives to the exercise; and groups may be seen pounding from morning till night."

The natives' dependence on pandanus and sea-food is stressed by Father Montiton, who speaking about the Tuamotuans in general, says: "The amount [of tridacna shells] never seems to diminish, even though everyone is constantly out after his daily portion of it. Moreover, together with the pandanus it is the sole and scanty food of all our Indians, for their miserable plantations of taro, the roots of which hardly reach the size of a bottle stopper, are not worth anything."[2]

[1] I found several such on the island which are now in the Bernice P. Bishop Museum.

[2] "La quantité [de bénitiers] semble ne jamais diminuer, quoique tout le monde aille sans relâche y puiser la pitance de chaque jour. Au reste, c'est avec le pandanus,

Other accounts show still more clearly how difficult the food situation was. Father Fierens writes that on Fangatau "pandanus fruit and fish form their staple food. Moreover, as they say themselves, they are often forced to lie down and hug their bellies in order to alleviate the hunger pains. With what joyous eagerness did they take the dry coconuts I had brought them!"[1]

As late as 1918 Father Audran reports from Napuka that "there are very few fruit-bearing coconut palms, only ten or so. Food consists entirely of tridacna clams (pahua) and pandanus fruits, but since this tree gives hardly anything at this time of the year, we have to make do with ordinary molluscs and the fish that one does or does not catch. I have seen children picking up fish bones from the ground, sucking them for a long time, then crushing them between two stones and eating them thus with pandanus fruits."[2]

This general dependence on pandanus nuts as a staple food on coral atolls has frequently been overlooked in the literature and most anthropologists have also had a very low opinion of the nutritive value of the pandanus nut. It is therefore extremely interesting to find the following piece of information in Forest Brown's *Flora of Southeastern Polynesia* (I, pp. 32—34): "A quantitative determination of the sugar content of the *Pandanus* fruit (basal mesocarp) kindly made by R. H. King of the Hawaiian Sugar Planters' Association, led to the surprising discovery that 25 per cent of the dry weight of this tissue in one of the coral island species *(P. pulposus)* is composed chiefly of dextrose (grape sugar). His analysis shows that the dry weight content of sugar (chiefly dextrose) of *Pandanus* flesh is equal to nearly half the

[1] "Le fruit du pandanus et le poisson forment le fond de leur nourriture. Aussi, comme ils le disent eux-mêmes, sont-ils souvent obligés de se coucher et de se serrer le ventre pour moins sentir les douleurs de la faim. Avec quelle joyeuse avidité ils ramassèrent les cocos secs que je leur avais apportés!" (Fierens, 1872, p. 127.)

[2] "Il y a fort peu de cocotiers en rapport, une dizaine seulement. Toute la nourriture consiste en bénitiers (pahua) et en fruits de pandanus, mais cet arbre ne donnant presque plus rien à cette époque, il ne nous reste plus que le vulgaire mollusque et le poisson qu'on attrape ou qu'on n'attrape pas. J'ai vu des enfants ramasser à terre des arêtes de poisson, les sucer longuement, puis les écraser entre deux pierres et les manger ainsi avec des fruits de pandanus." (Audran, 1918, p. 129.)

l'unique et chétive nourriture de tous nos Indiens, car il faut compter pour rien leur misérable culture du taro, dont les pieds ici atteignent à peine les dimensions d'un bouchon de bouteille." (Montiton, 1874, p. 503.)

sugar content of sugar cane (50 per cent sucrose, 2 per cent dextrose) but entirely different chemically, being chiefly dextrose in *Pandanus* and chiefly sucrose in *Saccharum (sugar cane)*. On analysis of living weights he found 3.75 per cent sugar (dextrose) in *Pandanus* as compared with 13 per cent of sugar (sucrose and dextrose) in sugar cane.

The starch content of the fruit varies greatly in amount, being absent in some storage parenchyma cells and abundant in others cut from the same piece of tissue. Doubtless the relative proportion of starch and dextrose changes as the fruit ripens ... Although the taste of the raw fruit of *Pandanus* is not disagreeable, the irritation to the mouth and throat, doubtless caused by the presence of needle-shaped crystals of calmium oxalate, makes its use as a raw food even in times of famine more or less annoying or even impossible. This irritating effect while somewhat like that produced by raw taro, is far less painful and is more pronounced in some species and varieties than in others. As with taro, cooking destroys the irritating agencies."

Unfortunately the pandanus tree does not bear fruit all the year round like the coconut palm but is seasonal. The harvest season lasts but 4—5 months, as a rule from August to December. This explains why the natives in pre-European times often went hungry in spite of the abundance of pandanus trees.

George Forster (II, p. 40) mentions that there were dogs on Takaroa in 1774: "As soon as we landed they embraced us, touching our noses, after the custom of New Zeeland, and began to bring coconuts and dogs for sale to the boats." Lucett (I, p. 247) says specifically about the Hao natives that: "They have no quadrupeds, save a few wretched dogs which they keep for eating, and a small species of rat which infests the islands in myriads." The great appreciation shown everywhere for such seasonal additions as turtle meat, sea birds and eggs is noted by Montiton (1874, p. 503) among others.

George Forster's remark above that the natives of Takaroa brought coconuts and dogs "for sale" is certainly his own interpretation of the ceremonial exchange the natives initiated. Wilkes was a keener observer, for he relates (I, p. 335) after his visit to Napuka in 1839 that the inhabitants of this island "had no idea of the principles of barter, and allowed any thing to be taken without opposition, receiving any articles in return with gratitude and delight".

57

That the wide-spread Polynesian taboo for women to eat certain foods also was upheld in the Tuamotus is confirmed by Father Fierens, who writes that "they were equally forbidden to eat what were considered to be delicacies, turtles, large fishes and generally everything destined for the gods".[1] A similar restriction, also sanctioned by the religion, excluded the young men, at least on Napuka, from the marae feasts, for the same author affirms that "the better part of the banquet was for the old men, who called themselves *raka,* i.e. saints or sacred ones. These so stuffed themselves with food that they were no longer able to walk, after which, lying down by the idols they waited for the food to be digested, in order to once more satisfy their gluttonous appetite."[2]

Of the Tuamotuan type of houses and huts there are several descriptions. Robertson (p. 117) who served under Wallis saw as early as 1767 on Nukutavake "three houses or rather shades without Door or sides but neatly thatch with Cocoa and palm tree Leaves". Montiton says that the natives "lived and slept higgledy-piggledy in hangars open to all the winds".[3] The small huts "are made of foliage and have the shape of a sugar loaf; to enter them you have to stoop".[4]

To the natives' clothing there are many references in the accounts of the early visitors. Forster (II, p. 40) tells us that in 1774 the men on Takaroa had only "a very small piece of cloth about their loins" whereas the women had a piece of cloth "enlarged to the size of a short apron". When the Spaniards called at Anaa two years earlier they saw (Corney, II, p. 37) women "draped from the waist to their knees with the same material as the men's breech-clouts". A century later Father Fierens remarked about the Tuamotuans that "these islanders are still in a state

[1] "Il leur était également interdit de manger ce qui était considéré comme nourriture de choix, tortues, gros poissons, et généralement tout ce qui était destiné aux dieux." (Fierens, 1872, p. 130.)

[2] "La meilleure part du festin était pour les vieillards, qui se disaient *raka,* c'est-à-dire saints ou sacrés. Ceux-ci se regorgeaient de viandes, à tel point qu'ils ne pouvaient plus marcher; après quoi, se couchant près des idoles, ils y attendaient que la digestion fût faite, pour satisfaire de nouveau leur appétit glouton." (Fierens, 1879, p. 438.)

[3] Autrefois ils "habitaient et couchaient pêle-mêle, sous des hangars ouverts à tous les vents". (Montiton, 1873, p. 281.)

[4] "Leurs huttes sont faites de feuillage et ont la forme d'un pain de sucre; on n'y peut entrer qu'en rampant." (Fierens, 1872, p. 130.)

of almost complete nakedness. As covering they have but belts made of pandanus leaves."[1]

There is little else to add to Te Iho's account of the material culture, and I shall therefore end my culling from the scanty literary sources with this unique glimpse of a Tuamotuan work-shop encountered in 1767 by Robertson (p. 124) on Nukutavake: "In two of thir Houses which appeard to be Carpenters Work Shops, we found several very fine pieces of Tortois Shell Carefully laid up, and several very large and fresh pearl Oyster Shells, some of the Oyster Shells was fixt in pieces of Wood and made very Sharp for Cutting with — at each house their was a pice of stone in a wooden frame, on which stone I supose they rub the Shells untill they bring it too a Sharp Edge—both stones appeard to have been used as Whitestones and they are of the same nature with portland Stone, which makes me think they are brought from some distant shore."

5. Comments and comparisons

Though meagre, the data presented in the previous parts of this chapter suffice for the general purpose of determining the main features of the pre-European social and economic system, and I shall here only try to make two clarifications.

The first is an attempt to achieve a more exact terminology in the field of social organization. Te Iho's account and the numerous gene-alogies preserved clearly show that Taneariki and his followers, who discovered Takume-Raroia thirty generations ago, divided up the atolls into sectors (*matakeinaga*) which later on, as the population gradually increased, were in their turn split up into still smaller sectors. In Te Iho's youth each sector was still inhabited by groups of what we now technically call "extended families", whose heads were all descended from the same ancestor. All persons, whether living or dead, who were descended from a common ancestor, formed a consanguinal group called *gāti*, which took its name from the founder. Each residential group of living persons with a common ancestor was, like the sector in which they lived, called a *matakeinaga*. Descent was bilateral but there was a strong

---

[1] "Ces insulaires sont encore dans un état quasi complet de nudité. Ils n'ont pour se couvrir que des ceintures faites de feuilles de pandanus." (Fierens, 1872, p. 127.)

tendency to trace it through the male line.[1] The group was neither exogamous nor endogamous, but agamous to use Lowie's terminology.

A comparison with the social organisation of the Maoris is illuminating. Firth (1929, pp. 97—98) describes it thus: "After a few generations, as the *whanau*[2] [extended family] increased in numbers, it became of sufficient importance to rank as a *hapu* ... Some men of influence would propose that henceforth the people be known as (say) Ngati-Kahu, naming a common ancestor Kahu from whom the members of the group all traced descent ... The *hapu* was in no sense an exogamous group. Marriage ... was encouraged within the *hapu* so long as the parties were not nearly related, but here again endogamy was not insisted upon. Again, the *hapu* was not a purely unilateral group. Descent through one parent only was necessary to establish membership in it, but an interesting feature of the system is that both mother and father were counted in tracing descent. Were they of different *hapu*, the children belonged to both; were they of the same *hapu*, the children had a double qualification for membership. Moreover, in the tracing of descent neither the matrilineal nor the patrilineal principle was rigidly followed; males and females might figure in the same genealogical line. As a rule, however, a person preferred to have his main line of descent from his most important ancestor following through males alone. Still, the names of women occur here and there even in some of the genealogies of the people of highest rank. The admission to membership through descent from either males or females—or both conjoined—shows that the *hapu* is not a unilateral group of the strict type."

The Maori *hapu* obviously corresponds to the Tuamotuan group called *matakeinaga,* whereas in both areas the descent groups including also preceding, deceased members have the same structure and name, *gāti (ngati).* This seems simple, but raises an intricate problem. For if we are to translate *matakeinaga* and *gāti* into modern anthropological terms, which are we to apply? The question is not purely academic, since we must be able to classify our anthropological data in order to mani-

---

[1] In Tonga this tendency has even been so strong that true patri-clans have emerged. No change of the marriage rule to exogamy has, however, yet taken place. (Murdock, 1949, p. 76.)

[2] The word *fānau* or *hānau* exists in the Tuamotuan dialect, too, but it means simply "to deliver".

pulate them, whatever the aim of our manipulation might be. The *gāti* is certainly not a lineage, for according to current usage this term denotes only a unilateral descent group, and then, of course, the *matakeinaga*, cannot be a clan, as it frequently has been called.

Firth feels (or felt at least in 1929) that owing to the strong tendency among the Maoris to trace descent through the male line, whenever possible, the word clan "may be retained for ease of reference and theoretical comparison, so long as its present connotation is remembered. To apply the term 'clan' to a non-exogamous, not strictly patrilineal or matrilineal group may seem to conflict somewhat with general usage; if its significance as shown in this context is borne in mind, however, no confusion need arise" (Firth, p. 98).

Later students of the social organization in Polynesia have not followed this suggestion, but have instead used the word "kindred". Unfortunately there has been a general vagueness about the definition of this term, and I was like Firth inclined to call the *matakeinaga* a quasi-clan, when I found Goodenough's excellent clarification of the matter in the February, 1955 issue of the *American Anthropologist*. Goodenough there shows (pp. 71—72) convincingly that the current confusion is due to the fact that in the literature the word kindred has two disctinct meanings. "Rivers (1926 a: 15—16) and Murdock (1949: 56—62) both treat the kindred as a group of persons who have a relative in common, regardless of whether kinship is traced through men or women. Such people cannot all be related to one another ... As defined in *Notes and Queries* (1929: 55), on the other hand, the term kindred 'should be limited to a group of persons who acknowledge their descent, genealogically or by adoption, from one family, whether through their fathers or mothers'. Here, a kindred refers to people who have an ancestor in common as distinct from people who have a relative in common. In this sense a kindred has continuity through time and all its members are related to one another. As *Notes and Queries* defines it, a kindred is any nonunilinear descent group; as Murdock and Rivers define it, it is not a true descent group at all. The source of confusion has clearly been the feature common to both types of group: in both cases consanguineal connections are traced through either sex. The difference is that in the kindred of Rivers and Murdock these connections are traced *laterally* to a common relative, while in the kindred of *Notes and Queries* they are traced *lineally* to a common ancestor. I wish to suggest that the kindred in the latter sense must be added to the kindred in Murdock's sense as an element in the social organization or early Malayo-Polynesian society. Hereinafter, I shall reserve the term kindred for the bilateral group which Rivers and Murdock had in mind and shall refer to the group defined by *Notes and Queries* as a nonunilinear descent group."

"Nonunilinear descent group" does not seem to be a term with enough appeal to become generally accepted and it is tempting to try here to achieve immortality (at least in anthropological circles) by introducing a new term. As, however, competition is keen and success rare in this field I shall limit myself to the more modest task of combining terms already in existence and call the two groups simply *lateral kindred* (bilateral) and *lineal kindred* (nonunilinear). Both were obviously present on Raroia in pre-European times, the lineal kindred being the *matakeinaga,* and the lateral kindred corresponding to a still well-known group called *kave*. As for *gāti,* it must for lack of a shorter and more precise term be labelled "a bilateral or unrestricted descent group".[1]

No term seems to have existed for the extended family. My principal informant, Te Iho, used *utuafare,* "household", which is a recently introduced Tahitian word, when speaking of this important social unit, and when asked to give the ancient word he replied that there was none. This is not so surprising as it at first appears, since the Tuamotuan kindred was always small. (Compare the Maori kindred which comprised several hundred members and where a special term, *whanau,* existed for the extended family). The lack of such a term certainly did not involve practical difficulties, as the members of an extended family were and still are referred to by the name of the head, to which the suffix—*ma* is added. E.g. "Hurima" means all persons living in Huri's household. Goodenough's fifth kin group, *kainga,* "a nonunilinear descent group based on parental residence" (p. 73) may have existed in former times, for Te Iho knew the term. His only explanation was, however, that it was an "ancestral land" *(fenua tupuna),* which does not clarify the matter much more than the following references in Stimson's Tuamo-

---

[1] Murdock (p. 62) deplores the fact that no larger bilateral kinship groups "have received extensive theoretical consideration in the literature", but proposes (p. 63) only one new term, *deme,* which he wants to use for an *endogamous* non-unilinear descent group.

tuan manuscript dictionary: "Kāiga—Home land, inherited land (literally 'place of eating'), kāiga tupuna—1. Ancestral land, 2. Heritage."

Mühlmann, who has written an etymologic-historical study called *Die Begriffe 'Ati und Mataeinaa: Ein Beitrag zur politischen Entwicklung und Besiedlungsgeschichte Polynesiens*, thinks that the two words *matakeinaga (mata'eina'a)* and *kaiga (kainga)* stem from the same root. "The constructed original Polynesian form of *mataeinaa* is exactly *matakaianga-anga* oder *mata-kaiangānga*, contracted to *mata-kainanga*. Such a form may be expected in, for instance, Tong. or Fut. as the oldest Polynesian dialects. But the concept as a whole does not exist in Western Polynesia at all, at least not in the form containing the part *mata*. This part must therefore have some sort of differential sociological significance for Tahiti and Hawaii as opposed to Western Polynesia."[1] The observation on the limited distribution of the word *matakeinaga* is valuable, but it is very doubtful whether there is any etymologic relationship between this word and *kāiga*. According to Stimson's dictionary *matakeinaga* is derived from the word *kei* whose basic significance is "bone". This is only said in passing, as the etymologic and historical derivations of course, have very little importance for the sociological analysis here.

Not only Goodenough's distinction but also his explanation of the relationship between the land area and the Gilbertese *oo* descent group (= *gāti*) applies to the situation on Raroia. He writes (p. 80): "In any community where cultivable land is not over-abundant in relation to population, and all rights to land depend on membership in strictly unilinear kin groups, a serious problem must soon arise. Unilinear groups inevitably fluctuate considerably in size. The matrilineal lineages on Truk, for example, readily double or halve their membership in the space of one or two generations. As a result, one lineage may have twice as much land as its members need while another has not enough to go around. Unless devices are developed to redistribute land rights to persons outside the owning group, intracommunity conflict is inevit-

---

[1] "Die konstruierte polynesische Urform für *mataeniaa* lautet exakt *matakaianga-anga* oder *mata-kaiangānga*, abgeschliffen *mata-kainanga*. Eine solche Form dürfen wir etwa im Tong. oder Fut. als den ältesten polynesischen Idiomen erwarten. Aber der Begriff als Ganzes findet sich in Westpolynesien überhaupt nicht, wenigstens nicht in der Fassung, die den Bestandteil *mata* enthält. Dieser Bestandteil muss also irgendwie differentiell-soziologisch für Tahiti und Hawaii gegen Westpolynesien bedeutsam sein." (Mühlmann, p. 748.)

able ... One of the simplest possible devices for achieving this end is to keep the land-owning groups nonunilinear. With the *oo* type of group a person has membership in as many *oo* as there are distinct land-owning ancestors of whom he is a lineal descendant. While he can expect a lot of land from those which have few surviving members. The overlapping memberships inevitable with unrestricted descent groups make them an excellent vehicle for keeping land holdings equitably distributed throughout the community."

The second comment I wish to make has to do with the subsistence economy. Te Iho stated repeatedly that though the Raroians greatly appreciated coconuts, there were in pre-European times—and even in his youth—very few palm trees on the island. The words "very few" I was for a long time inclined to regard as really meaning a considerable number, as even, let us say, some thousand palm trees undoubtedly would be "very few" compared with the 150,000—200,000 palm trees on the atoll to-day. As each palm tree produces 50—100 nuts a year, (which means that 20—25 palm trees amply provide for an individual's needs) and the population was only some hundred persons, I thought that around ten thousand palm trees in pre-European times was a fair guess.

But the unanimous testimonials of the missionaries who visited the group in the 1870s first made me doubt that there were even that many palms on most atolls, and later findings seem to indicate that Te Iho's statement must probably be taken literally.

The earliest visitors to the group are unfortunately all very vague about the extent to which the atolls were planted with coconut palms and the first to give us any detailed information is Lucett who made several cruises through the group in the 1840s. (His interest is easily explained by the fact that he bought up coconuts.) During a cruise in 1842 he saw, for instance, only "a few groves of cocoa-nut trees" on Amanu (I, p. 242) and adds that "the cocoa-nut is not abundant, and the fruit is only partaken of on rare occasions". (I, p. 247.) He seems surprised that Takume "has some beautiful groves of cocoa-nut trees" (I, p. 256) and only Anaa was found to be "densely covered with cocoa-nut trees" (I, p. 238). How exceptional this was is shown by the remark that the Anaa natives "are alive to the advantage the cocoa-nut tree gives them over their neighbours". (I, p. 260.) During a voyage in 1844 Lucett says that on Akiaki "two cocoa-nut trees were all that could be

Te Iho a Te Page, the last native *tahūga* historian and my main informant about the ancient culture and pre-European history of Raroia.

When making copra outside the modern village of Garumaoa the Raroians revert partly to ancient customs and live in palm leaf huts of pre-European type.

PLATE 2

PLATE 3 Russian naval officers exchanging gifts with Tuamotuan natives during Bellingshausen's passage through the group in 1820, when, among other atolls, Takume and Raroia were discovered. (Engraving from Bellingshausen's account, plate XII.)

The devastation of the 1903 cyclone on Hikueru atoll immediately south of Raroia, which was also situated directly in the path of the cyclone and greatly ravaged. (Photo by courtesy of J. Mervin, Papeete.)

seen above the low intricate scrub". (II, p. 57.) A reference to Ravahere runs (II, p. 59): "On the west end of the south extreme we noted a solitary cluster of cocoa-nut trees." Even in 1848 "there were only three or four cocoa-nut trees to be seen" (II, p. 199) on Ahe, one of the westernmost atolls, and on Tikahau Lucett noticed only "a few cocoa-nut trees on its north-west side". (II, p. 203.) These quotations should suffice to prove that the number of coconut trees in the Tuamotus was actually, as Te Iho claims, very small in pre-European times.[1]

How can this undeniable scarcity of palm trees be explained? Father Fierens gives us an important clue when he says that "their religious superstitions were also the reason why almost all these populations starved to death. When it happened that a man died all his possessions were immediately burnt, his plantations destroyed and his coconut palms mercilessly cut down in order to offer their core to his manes."[2]

A still more important reason for the scarcity of palm trees was that they were also deliberately cut down during the frequent wars or raids. Moerenhout (II, p. 371) mentions such instances and Lucett writes specifically that the Anaa warriors "some years ago ... overran nearly every island in the group, burning and slaying all before them; rooting up, and destroying every cocoa-nut tree standing, which accounts for their scarcity at the other islands". (I, p. 260.) The number of coconut palms must, however, obviously have been rather limited already before this wanton destruction, otherwise it would certainly not have been possible for the raiding parties to diminish the number of trees so rapidly and thoroughly.

Before finishing this short chapter I should like to extend the horizon for a moment and add a few words about the place of the

[1] On none of the *uninhabited* atolls that Lucett visited (see e.g. I, pp. 240, 286, 331, 340) did he find any coconut trees. Pickering (p. 60), who made the same observation, says: "So invariably is its presence attributable to human operations, that it has become a guide to the traders in seeking for natives." These facts hint that the coconut palm may have been carried to the Polynesian islands by human agents to a greater degree than hitherto realized, as suggested by Heyerdahl (p. 460).

[2] "C'étaient leurs superstitions religieuses qui étaient aussi la cause que presque toutes ces populations mouraient de faim. Un homme venait-il à mourir, aussitôt on brûlait ce qui lui avait appartenu, on détruisait ses plantations, et on coupait impitoyablement tous ses cocotiers, pour en offrir le cœur à ses mânes." (Fierens, 1872, p. 136.)

CHAPTER II: *Aboriginal culture*

Tuamotu group in Polynesia. That Tuamotuan culture had all the basic traits in common with the other eastern groups and New Zealand—and very few in common with western Polynesia—is clearly shown by Burrow's detailed study (1938) of cultural sub-areas in Polynesia. How great the cultural homogeneity actually was in pre-European times is best expressed in a later paper by Burrows (1940, pp. 350 —351) where he says that "many of the cultural differences within Polynesia do not coincide with differences in geographic environment. According to geographic environment, New Zealand would be set off from the rest of Polynesia by its cooler climate and different flora and fauna. The rest of Polynesia would be subdivided into high islands and atolls, because the two differ in soil and water supply, and hence in flora and fauna. Since high islands are as a rule not only richer in natural resources than atolls, but also larger in area, they can support far larger populations. Correlated with these differences are some differences in culture. So it would be possible to subdivide Polynesian cultures according to these geographic considerations. But the main regional variations within Polynesian culture do not coincide with geographic differences. The areas and centres ... will follow differences that seem most satisfactorily explained in terms of invention and diffusion."[1]

Murdock has in his recent epoch-making study, *Social Structure,* summarized (pp. 228—231) the available data on Polynesian social organisation and finds (p. 228) that "this structural type embraces all societies possessing cousin terms of Hawaiian type and lacking exogamous unilinear kin groups. In addition, it is characterized by the exceedingly frequent appearance of limited polygyny, the bilocal extended family, generation terminology for aunts and nieces, bilateral extension of incest taboos, and bilateral kindreds or demes." No data from the Tuamotus

---

[1] Whether we can speak about cultural differences or not in specific cases, evidently depends on the "scale" used, as the same author rightly points out (Burrows, 1940, p. 350): "There have been several attempts to apply the culture-area and culture-centre concepts to Polynesia. In any such attempt the first question to decide is what scale to use. If the criteria are of an order of magnitude like those that differentiate Wissler's culture-areas of North America, then Polynesia is emphatically all one culture-area. If comparatively minute differences are chosen, culture-areas and -centres will, of course, multiply in number. Thus, Skinner has outlined several culture-areas within New Zealand."

were available to Murdock, but judging from the evidence presented in this chapter the social organisation obviously conformed to the general Polynesian pattern.

As for the Tuamotuan economic system we can on the basis of the same evidence conclude that it was as everywhere else in Polynesia a food-gathering and planting economy without any surplus. A peculiar and important feature of this system has been pointed out by Herskovits (1952, p. 225): "Only in Polynesia, of all the principal areas of the world, do we find the exchange of goods on a non-ceremonial basis almost entirely lacking ... Markets, as such, are thus practically unknown. The subsistence needs of all are satisfied by their own economic self-sufficiency, while the acquisition of prestige is cared for by the lavish gift-giving that marks the feasts given on occasions of special importance."

CHAPTER III · **History of culture contacts**

Though most of the other Polynesian groups have attracted the attention of competent historians, no comprehensive and reliable history of the Tuamotu group has yet been published. The only attempts so far are a paper by Beltran y Rozpide, *Las Islas Tuamotu*, a chapter by Eugène Caillot in his *Histoire de la Polynésie Orientale*, and a book entitled *Histoire des religions de l'archipel Paumotu* by the same author. Beltran y Rozpide gives, however, only an incomplete list of the early visitors to the group, and Caillot's accounts, which are rather biased, deal principally with pre-European beliefs and the efforts of the Catholic missionaries from 1849 onwards. Lacking a general account dealing with both the political, economic and religious history of the group I have here gathered the scattered references found in the relations of various sea voyagers, official documents and missionary correspondences, and tried to discern the main trends.

1. Occasional visits by exploring ships, 1606–1816

Quiros must be considered the discoverer of the Tuamotu group, though it should be borne in mind that he naturally only sighted a few of the 78 atolls when he passed through the archipelago early in 1606 while searching for Terra Australis Incognita, the fictive continent which at that time tempted all explorers. The first atoll discovered by Quiros was probably South Marutea. Between this and Anaa he saw about another half a dozen, but it is impossible to say which they were since longitude at that time could only be determined by dead reckoning, a very unreliable method.

Anaa was sighted on the 10th February and smoke showed clearly that the island was inhabited which led Quiros to attempt a landing for the first time. Four members of the crew swam ashore through the surf and found a friendly reception. Quiros therefore stayed all night outside the island, which has no pass, and next day sent a group of men ashore in a boat to look for drinking water. Having replenished his water supply and gathered some coconuts Quiros departed the same evening. Before he left the Tuamotu group he sighted a few more atolls, one of which, Makatea, is easily identifiable while the others were probably Niau and Mataiva. No attempts were made to go ashore, however, and no contact was established with the inhabitants of any of these islands.

Previous to this first recorded visit to the group some sort of contact must have been made, for Quiros tells a strange tale of an old native woman who came aboard his ship wearing a "gold ring with an emerald on one of her fingers. She was asked for it, but replied by signs that she could not give it without cutting off her finger, and she seemed sorry for this. She was offered one of brass, which she did not care for" (I, p. 201). According to another chronicler the Spaniards also found on the island "half of a cedar pole, which had been worked on the coast of Nicaragua or Peru". (Quiros, II, p. 337.) The most probable explanation is that the ring was part of some flotsam, which like the cedar pole had drifted with the south equatorial current from the South American coast. With our present knowledge of the force and constancy of this current, we may presume that wreckage can also occasionally have been washed ashore on other atolls of the Tuamotu group. During my repeated stays on Raroia it happened more than once that I found glass floats for fishing nets of Peruvian origin. The influence of such wreckage on the native culture cannot of course have been anything but very slight, but it must at least have made the natives conscious of the existence of other peoples and cultures at a very early date.

Ten years after Quiros' hurried passage though the Tuamotus the Dutchmen Le Maire and Schouten sailed through the northern part of the group while on a trading voyage around the world. In contrast to Quiros they went ashore on almost every atoll they discovered. The first island they visited was Pukapuka, which they sighted on their east-to-west course on the 10th April 1616; it was uninhabited and they did not investigate it more closely. On the evening of the 14th April they came to the next atoll, Takaroa, after having passed almost within sight of Takume and Raroia. At some distance from the beach they were met by two canoes manned by natives. These "kept motioning us to the land and we them to the ship", says the chronicler (Le Maire, p. 193), but no closer contact than this was established. Since it was late in the day the Dutchmen immediately continued to the neighbouring atoll of Takapoto, where at dawn next day they discovered a group of armed men on the reef. After a while a few natives came out in a canoe but did not dare to go aboard the ship. However, they allowed an officer and some men, who rowed out to them in the ship's shallop, to approach, and the Dutchmen presented them with some beads and knives as a sign of their friendly intentions. The natives eventually came alongside the ship, and one of them "got into the gallery and pulled out the nails in the port-holes of the cabins belonging to the supercargo and the skipper, hiding them away and concealing them in his hair; they were very greedy after iron, indeed, they pulled at and thought they could drag out the bolts in the ship". (Le Maire, p. 194.) This behaviour seems to point to a previous acquaintance with iron and confirms the opinion just expressed that wreckage and other objects had repeatedly reached the Tuamotu group at an early period.

Le Maire and Schouten sent a group of sailors ashore, but no sooner had they landed than about 30 natives broke out of the bush and tried to snatch their weapons and seize the boat. The Dutchmen opened fire and killed or fatally wounded "a few". (Le Maire, p. 194.) The natives threw stones at them, but no one was injured. After this failure to establish peaceful contact with the natives, Le Maire and Schouten continued their journey westward. On the 18th April they discovered an island which judging by the latitude they give must have been Manihi or Ahe, where the crew with great difficulty succeeded in filling and taking aboard four barrels of water and a sack of "herb".[1] (Le Maire, p. 196.) "Shortly after" (Le Maire, p. 196) they sighted still another atoll, which most geographers have identified as Rangiroa, but their

---

[1] This herb which later visitors usually called scurvy grass was certainly the *nau* or *horahora* of the natives. The scientific name is *Lepidium bidentatum*.

visit there was of short duration, as the Dutchmen were put to flight by intolerable swarms of flies. Thereupon Le Maire and Schouten left the Tuamotu group.

The next European visitor arrived in the group more than a century later, in 1722. He too was a Dutchman, Roggeveen. Intentionally he followed the same route as Le Maire and Schouten. After having sighted and coasted a small atoll, probably Tikei, on the 18th May, Roggeveen's little fleet of three ships continued the following day due west. During the night one of the vessels, the *Afrikaansche Galei,* separated from the others and was wrecked on the reef of an island which Roggeveen for this reason called Pernicious (Schadelijk) Island. After many hardships the lifeboats of the remaining ships succeeded several days later in saving the crew of the *Afrikaansche Galei.* In connection with this rescue there was one remarkable event. Roggeveen gives this account of it: "The loss of such a good and seaworthy ship is the greater, since most of the bread and groats supply in barrels, which was still as good to eat as when it left home, was lost, as the ship aground on the sharp coral reef immediately sprung a leak and was filled with water; so that the crew could only save enough food and strong liquor to last them for a few days: which liquor is possibly also the reason why two sailors from the *Arend* and three from the *Thienhoven* have decided to stay there; for when the last vessel left the shore these hasty hands appeared, calling: 'We wish you a prosperous journey, say good night to our friends in Amsterdam, we are staying here!' Further the chief carpenter of the *Galei* and two or three others of the crew say that the crazy deserters had asked them to stay there too, which resolve is all the more incomprehensible, since they cannot be ignorant of the fact that no shipping touches the place, so that they cannot at any time (when they change their minds) return to their own country. They also know that the island is inhabited, and if driven by intoxication or lust they try to have intercourse with the women of the Indians[1] they will surely be murdered."[2]

[1] Most European visitors called the Polynesians "Indians" until the end of the 19th century.

[2] "Die verlies van soo een goed en welbeseyld Ship is des te grooter, aangesien de voornaamste levensmiddeln van brood en gort, in vaatwerk, en nu nog soo deugtsaam als wanneer hy uyt 't Vaderland vertrocken was, al te samen, sonder iets te hebben konnen salveeren, verloren sijn, vermits het Schip, op de scherpe Coraalklippen stootende,

The historians who have touched upon this episode differ in their opinions regarding the identity of Roggeveen's Pernicious Island. But one important fact strongly points to Takapoto; Moerenhout records how on his visit to Takapoto in 1830 the natives "spoke of cannons. At first I did not know what they meant and I thought they were asking if there were any aboard, but at last I understood that they were speaking of cannons that they had ashore. Curious to see them I had them shown to me at once; but I found them in such a state that nothing could be distinguished. The natives told me that they came from a vessel that had foundered on their shores a very long time ago."[1]

Whatever may be the truth about the identity of Roggeveen's Pernicious Island, the fact that at this early date five Europeans stayed behind on one of the atolls together with some equipment from the wrecked *Afrikaansche Galei* is of some interest. To what extent these Dutchmen may have influenced the native culture is of course a matter of conjecture, but I at all events think it much more likely than did Roggeveen that their lives were spared. The Tuamotuans sometimes gave shelter to shipwrecked persons and, like all other Polynesians, they greatly admired the white complexion and were therefore especially inclined to treat Europeans with a certain veneration.

[1] Les Indiens "me parlèrent de canon. Je ne savais pas d'abord ce qu'ils voulaient dire, et je croyais qu'ils s'informaient s'il y en avait à bord; mais je compris enfin qu'ils parlaient de pièces de canon qu'ils avaient à terre. Curieux de les voir, je m'y fis conduire de suite; mais je les trouvai en tel état, qu'on ne pouvait rien distinguer. Les naturels me dirent qu'ils provenaient d'un bâtiment qui s'était perdu sur leurs côtes, il y avait bien long-temps;" (Moerenhout, I. pp. 204–205.)

---

in 't kort geborsten en vol water was; soo dat het volk alleen voor eenige weynige daegen van spijs en sterken drank in staat is geweest te konnen bergen: welke sterken drank mogelijk ook de oorsaak is, dat twee Matroosen van 't Schip den Arend, en drie van Thienhoven, goedgevonden hebben aldaar te blyven; want het laetste vaartuyg van de wal vertreckende, quamen die onbesonne gasten te voorschijn, roepende: Wy wenschen u een behoude reys, segt onse vrinden t'Amsterdam goede nagt, wy sullen hier blyven. Voorts segt den Oppertimmerman van de Galey en nog twee à drie andere van 't volk, dat die uytsinnige weglopers haar aangesogt hebben om insgelijx aldaar te blyven: welke resolutie des te onbegrypelyker is, alsoo haar niet onbekent kan sijn, dat die plaats van alle scheepvaart ontbloot sy, om dus t' eeniger tijd (wanneer sy sullen resipeeren) weder in hun Vaderland te konnen keeren. Ook is haar kenlijk dat het Eyland bewoond word, en door dronkenschap of dartele wellust gedreven werdende, om met de vrouwen der Indianen vleeschelyke gemeenschap te hebben, sy sekerlijk sullen vermoord worden." (Roggeveen, pp. 145–146.)

During the rest of his journey through the Tuamotu group Roggeveen encountered further difficulties. After having at the last minute avoided running aground again—probably in the narrow strait between Kaukura, Toau, Arutua and Apataki—he landed on Makatea on the 2nd June in order to collect scurvy grass. The natives seemed hostile and brandished their spears, but after the Dutchmen had fired a volley of musketry and given mirrors and other trinkets as tribute, they helped the sailors to collect scurvy grass. The next day the Dutchmen returned, but when they had moved halfway up to the plateau (Makatea is a raised coral atoll) they met the islanders and their chief, who signed to them not to continue. Since the Dutchmen paid no attention to the warning, the natives attacked with their stones slings. The Dutchmen opened fire, killing many natives and injuring the chief. The islanders were now seized with frenzy and pelted the intruders with such a rain of stones that they were eventually forced to retreat. Several Dutchmen were killed.

The next white man to sail through Tuamotuan waters was Byron, commanding the *Dolphin* and the *Tamar,* who discovered Napuka and Tepoto on the 7th June 1765, but was unable to land owing to the high breakers and hostile attitude of the inhabitants. On the 9th June Byron arrived on Takaroa; he, too, was obviously unwilling to leave the track of Le Maire and Schouten. In desperate need of scurvy grass and fresh fruit, the Englishmen tried to land the next day, but the inhabitants showed them by every means that they were not welcome. When the natives went so far as to send out some large canoes to chase the ship's boat, the English attacked and opened fire on the fleeing aggressors. Two or three of these were killed. Later, when the natives were gathering around their canoes on the beach, they were fired on again. They fled in terror, and when the English went ashore next morning they found all the huts abandoned and could collect coconuts and scurvy grass undisturbed. (Byron, pp. 97—101.)

While investigating the huts Byron's men were surprised to find "the carved head of a rudder, which had manifestly belonged to a Dutch longboat, and was very old and worm-eaten. They found also a piece of hammered-iron, a piece of brass, and some small iron tools, which the ancestors of the present inhabitants of this place probably obtained from the Dutch ship to which the longboat had belonged, all which I brought away with me." (Byron, p. 102.) This rudder certainly belonged to the *Afrikaansche Galei,* and further strengthens the theory that the wreck occurred on the neighbouring island Takapoto, with which Takaroa formed a political unit similar to that of Takume and Raroia. After a short call at Takapoto, where the inhabitants were unafraid and friendly and some gifts were exchanged, Byron quickly left the Tuamotu group.

During the ten years immediately following Byron's visit, a surprisingly large number of ships found their way to the Tuamotu group. During his circumnavigation of the world, which led to the discovery of Tahiti, Wallis sighted six atolls in the Tuamotu group. He sent exploring parties ashore on two of them, Pinaki and Nukutavake, but only on the latter atoll did the Englishmen make any contact with the natives. After the ship had fired a nine-pounder the landing party exchanged gifts with them for some hours. When a musket was fired next day in order to induce the natives to continue the barter, they left, however, and sailed across to a neighbouring island. (Robertson, pp. 118 —122.) Wallis's companion Carteret on the *Swallow,* with whom he had lost contact immediately after the passage through the Straits of Magellan, sighted three of the southernmost atolls of the group. Bougainville in the following year, 1768, saw eleven atolls and skirted the coasts of several so closely that he could distinguish groups of natives. He considered however, that the islands were not worth wasting time on and steered a more southerly course in order to get out of the group as quickly as possible. (Bougainville, p. 182.)

During his first voyage Captain Cook sighted seven atolls in the southern part of the Tuamotu group in April 1769. Several of these were previously unknown, but no contact with the natives was established anywhere. During his second voyage he discovered three new atolls while cruising through the group in August 1773. In April the following year he saw a few more but stopped only at Takaroa and Takapoto, where gift exchanges took place. The natives seemed to resent his visit (Cook, 1777, I, p. 313), which is not surprising, as the calls of European ships at Takaroa and Takapoto had by now become quite numerous. George Forster (II, p. 43) mentions that Cook fired a cannon shot over the head of the natives to take the conceit out of them before he left. This was Cook's last call in the Tuamotu group, for his third voyage took him to other parts of the Pacific before he finally met his death on Hawaii in Kealakekua Bay.

Disturbed by the British penetration of the Pacific, which they regarded as their sphere of interest, the Spaniards sent a number of expeditions to Tahiti at the same time as Cook's second voyage, so as to assure themselves of a foot-hold. But they showed surprisingly little interest in the six atolls of the Tuamotu group which they saw or discovered during their three expeditions to Tahiti, and only once during the second expedition, late in 1774, did they go ashore on Anaa. The natives met them with a rain of stones, but when the Spaniards had let off a few warning shots they calmed down and an exchange of gifts took place. (Corney, II, pp. 112—114.)

After the last Spanish expedition under Langara had passed through the Tuamotu group in 1775 fifteen whole years went by before a European vessel was once more seen in these waters. This was the British man-of-war *Pandora,* which on her outward voyage to Tahiti in March 1791 passed South Marutea and Tureia. At the beginning of 1792 the whaler *Mathilda* was wrecked on a desert atoll, Mururoa, but the crew managed to reach Tahiti in the lifeboats. (Wilson, p. 34.) A few months later Captain Bligh on his second voyage to Tahiti discovered another of the southernmost atolls, Tematangi. Neither Edwards on the *Pandora* nor Bligh tried, however, to explore the new atolls they discovered.

In 1797 Captain Wilson on the missionary ship *Duff* twice passed through the Tuamotu group and sighted South Marutea and Pukarua the first time and Takaroa, Takapoto, Arutua and several other neighbouring islands the second. Only on Pukarua, however, did he send ashore a party of his men, but they found the island uninhabited. (Wilson, pp. 119—126).

The English trader Turnbull made two unsuccessful attempts to start bartering, when coming from the south he passed through the group in March 1803. The first attempt occurred on Nukutipipi, previously discovered by Carteret, and the second on Manihi. Between the visits to these two islands Turnbull discovered two new atolls, Makemo and Taenga, immediately east of Raroia. Later the same year he lost his ship—which he had over-optimistically sent out from Tahiti in order to buy pigs—"on a low reef of rocks and sand-banks, in the vicinity of a cluster of islands called the Pallisers, in latitude 15° 38′ south, and longitude 146° 30′ west". (Turnbull, p. 302.) This position corresponds to the northern shore of Kaukura, which is one of the islands in the cluster where Roggeveen got entangled, and as no other under-water reefs exist here, the ship must have been wrecked on the rim of the atoll itself. The crew were forced to put up a continuous defence against the natives until eventually they were able to return to Tahiti on an improvised barge. After this unfortunate incident no further visits are recorded before the Russian Kotzebue appeared in 1816—an interval which must have been due in some degree to the state of anarchy and civil war existing through almost all that period in Tahiti, where the only safe harbour in this part of the Pacific is to be found. Kotzebue sighted half a dozen atolls in the Tuamotu group, but sent ashore a landing party only on Pukapuka, which at that time was still uninhabited.

It is not altogether impossible that some whaler, merchantman or other type of vessel, about whose voyages accounts are rarely published, also passed through the group at the end of the 18th or the beginning of the 19th century. Whaling had begun in the southern part of the Pacific in 1787, and before the turn of the century trading ships began to buy up sandalwood in Polynesia. (Kuykendall, p. 82.) But the whalers sought protected harbours, plentiful supplies of fresh food and willing women, and in eastern Polynesia these were not to be found in the Tuamotu group but only on high islands such as Tahiti and Nukuhiva. Sandalwood, too, was only found on the high, mountainous islands. There was therefore no reason to visit the Tuamotu atolls, especially as the surrounding waters are difficult to navigate. Finally, it must be remembered that the number of whalers and merchantmen in the southeastern Pacific during this period was still very small (for instance, only a score of calls of such ships at Tahiti are listed during the period 1797—1816 in the missionaries' correspondence in *Transactions of LMS*). The influence of such possibly unrecorded visits to the Tuamotu group need not therefore be considered.

To summarize, of the fourteen known European visitors between 1606 and 1816, six did not bother to land or landed on uninhabited atolls. Of the remaining eight only the first visitor, Quiros, seems to have had exclusively friendly relations with the natives. All the others were involved in skirmishes and obliged (or at least they pretended so) to make a show of force. In spite of the hostilities gifts were often exchanged, and the European articles given the natives are specified in two cases. Byron (p. 106) traded with beads, nails, hatchets and bill-hooks, and Wallis (pp. 425, 428) with beads, nails, ribands, knives, hatchets, glass bottles, shillings and sixpences! The effects on the natives of these contacts were of course slight, and only two are worth mentioning. In the first place the skirmishes probably confirmed the natives in their previous belief that a stranger invariably is an enemy. In the second place the size of the ships and the superiority of the articles they got in exchange must clearly have indicated that these white men were very powerful. As for Raroia, no ship called there during this period, but a friendly alliance existed between that island and Takaroa-Takapoto, which were visited by several ships, and the Raroians were therefore certainly at an early date well informed about the occurrences in that part of the group.

2. Missionary fore-runners and traders, 1817–44

From the year 1817 onwards a marked religious and political influence from Tahiti began to make itself felt in the Tuamotus. Before that year the various atolls, with the possible exception of Makatea (Turnbull, p. 262), were all independent of the Tahitian rulers, but gradually ties of an increasingly more complex character were formed.

What paved the way for the recognition of Pomare II in certain parts of the Tuamotu group were the devastating raids that took place there between 1800 and 1815. Warriors from Anaa, the most fertile and populous of the atolls, started a violent expansion, plundered the surrounding islands, cut down the coconut palms, killed the men and took home the women and children as slaves. Moerenhout says (II, p. 371), that the Anaa-warriors eventually ruled over all the islands up to the "Palliser group" and "Tiooka" (Kaukura, Arutua, Apataki and Takaroa) in the North and as far as the "Two groups" (Marokau and Ravahere) in the East. According to Te Iho, Takume and Raroia were also raided by Anaa-warriors during this period, but the inhabitants managed to keep their independence.

The Anaa-warriors, who were appropriately called *parata* (the name of a man-eating shark) by the other natives, were especially barbarous to-

77

wards the inhabitants on Kaukura, Arutua, Apataki, Takaroa and Taka-poto, whom they "finally expelled and whom they had the audacity to pursue as far as Otaiti; but Pomare stopped the slaughter by offering the vanquished his hospitality and protection. He even ceded them some land in his district and forbade their embittered enemies to attack them or pursue them in his domains."[1] (See also Ellis, III, p. 305.)

When Pomare's own subjects renounced their ancient faith, the fugitives also "cast away the gods they had brought with them, and were instructed by the Missionaries". (Ellis, III, p. 305.) Among these Tuamotuan neophytes there were also some men from Anaa, and one of them, called Moorea, returning home in 1817, "began to instruct the people with such success, under the Divine blessing, that, with the exception of the inhabitants of one district, the population agreed to renounce heathenism. Moorea was subsequently charged with having deceived his countrymen in the accounts he had given of the change at Tahiti, and was obliged to leave the island, as his life was threatened." (Ellis, III, pp. 305–306.)

Hostilities evidently flared up afresh, for according to a reliable source Pomare II at last negotiated a peace in 1821 shortly before his death. At that time Pomare was at the height of his power. He had vanquished his last political and religious opponents in Tahiti and was the un-challenged ruler of the whole island. The entire population had been converted to the type of Christianity represented by the London Mis-sionary Society and all the missionaries, whose number had greatly increased between 1816 and 1820, were wholly on his side and supported him. It was therefore not surprising that Pomare could now act as a sort of arbiter between the various rulers on the most westerly atolls of the Tuamotu group. It should also be remembered that Pomare himself had Tuamotuan chiefs among his ancestors. (Corney, II, pp. XXXVI–XXXVII.)

The event is recorded as follows by two visiting inspectors from the London Missionary Society: "King Pomare, we found, when we arrived,

---

[1] Qu'ils "finirent par expulser, et qu'ils eurent l'audace de poursuivre jusqu'à O-taïti; mais Pomaré arrêta le carnage, en accordant l'hospitalité et sa protection aux vaincus. Il leur céda même quelques terres dans son district, et refusa à leurs ennemis acharnés la permission de les attaquer et de les poursuivre jusque dans ses domaines." (Moerenhout, II, p. 371.)

CHAPTER III: *History of culture contacts*

was on the adjacent island of Eimeo. Here a very interesting scene took place about six weeks before our arrival. A number of the Anaa people, or inhabitants of Chain Island, and Paumotans (both subjects of Pomare) assembled here. These tribes had long indulged towards each other the most rancorous hatred, and their islands being adjacent they were continually at war, in conducting which neither side gave quarter. The King determined, if possible, to subdue this enmity, and establish permanent peace between them. He therefore convened a meeting of the chiefs and principal personages, unarmed, on both sides. These were separately ranged in the two courts above mentioned, divided by a low fence. There stood Pomare, between the two parties, and in an impressive speech exhorted them to reconciliation. His arguments and his authority prevailed, and the representatives of both islands entered into an agreement upon the spot, that there should be no more war between their respective people, but that friendly intercourse should take the place of perpetual strife." (Tyerman and Bennet, I, p. 61.)

According to Teuira Henry, who confuses Pomare I with Pomare II, the king is also said to have "sent as representatives to his new islands two members of his family, whom he named Vaira'a-toa after himself, and Ari'i-Paea". (Henry, p. 111.) I infer from the sources quoted by Teuira Henry (probably Orsmond's notes) that the old rulers, Tepeva with his headquarters on Fakarava and Tufariua with his on Takaroa, continued to rule over Tapuhoe and Vahitu respectively (cf. Map A) while of Pomare's men Vaira'atoa became ruler of Taravaia with Kaukura as headquarters and Ari'ipaea ruled over Putahi (i.e. Anaa) with that island as headquarters. About the easternmost islands Henry says nothing, whereas a manuscript book from Raroia, which gives an identical account of the partition of the eastern half of the archipelago, adds the following interesting information: "From the border line of Pomare's part, from Hao and all the way windwards, [the part] is called Maragai. From the [same] border line and to Fagatau, Fakahina, Pukapuka, or Mahina-i-tetahora, Napuka and Tepoto, [the part] is called the Topitimaoake nation."[1]

---

[1] "O te otia ia o ta Pomare tufa raa, mai Hao e haere atu i te pae i nia, ua parau hia e Maragai. Mai te otia e haere atu i Fagatau, Fakahina, Pukapuka, oia hoi Mahina-te-Tahora, Napuka e Tepoto, ua parau hia nunaa Topitimaoake." (Paea, Book IV, p. 8.)

There was never any question, however, about effective sovereignty over the western islands, and I even doubt that Pomare's so-called "representatives" ever settled down in their domains, for they are never mentioned again in the narratives of sea captains, traders and other visitors to this part of the Tuamotus.

Missionary work progressed rapidly. "Early in 1822, Moorea and Teraa were publicly designated, by the members of the church in Wilkes' Harbour, as Christian teachers, and sailed for Anaa. Shortly afterwards a canoe from this island, which is situated in 17. S lat. 145. W. long. arrived at Tahiti. These dauntless sailors, who, in order to procure books, had traversed, in their rudely built vessels, a distance of three hundred miles, brought the pleasing tidings, that the inhabitants of Anaa were willing to receive Christianity, were building a place of worship in every district, that war, cannibalism, and other atrocities of idolatry, had ceased. Two other teachers, Manao and Mareuu, were afterwards sent to these [Tuamotu] islands." (Ellis, III, p. 306.)

We can therefore assume that from 1822 the inhabitants of the western atolls were nominally Christians and recognized Pomare's authority at least in principle. In 1825, when the missionary Crook visited the Tuamotu group, native missionaries had even reached Amanu, *southeast* of Raroia, but had been attacked. (Ellis, III, p. 307.) No later than the following year, Beechey reports (I, p. 243), however, from the neighbouring island of Hao, that he found a native missionary there who had "succeeded in persuading the greater parts of the islanders to conform to the ceremonies of Christian worship". As the new doctrines spread, a trend towards recognizing the suzerainty of the Pomare family, without accepting any restrictions in local government, gradually grew stronger in the western part of the group during the 1820s and 30s.

The relative pacification of the Tuamotus, which was the consequence of this religious and political expansion, also at last caused many traders to try their luck, and soon several schooners with Papeete as home port penetrated the group. What first tempted the traders were exclusively the large quantities of pearls and mother-of-pearl shells to be found in the lagoons of most of the atolls. The first European to notice the abundance of pearls and shells seems to have been Behrens, who served under Roggeveen. He writes: "We also found lots of mussels, shells, mother-of-pearl and pearl oysters, so that it seems that a profitable pearl fishing industry could there be established; forasmuch as we also found pearls in some oysters that the inhabitants had torn off the rocks."[1] Turnbull (p. 261) tried to land "two expert divers from the Sandwich Islands" on Manihi in 1803, but the inhabitants opposed the attempt.

The next writer to mention pearl fishing is Ellis, who relates that the missionaries on Tahiti together with king Pomare II even before 1820 thought of building a trading vessel and that "it was intended to employ the vessel in the pearl-fishery, among the Paumotu Islands to the eastward". (Ellis, II, pp. 239—240.) For some reason the plans were never put into action, but soon afterwards others began to collect mother-of-pearl shells in the group with the aid of native divers. As early as 1823 Lesson says (I, p. 253) about the Tuamotu group that it was the meeting place of British and American pearlfishers. In Papeete harbour he talked to the mate of a pearl-fishing vessel, who informed him that a trader employing thirty native divers could count on their collecting 1 ton of mother-of-pearl shells a day and that 20 tons of shells yielded 1 lb. of pearls on the average. (Lesson I, p. 254.) In 1826 Beechey (I, p. 229) encountered a pearlfishing brig as far east as Hao, and Moerenhout, who himself was actively engaged in pearlfishing in the 1830s, confirms (II, pp. 354—369) that other pearlfishing boats than his own visited the group, and mentions for instance (II, p. 323) that a Swedish captain had hired divers in the group already before 1827.

About the mother-of-pearl shell fishery Wilkes (II, p. 37) remarks that "from 1832 to '38, it had been very productive" and adds that the amount obtained was "about nine hundred tons", evidently referring to the annual production. Other products were not yet sought after in the Tuamotus during this period (Wilkes, I, p. 359), but the number of whalers calling at Papeete had increased to about fifty by the end of the 1830s (Wilkes, II, p. 51), and it is possible that some of them occasionally made short stops in the Tuamotus.

The exploring ships that visited the Tuamotu group during the 17th and 18th centuries had been too well armed and stayed too short a time

[1] Nous y trouvames aussi beaucoup de moules, de nacres, de mere-perle & d'huitres perlieres; de sorte qu'il y a beaucoup d'apparence, qu'on pourroit y établir une pêcherie de perle très-avantageuse; d'autant que nous trouvames aussi des perles dans quelques huitres, que les habitants avoient arrachées des rochers." (Behrens, pp. 148—149).

to be really endangered by the attacks the natives occasionally launched upon them. The pearl fishing ships cruising around the archipelago from the 1820s onwards were on the contrary unarmed, their calls often lasted for months and they were forced to transport and take aboard numbers of native divers. If we moreover bear in mind that these ships usually had large stocks of bartering goods on board, we easily understand that the natives were sometimes tempted to capture them. Such attacks were very common during the 1820s, and Beechey (I, pp. 281–283) gives the following unexpected explanation for them: Queen Pomare, "seeing the estimation in which the pearl oyster-shells were held by Europeans, imagined that by levying a duty on them she would greatly increase her revenue. Orders were accordingly issued to all the tributary islands to seize every vessel trading in shells, which had not previously obtained the royal licence to procure them. The Chain Islanders, who, from their enterprising and marauding habits, may be considered the buccaneers of the eastern South Sea archipelago, were too happy to find themselves fortified with a plea for a proceeding of this nature, and instantly sent one of their double canoes to Tiokea [Takaroa], where they found the Dragon, an English brig, taking in pearl shells. These people behaved in a very friendly manner to her crew, and allowed her quietly to take her cargo on board; but the Dragon was no sooner ready to put to sea, than several of the islanders went on board with the ostensible purpose of taking leave, but suddenly possessed themselves of the vessel, overpowering the master and crew, binding their hands, and sending them on shore as prisoners. A general plunder of the vessel ensued, in which every thing moveable was carried away. The natives, after this atrocious act, went to church to return thanks for their victory; and to render their prayers more acceptable, transferred the bell of the ship to their place of worship. During several days they detained the master bound hand and foot, and debated whether he should not be put to death and eaten; a fate which we were informed he would in all probability have encountered but for the interference of one of their chiefs, for the Tiokeans are still reputed to be cannibals, notwithstanding they have embraced the christian religion. The crew, more fortunate than their commander, very soon obtained their release, upon condition of fitting the brig for sea, the natives imagining they could navigate her themselves. The vessel being ready, the master, under some pretext, obtained permission to go on board, and having speedily established an under-standing with his crew, he cut the cables and carried her out to sea.

The stolen property was of course never recovered, and the vessel was so plundered of her stores that the object of her voyage was lost. When she reached Otaheite the master stated the case to the consul, whose representation of the outrage to the queen was, as has already been said, treated with derision. The consul availed himself of the present occasion to obtain restitution of the stolen property, or remuneration for the owners, and a repeal of the objectionable order, the execution of which it is evident could not be safely confided to a barbarous people, at all times too prone to appropriate to themselves whatever might fall within their reach. Her majesty was exceedingly unwilling to abandon this source of revenue, and strenuously urged her indubitable right to levy taxes within her own dominions, maintaining her arguments with considerable shrewdness, and appealing finally to the chiefs. Finding them, however, disposed to accede to the demands of the consul, she burst into tears; but at length consented, by their advice, to send a circular to the Pamoutas, or Low Islands, directing that no molestation should be offered to any vessels trading in shells, or touching at those islands for refreshment; but on the contrary that all necessary aid and assistance should be afforded to them; and that in the event of any dispute, the matter should be referred to the authorities at Otaheite."

The quotation clearly reveals the extent of the religious progress in the group and the true nature of Queen Pomare's sovereignty.

Later, too, occasional attacks on pearl fishing boats were made. Moerenhout (II, pp. 358–368) relates that one of his own pearl fishing ships was attacked in 1832 by hired divers from Anaa in collusion with the inhabitants of Hao. The ship was sacked completely after the whole crew had been taken prisoner. The captives were not rescued until some months later by a schooner despatched for that purpose, whose captain avenged the attack by taking two or three prisoners and burning all the canoes on the atoll. The following year a similar conspiracy was di-rected against another vessel during its call at Hao, but the plot was discovered in time and the ship managed to make a getaway. (Moeren-hout, II, p. 368.) Darwin notes in his diary (p. 399) on 22nd December 1835 that "about two years ago, a small vessel under English colours was plundered by some of the inhabitants of the Low Islands". Stories about seizures of this sort are still told on many islands. After the end of the 1840s, when the French had gained effective control over the greater part of the group such piratical incidents ceased completely, however. The last occurred in 1856, when the crew of the schooner Sarah-Anne were massacred by the natives of Tematangi. (Rey-Lescure, pp. 222—234.)

Let us now turn to the history of Raroia, which during the whole of this period played a very negligible part in the commercial and cultural exchanges. The island was evidently not mentioned or known by the Tahitian Tupaia, who as early as 1773—74 gave Cook valuable information about other atolls in the Tuamotu group (see map in J. R. Forster at p. 513), nor does it appear in the list which the Spaniards compiled with the aid of some Tahitians in 1774—75. (Corney, II, pp. 187—189.) Several of the earliest European sea captains passed close to Takume-Raroia during the period 1606—1816, but it was one of the last atolls in the group to be discovered. It was in fact found on the 12th July 1820 by the Russian naval officer Bellingshausen during his Antarctic journey. Bellingshausen has left us the first known map of Takume and Raroia, but he did not go ashore on either of the atolls, and his observations about Raroia are limited to the following brief remark in his account of the journey: "We soon sighted ahead another island bearing S.28°W. from the southern extremity of Prince Volkhonski Island and separated from it by a strait 4 miles wide. Proceeding towards it, we lay at noon off the north-eastern side of this island a mile from the shore. From observations we fixed the position of the *Vostok* at Lat. 15°57′52″S., Long. 142°12′11″W. From noon until nightfall we proceeded along the narrow eastern coral shore at a distance of from ½ to 2 miles; it is covered with scattered undergrowth and low trees. Surf was breaking heavily on this coral shore. The northern and western sides from which the lagoon was visible were quite covered with trees, and at various points on the north-western shore we could see smoke rising up out of the trees, which showed that the island was inhabited. Mr Lazarev informed me that he could see people and canoes on the shore.

The northern extremity of the island lies in Lat. 15°55′45″S., Long. 142°15′19″W. The southern extremity lies in Lat. 16°13′35″S., Long. 142°24′32″W.; the centre in Lat. 16°05′35″S., Long. 142°19′00″W. The island lies along a N. by E.½E. and S. by W.½W. direction. I made the length 21 miles, but Mr Lazarev found it to be only 16 miles and 7 miles wide at its greatest width, with a circumference of 44 miles. I called this island "Field Marshal Prince Barclay de Tolly[1] Island"." (Bellingshausen, I, pp. 235—236.) Bellingshausen discovered altogether eleven new atolls in the group and exchanged gifts with the natives of several of them.

Of the visitors to the group during the next 25 years who left accounts of their journeys (i.e. Tyerman & Bennet, Duperrey, Lesson, Kotzebue, Beechey, Downes, Moerenhout, Fitz-Roy, Darwin, Russell, Dumont d'Urville, Du Petit-Thouars, Wilkes, Belcher, Lucett) none landed on Raroia or published any information about the island.[2] But some inferences can be drawn from various general accounts. On his map of 1839 Commodore Wilkes (I, between pp. 316 and 317) places both Takume and Raroia just west of the line dividing the Tuamotu group into an eastern, still cannibalistic half and a western more civilized half. That this border actually ran between Takume-Raroia and Fangatau is confirmed by Lucett's account of the different receptions he met with on these islands in 1842. (I, pp. 249—257.) The natives on Fangatau were hostile and completely untouched by Western culture, and Lucett (I, p. 253) goes as far as to say that he was "the first white man they had ever touched". But on Takume, where incidentally he met natives from Anaa who had just completed a raid on Fangatau, he was well received, and stayed "four or five hours, trading for pearls and other island productions". (Lucett, I, p. 257.)

Wilkes' map of 1839, to which I have just referred, also includes another line of demarcation running from north to south immediately east of Takaroa-Raraka-Tahanea-Anaa and marked: "To the East of this line the missionaries have not extended." If by the term "mis-

---

[1] After Barclay de Tolly, Michael Andreas, 1761—1818, who was several times Russian Commander-in-Chief and minister of war. He is in Sweden principally known for his march across the ice-bound Gulf of Bothnia and capture of the Swedish town of Umeå in 1809, which feat brought the Finnish war to a victorious end for the Russians. This name is unknown to the Raroians to-day, and like the European names of the other atolls in the group never used in French Oceania.

[2] Both Meinicke (p. 366) and Buck (1953, p. 108) state erroneously that Lieutnant Ringgold of the US Exploring Expedition visited Raroia during the second survey of the Tuamotus in 1840. All Wilkes says (IV, p. 283) is that Ringgold's party on December 26 "made the island of Raroia, or Barclay de Tolly, and passed close to it".

sionaries" "European missionaries" is meant, the statement is true in so far as these had previously made only a few voyages through the group. However, in this case no clear line of demarcation is possible at all. If on the other hand the term "missionaries" refers to "native missionaries", the line must be shifted much further east and would probably even coincide with the "cannibal demarcation". It has already been related that a native missionary was active on Hao as early as 1826, and as regards Raroia, Te Iho maintains that native missionaries from Anaa had already spread the new gospel among the inhabitants "several years" before "Hau Farani" (i.e. the French Protectorate) was established in 1842. Even before the protectorate, which also included the Tuamotu group, the Raroians had formally recognized Queen Pomare's sovereignty, and Te Iho's father's office as a judge was, for example, confirmed by her.

It may be assumed that during the 1830s Raroia began to be visited by occasional schooners buying up mother-of-pearl shells or employing some islanders as divers. About Takume Lucett remarks that at the time of his visit in 1842 the natives already had "frequent intercourse with Anā, and vessels from Tahiti have had boats diving here". (Lucett, I, p. 256.) This statement is certainly also true for the neighbouring Raroia with which Takume, as previously mentioned, formed a political and cultural unit.

3. French penetration of the group, 1845–79

During the months from May to August 1842 a French squadron under Dupetit-Thouars took possession of the Marquesas Islands and on the 9th September of that year the Society Islands were declared a French protectorate. Since Queen Pomare considered herself to be the ruler of the whole Tuamotu group as well, Dupetit-Thouars did not take the trouble to make the chiefs of the various atolls sign deeds of cession, but considered them ceded with the Society Islands. The French stationed troops and naval squadrons in both the Marquesas Islands and Tahiti, but the inhabitants of the Tuamotus, who in most cases were completely unaware of the fact that they were now under French protection, were to discover only gradually what it meant to have representatives of a European power in the neighbourhood.

Since at the outset the political and military problems in Tahiti kept the French fully occupied, it was a long time before they began to try to organize the administration of the Tuamotu group, and as a rule the missionaries everywhere preceded the civil authorities. (This tendency has been very common in the Pacific as Koskinen has shown in his study *"The Missions as a Political Factor in the Pacific Islands"*.) But curiously enough, the first missionary to establish himself in the Tuamotu group was not a Frenchman but an American Mormon.

As early as May 1843 Joseph Smith decided to send missionaries out to the South Seas, and on the 9th October the men he had appointed, Noah Rogers, Benjamin Grouard, Addison Pratt and Knowlton Hanks left Boston. Hanks died soon after their departure, but the others reached their destination the next year. Pratt settled down on Tubuai and Rogers and Grouard on Tahiti. (Butterworth, p. 52.) On the 1st May 1845 Grouard arrived on Anaa, where his success was immediate. "Grouard remained on Anaa and began immediately to preach the gospel. On May 25, less than a month after he had landed on the island, he baptized his first six converts. By June 15th he had baptized about 24, all from the village where he lived. He toured the island of Anaa which took him fifteen days because he preached and lectured on the way. He preached 31 sermons in public, held countless discussions on religion and baptized 29 persons. From then on he baptized people almost daily. On September 21, 1845 the first general meetings of the church were held. Five branches were organized, and seventeen officers were set apart by ordination. From the time that Grouard had arrived on Anaa (a period of 4 months, 21 days) he had baptized 620 persons with bright prospects for many more." (Butterworth, p. 56.)

During the period 1846—1850, when Grouard was the only missionary of the Latter Day Saints in French Oceania he visited Anaa several times. In 1852 he returned to America and for the next 20 years the French authorities did not grant permission to him or any other of the missionaries of the Latter Day Saints to visit the islands in the new protectorate. During these years the Latter Day Saints mission in Tahiti was directed by a local American resident called John Hawkins, but the membership was small and no further attempts were made to spread the faith in the Tuamotu group. The new converts on Anaa did not hesitate to continue the mission work, however, and during the years immediately after their own conversion they visited practically all the atolls in the western half of the group, where they succeeded in converting a considerable number of natives, both heathens and those who had been converted to Protestantism by earlier native missionaries. The particular appeal of mormonism to the natives might to some extent be explained by the doctrine of polygamy.

This Mormon advance greatly alarmed the Catholic missionaries, who had already won a firm foothold in the neighbouring groups, Mangareva and the Marquesas. Not unexpectedly the initiative was taken by the oldest and most successful Catholic mission station, the one on Mangareva, which had been established as early as 1834. In a letter addressed to the superior general of his congregation the head of the Mangareva Mission, Father Laval, relates (1851, p. 398) that he, a colleague, Father Fouquet, and a young native from the Tuamotus, Makipotero or Pierre Maki, arrived at Faaite via Tahiti on the 19th May 1849 in order to start mission work.

Laval and Fouquet went on by canoe from Faaite to Fakarava, the home of their native assistant. The considerable influence of Pierre Maki, who belonged to one of the principal families of the atoll, contributed to the progress of the mission and in the district of Tetamanu particularly a large number of neophytes had soon been made. Now and then the missionaries visited the neighbouring island of Faaite, where also a good many souls were saved. (Terlyn, p. 188.) Without winning Anaa, which now as previously held a key position in the group, the chances of complete success were small, however, and the Catholic mission therefore decided to concentrate on gaining a foothold there as soon as possible.

In 1851 the first Catholic missionaries arrived on Anaa and by 1853 they were four in number. In the latter year quarrels between the natives who remained faithful to Mormonism and those who had gone over to the new faith broke out; the recently installed French gendarme was killed and two of the Catholic missionaries were badly manhandled. Naturally, the French governor in Tahiti could not tolerate such agression in a district which since 1842 had been considered part of the French Protectorate. He dispatched a punitive expedition, and three or four of the ring leaders were hanged on Anaa, while many others who had taken part were conveyed to Tahiti for trial and punishment.

(For a Catholic version of the event see Terlyn, pp. 189–190, for a Latter Day Saints version see Butterworth, pp. 60–61.) Thereafter, mission work continued in a peaceful manner, and the Fathers concentrated in the first place on teaching and converting the young. (Terlyn, p. 190.) But no serious attempt to proselytize other islands than those already won, Fakarava, Faaite and Anaa, was made for the next fifteen years, though converted natives from these islands slowly spread Catholicism as they travelled through or settled down in the group.

The punitive expedition to Anaa in 1853 was not the first demonstration of the governor's firm intention to enforce respect for French sovereignty over the Tuamotu group. In 1848 the government vessel *La Sirène* had been dispatched to Anaa "to restore order" (Lucett, II, p. 254), and as early as 1847 the same vessel visited Raroia in order to administer justice for an attack made by the Raroians on a French trading schooner. Of this event, too, there are several versions. The French one is contained in a "memoir" of Captain Ribourt, who was aide-de-camp to the governor from 1847 to 1849. "He [Ribourt] commanded the expeditionary force that I sent (on the 4th August 1847) on the *Gassendi* with orders to disembark on the islands Barclay de Tolly and Volowschi in the Pomutoo archipelago in order to obtain satisfaction from the peoples who had some time previously massacred the crew of the French schooner *La Sérieuse*. Having established control over the population, he treated them with generosity and made them give up the culprits, who were taken to Tahiti, tried and executed."[1]

The Englishman Lucett, who had on several occasions been in trouble with the French authorities for smuggling and therefore had a grudge against them, records (II, pp. 216–17) how on 16th June, 1848, on North Marutea he "fell in with eight or ten natives, all the rest being engaged in diving for mother-of-pearl shell, to work out a penalty inflicted upon them by the French government of Tahiti, for the murder of a Mr. Riccardi and his crew, who were killed at the island of Raroia (Barclay

---

[1] "Il [Ribourt] a commandé la colonne expéditionnaire que j'ai envoyée (4 août 1847) sur le *Gassendi* faire le débarquement aux iles Barclay de Tolly et Volowschi, dans l'archipel des Pomutoo, afin d'obtenir satisfaction des peuples qui avaient quelque temps avant massacré l'équipage de la goélette française *La Sérieuse*. S'étant rendu maître de la population, il a usé de générosité et s'est fait remettre les coupables qui ont été conduits à Taïti, jugés et exécutés." (Kroepelien, p. 139.)

de Tolly Island) twelve months ago, and the vessel they were in plundered and burnt. The natives who committed the sanguinary deed affirmed that they only revenged upon Riccardi the cold-blooded murder of some of their own countrymen; for that, about six years ago, Riccardi wantonly ran down one of their canoes, by which piece of cruelty five lives were lost, and he also killed one or two others by firing at them with muskets. The governor dispatched the steam frigate Gassendi, with troops, to apprehend Riccardi's murderers. They had dispersed, it appears, immediately after they had inflicted their savage vengeance, and had fled to different islands; but the relentless *pahi anahi* (fire ship) pursued them, nor abandoned the pursuit till she had them all in irons under hatches. They were tried in Tahiti; and some were hung, others doomed to work for the remainder of their days in irons, and the rest sentenced to pay 200 tons of mother-of-pearl shell, with the pearls therefrom, to the owner of the little vessel, which is more than ten times her equivalent value. But what had the natives of Marutea to do with the fine you will ask? Why, as there was but little prospect of the unhappy remnant of Raroians being ever able to accomplish the fine, the natives of Marutea were brought in as accessories after the fact, because, as is the wont of the migratory Paumutuans, they happened in their wanderings to touch at Raroia subsequent to the massacre. In like manner, some of the natives of Hikueru were brought in guilty of a similar offence, and were condemned to pay, the men three tons of shell each, and the women one ton and a half each."

Finally, Te Iho describes the event in the following manner: "One day during my father's time there came a ship with two masts and with Frenchmen and Tahitians aboard. The captain wished to hire some men to dive for shells for him and also wanted us to collect sea slugs. The vessel lay for some days at Tetou [see end map] which was the biggest village at that time. With him on board the captain had a woman from Papara [one of the districts in Tahiti] and a Raroian man called Piki fell in love with her. The woman left the captain for Piki's sake. Several Raroian women started to keep company with the crew instead. For these reasons a quarrel between our men and the crew broke out. The Frenchmen also had many new things which the men on our island desired. The following Sunday when the chief, Tatoa, and most of the others on the island were in church, some men slipped aboard the ship and killed the Frenchmen and the whole crew altogether nine men, I think. They took all they wanted aboard, but flour and rice they did not know what to do with, so they threw the sacks into the sea. Then they sailed the ship down to the southern part of the lagoon and set fire to it. Several moons later there came a French ship with soldiers. The soldiers hanged three men here in the village, on the beach near the marae Tumahoehoe. They took 20 men, I think it was, with them to Tahiti. Another three were hanged there and the rest were made to work on the roads as a punishment. My father's brothers, whose names were Temarutaitai and Mahinui were both among those who were sentenced to work on the roads on Tahiti, and therefore they changed their names and were afterwards called Teahutaga and Ho'omoni."[1]

The three sources seem to differ greatly about the punishment of the culprits, but the main facts appear to be clear: the Raroians attacked a French trading schooner and killed the crew some time in 1847, for which they were severely punished by the French authorities. That this event influenced their attitude to the French thereafter is evident.

What happened also shows that the French authorities were firmly resolved to teach the natives on *all* the atolls in the group to respect their sovereignty. But they did not yet make any real attempt to establish effective control over the islands, and their policy seems rather to have been to wait until the Catholic missionaries had penetrated the group, before they appointed chiefs or administrators. Laval says (p. 396) that the governor had even asked him to become the representative of the government on Faaite and Fakarava, but that he turned down the offer.

The first French representative to settle in the Tuamotu archipelago was the gendarme who was sent to Anaa soon after the arrival of the Catholic missionaries. He was succeeded by a native chief from Kauehi, Paiore, who was pretentiously called "regent (auvaha) for the Tuamotus". (Emory, 1940, p. 573.) Paiore had his headquarters on Anaa and retained his office until 1861. From 1864 onwards a French administrator resided in the group, with his headquarters first on Anaa and later on Fakarava. The authority of Paiore and his immediate successors did not extend

---

[1] Teahutaga means "heap" or "mound" and refers to Temarutaitai's digging work. Ho'omoni, or Hokomoni in Tuamotuan, means "exchange of money". Mahinui was the first Raroian to use money.

very far, however, and the entire north-eastern part of the group, at least from Takume and Raroia, was long to remain completely independent. Paiore's only attempt to extend his power was made in 1860, when he visited a few of the north-easterly islands, but this came to a bad end. Six members of Paiore's party, who had evidently behaved in a provocative manner and had defiled a *marae* (cult-place) on Fakahina were killed by the inhabitants, and the rest had a narrow escape. A punitive expedition of over 300 natives from Tahiti and the western part of the Tuamotus was immediately dispatched to Fakahina. Ten men were killed during the pursuit and the whole of the remaining population, 21 men, 33 women and 50 children, was arrested. (Anonymous, pp. 409–415.) The accused were brought to trial in Tahiti, but since the ringleaders had escaped and the victims evidently had behaved in a provocative way, they were eventually released. The women and children spent some time on Anaa and Fakarava before they were taken back to their homes.

As with other parts of the group, the north-eastern atolls were not brought under civil control until their inhabitants had been converted to Christianity. The Catholic missionaries, who had been increasingly successful in the western part of the group, at last decided in 1869 to penetrate the eastern part. At that time there were still six pagan islands in the eastern region (Terlyn, p. 191), and these must have been Reao, Vahitahi, Takoto, Fangatau, Fakahina and Napuka. Terlyn also mentions five Mormon islands (p. 191), and amongst these were both Takume and Raroia. According to Te Iho, several Raroians had already been converted to Mormonism by native missionaries from Anaa before the attack on *La Sérieuse* in 1847, and I have had a unique opportunity of studying how this faith—as it was interpreted and practised by the natives themselves—gradually grew on Takume-Raroia during the period that followed. During my second stay on Raroia 1949–51 I happened to find an old church register among a pile of lumber in an abandoned house. It had been kept by the native Latter Day Saints minister during the 1860s, and it clearly shows that at least three quarters of the population were Mormons when the first Catholic advance was made in 1869. (I later presented the register to the Rev. Edward F. Butterworth of the Reorganised Church of the Latter Day Saints.)

When in 1869 the Catholic Bishop of Tahiti was shown plans for an extension of the mission he "willingly consented thereto; a schooner was chartered and Father Albert [Montiton] set out. His voyage to the islands was of short duration: for he could only spend one day on certain islands and no more than three or four days on the others. This Father had taken along four catechists; he left one on each of the four important islands of the group: Alain Fatuga was left on Raroia in order to instruct the people of that island and lead them to Catholi- cism."[1] The other catechists were left on Takoto, Hao and Fakahina. Towards the end of 1869 another missionary, Father Fierens, replaced these catechists with others. (Montiton, 1873, p. 276.)

As many inconveniences attended the use of the trading schooners whose captains cared only for their own business, the Catholic mission purchased a schooner of between 18 and 20 tons. The possession of a schooner meant a great deal, for the missionary was now master of his route, free to multiply and prolong his stays according to the demands of his work. On the 2nd February 1870 Father Montiton left Tahiti. "Our first stop after Anaa was at Raroia, where I spent eight days catechising and baptizing the small Christian community which survives and keeps its place among the Mormons. I consecrated two marriages and baptized six persons, among them a blind, old invalid woman, but not including a new-born child who went to Heaven a few days after my departure ... I spent another eight days on the neighbouring island, Takume, where every Sunday for some time one of our pupils from Anaa has been teaching the catechism to the children in the little chapel that had previously been built of limestone plastered plaiting by my orders."[2] This catechist was probably one of those whom Father

[1] Sa Grandeur "y consentit volontiers; on fréta une goélette et le P. Albert [Montiton] partit. Son voyage aux îles fut de courte durée: car il ne pouvait séjourner qu'un jour dans certaines îles et dans les autres trois ou quatre jours seulement. Ce Père avait amené avec lui quatre catéchistes; il en laissa un dans chacune des quatre îles importantes du groupe: Alain Fatuga fut laissé à Raroia pour instruire les gens de cette île et les amener au catholicisme." (Terlyn, p. 191.)

[2] "Notre première relâche, après Anaa, eut lieu à Raroia, où je passai huit jours à catéchiser et à baptiser la petite chrétienté qui se conserve et se maintient au milieu des Mormons. Je bénis deux mariages et baptisai six personnes, dont une vieille femme aveugle et infirme, sans compter un nouveau-né qui s'envola au ciel quelques jours après mon départ ... Je passai également huit jours dans l'île voisine, à Takumé, où chaque dimanche, depuis quelque temps, un de nos élèves d'Anaa enseignait le caté- chisme aux enfants dans la petite chapelle que j'avais précédemment fait bâtir en clayonnage de chaux." (Montiton, 1873, p. 277.)

Fierens had left behind in November the previous year, and who evidently alternated between Takume and Raroia.

For two and a half years, i.e. up to July 1872 (Montiton 1873, p. 384), Father Montiton toured the eastern islands and succeeded in converting the majority of the population of the remaining heathen atolls, Fangatau, Fakahina, Vahitahi, Takoto, and a good many people on the Protestant and Mormon islands Hao and Amanu. While Father Montiton was busy evangelizing in the most easterly islands, Father Fierens made another journey to Raroia-Takume and some other central islands. In a letter to Father Fouquet, a colleague who was one of the first Catholic missionaries on Anaa, Father Fierens says that on these two islands they had "several Catholics whom you have formerly baptized on Chain Island [Anaa]. They have built two school-houses, which are also used as chapels: they are at present assembling material with which to build their churches later on."[1]

Exhausted and sick, Father Montiton left French Oceania in 1872, and until 1891 the mission work in the eastern part of the Tuamotus was carried on by Father Fierens and Father Terlyn alone. Terlyn wrote a short account of the work of the Catholic mission in the Tuamotu group, but gives no further information about conditions on Raroia. But the events connected with the conversion and the erection of the church there are preserved in the oral traditions of the Raroians and Te Iho relates that it took three years to build the church and that it was finished in 1875 (which is written in large figures over the door). "To begin with no one would go to the church. Everyone said: 'No doubt the new religion is better, but why should we shut ourselves into a big house to worship the *popaa* god?' So they continued to go to the great stone-built *marae*, or cult site, which lay down by the landing place in the bay. One of *Metua Apereto's* [Father Montiton's] successors, however, hit upon a shrewd way of changing this. He had the biggest stone of the *marae* broken loose, transported it up to the church, and used it as a step outside the entrance. After that the church was always full." (Danielsson, 1953 a, p. 130.) Also according to Te Iho, the Raroians built

[1] "Nous avons plusieurs catholiques que vous avez baptisés autrefois à l'île La Chaîne [Anaa]. Ils ont bâti deux maisons d'école, qui servent aussi de chapelles; ils réunissent en ce moment des matériaux pour construire plus tard leurs églises." (Fierens, Lettre 1872, p. 126.)

a prison next to the church, but it looked so gloomy and depressing when it was finished that they seldom used it. The prison roof disappeared during the cyclone of 1903 but the broken walls are still standing.

Around 1880 the population of all the eastern islands was converted; the only exception was Tematangi, where the natives clung to their old faith until 1888 when they finally embraced Catholicism. On the western islands, too, the Catholic missionaries had won many souls during this period. (Fierens, 1872, p. 125.)

Everywhere the missionaries taught the almost naked natives to dress and showed the superiority of European articles. Montiton writes for instance that in order to reward the natives in Fangatau, who had helped him to construct the church, he dressed them "with frocks, shirts, trousers, bought or received as alms in Tahiti, and I enriched the men with fishing harpoons, iron wire, hooks and various other articles useful in these islands".[1] This gradually created new needs among the islanders and must be regarded as one of the causes for their eagerness to earn money by diving for mother-of-pearl shells or making copra.

The diving for mother-of-pearl shells, which had already started around 1820, greatly increased during the years between 1845 and 1879 and an ever greater number of natives periodically took part in this remunerative occupation. But as no reserve zones from which the lagoons could be repopulated were established, and as diving took place too frequently, the lagoons were, of course, gradually emptied of shells. Cuzent writes (p. 69) that in 1861 the pearl fishery was very profitable and that the value of the total production in the group that year was 100,000 francs. Then he goes on to say that by the 1880s the situation had completely changed. The natives had then to dive to great depths to find shells, and only a few lagoons in the east, where the inhabitants were still completely savage, had not yet been exhausted. The figure 100,000 francs for 1861 means a production of 1,000 tons, since the price then was 0.10 fr. per kg. (Cuzent, p. 70.) It has already been recorded that, according to Wilkes, production in 1839 amounted to 900 tons. Even though Cuzent gives no figures for 1880, we can certainly trust him

---

[1] "En récompense, j'habillais les femmes et les enfants de robes, de chemises, de pantalons achetés ou reçus en aumône à Tahiti, et j'enrichis les hommes de harpons de pêche, de fil de fer, d'hameçons et de différents autres articles utiles dans ces îles." (Montiton, 1873, p. 282.)

when he says that production had decreased considerably, for in 1889, the first year for which we have reliable statistics, the figure was 602 tons.

Some time about 1840 the natives on Anaa and a few other atolls in the western part of the group had begun to manufacture coconut oil for export. (Previously they had only made small quantities for home consumption and occasional trading trips to Tahiti. See Wilkes, I, p. 359.) Lucett, for example, notes in his diary on the 15th February 1844 that "four white men were staying at the settlement [on Anaa], and they had collected between them nearly sixty tons of oil". According to the French governor De la Richerie (quoted by Meinicke, p. 401) the annual production of coconut oil about 1860 was on Anaa 200 tons, and the same author gives the following figures for the other western islands where oil was manufactured at this period: Takaroa 30, Manihi 20, Apataki between 15 and 20, Kaukura 15, Taiaro 15, Marokau between 10 and 15, Takapoto between 10 and 12, Tikei, Toau, Aratika, and Faaite, each 10, Arutua and Fakarava, each between 7 and 8 tons. The total for the whole group was about 400 tons.

Up to the 1870s only the oil was exported, and the method of preparation was laborious and most ineffective. "When the nuts are ripe enough they are grated by means of a serrated iron-blade fixed on a trestle. The pulp thus obtained is put into a canoe fixed one metre above the ground so that the pigs cannot eat the contents. A little cavity is hollowed out inside and at one end of this canoe. Then the pulp is watered with the liquid contained in the fruit (coconut-water), and if this coconut water does not suffice seawater is added. The whole is left to ferment in the sun, care being taken to cover the canoe with leaves plaited into mats when rain is expected or the air becomes too misty. As the oil exudes from the tissues, it flows into the cavity, where it is gathered and stored in the trunks of hollow coconut palms. At the end of twenty-five to thirty days the pulp has yielded its entire oil supply; the residue is then pressed. When it is exhausted it is burnt, for when the animals, which are fond of it, eat it, they immediately sicken."[1]

---

[1] "Quand les noix sont assez mûres, on les rape à l'aide d'une lame de fer dentelée qu'on fixe à un chevalet. La pulpe qui en provient est mise dans une pirogue, élevée d'un mètre au-dessus du sol, afin que les porcs ne puissent en manger le contenu. Un petit réservoir est creusé à l'intérieur et à l'une des extrémités de cette pirogue. Alors on arrose la masse pulpeuse avec l'eau contenue dans le fruit (eau de coco), et si cette

Not until the 1870s did the new German method of drying the kernels whole and exporting them in that form begin to be used. In this way the process was greatly simplified and much labour saved, especially as the dry air on the Tuamotu atolls made it unnecessary to build drying platforms, as in the Society and Marquesas islands, and the nuts could thus be left to dry on the ground. In spite of this improved processing method the immediate increase in copra production was very small. The reason for this was simply that with the exceptions mentioned above the islands did not yet possess more coconut palms than were needed for the islanders' own immediate needs. (See Chapter II, part 5.)

A third island product which began to be exploited in the 1840s was the sea-slug (trepang, bêche-de-mer), for which there was a great demand in China, since the wealthy classes there considered it a "great luxury, believing that it wonderfully strengthens the system and renews the exhausted vigor of the immoderate voluptuary". (Morrell, p. 401.) I think that we can safely assume Lucett to be the originator of this trade in the Tuamotus. Before him it is not mentioned in literature and Lucett describes it in 1848 as being an entirely new enterprise. He is for instance very bitter about the fact that a rival on Kaukura "had succeeded in obtaining from the natives the first important parcel of biche de mer, which, after two years' perseverance and instruction from us ... they had collected". (Lucett, II, p. 205.) On the next page he further informs us that he had used "white men to instruct the natives how to cook and cure the biche de mer". On several islands Lucett also left pots and pans in order to extend his business. During this trip he visited Rangiroa, Kaukura, Aratua, Apataki, Faaite, Fakarava, Hikueru, Motutunga, Tuanake, Raraka and Kauehi in order to check up on his workers. On Rangiroa he collected 12 tons, on Kaukura 320 baskets and on Faaite about 70 baskets (Lucett II, pp. 211, 226, 227), and appeared

eau de coco ne suffit pas, on y ajoute de l'eau de mer. On laisse le tout fermenter au soleil, en ayant soin, lorsqu'il vient à pleuvoir ou que l'atmosphère devient trop brumeuse, de couvrir la pirogue avec des feuilles tressées en forme de nattes. Au fur et à mesure que l'huile se dégage des tissus, elle se rend dans le réservoir, où on la recueille, et on la conserve dans des troncs de cocotiers creusés. Au bout de vingt-cinq à trente jours, la masse a rendu toute l'huile qu'elle pouvait produire; les résidus sont alors soumis à la presse. Quand ils ont été épuisés on les brûle, car lorsque les animaux, qui en sont friands, les mangent, ils deviennent aussitôt malades." (Cuzent, p. 65.)

to be quite hopeful about the future. As time went on other merchants also occasionally bought up sea-slugs, but as the demand for this product varied considerably it did not play as great a part as mother-of-pearl shell diving as a source of income for the islanders. Another reason why the production never reached any great proportions was the complicated curing process the sea-slugs required. "They are taken to the shore, where they are split at one end with a knife ... Through this opening the entrails are forced out by pressure ... the article is then washed and afterward boiled to a certain degree ... then buried in the ground for four hours; then boiled again for a short time, after which they are dried, either by the fire or the sun. Those cured by the sun are worth the most." (Morrell, p. 401.)

The Raroians' share of the Tuamotuan trade was always very modest, but at least from the 1870s onward the island was at frequent intervals visited by schooners that hired men for mother-of-pearl diving on other islands. A number of inhabitants also collected sea-slugs. The most noteworthy results of these contacts were the acquisition of sundry European articles and a host of new diseases. As the natives had no resistance through previous immunity and lacked all notions of modern hygiene, even such comparatively harmless diseases as measles and influenza were fatal. Many died and the decrease in the population was further accelerated by syphilitic sterility.

4. French colonial administration, 1880–

In 1880 an important event took place. King Pomare V, who had succeeded his mother, Queen Pomare IV, three years previously, ceded his possessions to France. The French home government ratified the cession on the 30th December 1880, and from that date onwards Tahiti and all the island groups that had previously belonged to the protectorate became a French colony. The entire administration passed into French hands and all the natives became French citizens. (Caillot, 1910, pp. 308–312.)

As far as the Tuamotus were concerned the most important consequences of this change of status were the reorganization of the local political administration and the appointment of committees on all the atolls to clear up land titles. Up to 1880 each island or even each district into which most of the islands were divided had been administered by a hereditary tribal chief. Sometimes on the western atolls a judge had been appointed according to the Tahitian pattern, but the duties and responsibilities of both the chief and the judge had been very vaguely defined. Now, however, the Tuamotu group was divided into new political districts (usually each island formed a district, but many smaller atolls were combined) and since they were now French citizens, the inhabitants of each district henceforth elected a council consisting of a chairman, a judge, a constable and two additional members. The chairman, who was given more or less the same functions as a French mayor was usually the most influential member.

French law also began to be applied in matters concerning land ownership, and in order to speed up the transition from the old collective system to the new French individual system committees for land questions were appointed on every island. (In practice these committees always consisted of the same men who made up the district councils.) On Raroia the first general meeting, attended by the entire adult population, was held on the 1st February 1883, according to existing copies of the minutes. In Chapter VII the complex problems arising from this change in land ownership will be discussed at greater length, and it will only be mentioned here that the temporary solution reached at this meeting served to stimulate many landowners, possessing what they thought were clear titles, to plant coconut palms to a previously unknown extent. In this enterprise they were encouraged not only by the traders, who frequently brought sprouting nuts from Tahiti, but also by the missionaries who many times even directed the planting themselves. The result of this intensified planting of palm trees did not seriously influence the statistics on exported copra before the end of the century, however, when the palm trees began to reach maturity and yield their maximum.

All this time the production of mother-of-pearl shell decreased steadily, as is shown by the following figures from the official statistics:

Year	Tons	Year	Tons	Year	Tons
1889	602	1893	570	1897	451
1890	656	1994	676	1898	437
1891	608	1895	295	1899	388
1892	593	1896	591	1900	443

99

Small amounts of sea-slugs were still being exported during this period, but the value of the total production was insignificant.

As for missionary activity, the other churches finally began a counter-offensive against the Catholic advances during the last quarter of the century. The delay was caused by both external and internal difficulties besetting the non-Catholic churches. The English Protestant missionaries active in Tahiti at the time of the establishment of the French protectorate in 1842 were discouraged by the difficulties which arose and but for a few exceptions left the island. Only isolated attempts were made to replace them with other English missionaries, and under these conditions the Protestant mission could naturally not attempt any work in the Tuamotu group either. After Grouard's departure in 1852 Latter Day Saints missionaries were no longer permitted to enter French Oceania and thus a vacuum ensued from which the Catholic missionaries benefitted.

The first French Protestant missionaries arrived in Tahiti in 1862 (Caillot, 1910, p. 301) but they concentrated their efforts on that island, the Leeward Islands and the Austral Islands, and therefore the Latter Day Saints missionaries were the first who seriously tried to renew the competition with the Catholics in the Tuamotu group. After having been turned away in 1878, the Latter Day Saints missionary William Nelson returned to French Oceania the next year and energetically revived missionary work. During the long period that the Tahitian Latter Day Saints mission had been without contact with America the well-known split in the original Church had occurred in 1852, and Nelson belonged to the Reorganized branch led by Joseph Smith III.[1] In French Oceania this branch—which now has its headquarters in Independence, Miss.—thus got a clear start of the Utah branch, led by Brigham Young, but gradually missionaries from the latter faction also arrived and in their turn claimed to be the true heirs of the original church that had sent Grouard to French Oceania as early as in 1843. The Protestant mission, which retained its strong position in Tahiti, returned too late to the Tuamotu group and never succeeded in regaining the dominant place it had occupied at the beginning of the century.

During the long interval, when the Protestant and Latter Day Saints

[1] The members of this church are called *kanito* all over French Oceania, a word probably derived from the English "saint".

congregations in the Tuamotus were left without foreign guidance many new hybrid sects arose—as elsewhere in Polynesia under similar circumstances (see e.g. Koskinen, pp. 101—104). Caillot mentions (1909, p. 38) the existence of Israelites (Itaraera), Sheep (Mamoe), and Whistlers (Hiohio) in 1900. The Mormons were called Israelites before the split in the mother church, and the name probably refers here to those older Mormons who did not join either the Utah or the Independence branch. What characterized the Sheep, it has been impossible to find out, but of the practices and beliefs of the Whistlers we have a good description by Stevenson (I, pp. 274—75): "Their meetings are held publicly with open doors, all being 'cordially invited to attend.' The faithful sit about the room—according to one informant, singing hymns; according to another, now singing and now whistling; the leader, the wizard—let me rather say, the medium—sits in the midst, enveloped in a sheet and silent; and presently, from just above his head, or sometimes from the midst of the roof, an aerial whistling proceeds, appalling to the inexperienced. This, it appears, is the language of the dead; its purport is taken down progressively by one of the expert, writing, I was told, 'as fast as a telegraph operator'; and the communications are at last made public. They are of the baldest triviality; a schooner is perhaps announced, some idle gossip reported of a neighbour, or if the spirit shall have been called to consultation on a case of sickness, a remedy may be suggested. One of these, immersion in scalding water, not long ago proved fatal to the patient."

A typically native element in these practices is evidently the deep-rooted belief in ghosts. All hybrid sects of this type have, however, completely disappeared now, and the present church affiliations of the Tuamotuan natives is as follows: Catholics 3,443, Kanitos (Independence branch) 1,346, Mormons (Utah branch) 510, Protestants 494, Adventists 6, Affiliation not declared 767. (Teissier, Table 1.)

An important part in the acculturation process was also played by the cyclones of 1877, 1878, 1903 and 1906. An unforeseen *direct* result of these cyclones was that they increased the supply of mother-of-pearl shells in practically all the lagoons. (Ranson, 1952 a, p. 5.) This seems strange, but as a matter of fact the previous decrease had been due not only to too frequent diving but also to the gradual formation of a layer of silt on the bottom of the lagoons. This had prevented the mother-of-pearl shell embryos from finding the hard surface they need to cling to, and most of them therefore immediately perished. The cyclones deposited coral stones and trees in the lagoons, and formed excellent foundations for the mother-of-pearl shell embryos. Henceforth and especially after the cyclone in 1903, the mother-of-pearl shell stock increased markedly everywhere in the group, only to fall again twenty years later, when the silting up process once more began to make itself felt.

A large number of *indirect* results of cyclones are given by Visher (pp. 115—118). He maintains for instance that the cyclones increase inertia, strengthen the natives in fatalism and communism, favour the spread of disease and tend to diversify plant and animal life. Further Visher thinks it likely (pp. 133—135, 141) that cyclones make businessmen sceptical of investing money in tropical colonies, take away the natives' incentive to save money and scare away talented white men from the tropics. I have unfortunately not been able to test any of these interesting hypotheses, but another important effect of the cyclones, overlooked by Visher, is clearly noticeable in the Tuamotus. On Raroia as on many other atolls in the group the cyclones, especially that in 1903, actually served to *accelerate the acculturation process.*

During this cyclone the *taro* pits were filled with gravel, and all ancient-style houses, canoes and implements were destroyed. After the calamity the Raroians did not think it worth while digging new *taro* pits (which was hard work) as they could buy flour aboard the schooners. It was of course also simpler and quicker to replace what had been lost with Western materials and objects than to try to imitate the work of their ancestors. Not only material but also spiritual values were lost with the disappearance of many old manuscript books. These contained genealogies and historical traditions, which the Raroians had recorded immediately after the first missionaries had taught them to write, and few men cared to make new copies. Several of the old political and religious leaders perished, too. The cyclone of 1903 constitutes therefore on Raroia as on many other atolls a serious break with the old culture. From now on the islanders lived, at least materially, in a Western world.

As may be easily understood the natives were very little affected by the first world war. A certain food shortage did occur, but it was soon alleviated, and a few Tuamotuans—among them the part-European trader on Raroia—enlisted in the volunteer corps that French Oceania sent to the European theatre of war. The influenza epidemic that occurred at the end of the war did, however, find its way to the Tuamotu group, where it claimed many victims owing to the fact that there were neither physicians nor medicines, and that the natives lacked all notions of modern hygiene. The number of deaths in the group is estimated to have been between 700 and 800, and Raroia was struck especially hard. According to surviving Raroians with personal memories of the epidemic, half the population was carried off and there were only four men on the entire island who were sufficiently well to bury the dead.

A catastrophe of quite a different nature was the economic depression occuring at the beginning of the 1930s. The Raroians had during the previous period become increasingly more dependent on the copra export until their whole economy was finally geared to a surplus production. When world trade now suddenly collapsed, the islanders were completely bewildered—especially since there was no substitute for the copra crop—and at first they did not know what to do. As time went on necessity forced them to try the only possible way out: to revert to the traditional economy of their forefathers, living on sea-food, coconuts and pandanus fruits. When the world, at least temporarily, returned to normal, however, the natives immediately began to clean up their neglected plantations and resumed copra production. This they did of course for the same reasons that had earlier induced them to plant coconut palms, and copra has ever since been their main source of income, while mother-of-pearl shell diving has gradually decreased in importance. No sea slugs have been collected since the civil war in China closed the important market there.

For a short time the last world war had the same effect as the depression at the beginning of the 1930s, since French Oceania was temporarily isolated by the fall of France, but when the colony ranged itself on the side of de Gaulle in September 1940, economic relations with Australia, New Zealand and America were soon re-established. Copra prices rose rapidly, but a certain shortage of most foreign goods lasted all through the war. The most noteworthy event after the war is the beginning of political activities culminating in the election of the first native deputy to the National Assembly in Paris. A branch of the new pro-native party has even been constituted on Raroia. Finally, it must also be noted that a school was opened on Raroia just prior to my study.

Compared to other islands in French Oceania the Tuamotus are the least affected by European culture, and strikingly few foreigners, White or Chinese, have settled in the group. This does not, however, mean that much of the old culture is left. On the contrary, the changes have been profound, and lovers of South Sea movies would not feel at home on Raroia. The material culture is almost wholly Western, and the natives use European tools exclusively, dress in the European way and frequently have such luxuries as radios, bicycles and refrigerators. Many houses are, however, still made of plaited palm leaves, and the canoes are in general of Polynesian model with outriggers.

The only trace left of the old religion is the general belief in ghosts and spirits. The political structure has also changed considerably with the emergence of new classes of leaders, i.e. elected chiefs, traders and catechists or ministers. Most atoll communities are, however, still fairly homogeneous with few social stratifications. Economically a whole re-volution has occurred with the rise of the copra trade, and to-day every-where in the Tuamotus the natives have abandoned the old subsistence economy in favour of a surplus production. Most of the natives still have enough land to secure a good living and many have a considerable income by any standard.

Even the language has undergone profound changes, and the Tua-motuan dialect is spoken to-day only by the old men and women. As a result of the frequent contacts with Tahiti, the local dialect will probably in the end be completely replaced by Tahitian.

The cultural situation, like the environment, is in its main charac-teristics similar throughout the group. There is a slight difference of degree, and as a rule it can be said that the impact of Western culture diminishes as the distance from Papeete increases. Raroia, situated at 142°30″ west and 16° south, occupies therefore not only geographically but also culturally an intermediate position in the group.

5. Summary of culture contacts

In order to get a clearer picture of the acculturation process I shall try, finally, to summarize the type and frequency of the culture contacts. This summary is, of course, very approximate and tentative.

Exactly what influences the Raroians are exposed to when visiting

Tahiti and the other atolls during diving seasons is not clear and merits a special investigation, which I unfortunately have not yet been able to undertake. The only influences worth mentioning in addition to the personal contacts listed below are the radio and the magazines. Their impact has, however, so far been very slight due to the fact that the islanders do not understand any other language than Tuamotuan and the closely related Tahitian dialect. The first wireless receiver was introduced by the part-native store-keeper in 1950 and a second was bought by a wealthy land owner two years later. When living in the central village, the whole population regularly listens to the news, church services and music during the Tahitian language program broadcast between six and seven o'clock every evening. Three or four men subscribe to two monthly magazines in the Tahitian language containing world and local news, official decrees and political articles. The only existing book in Tahitian is the Bible, which is frequently read by all the islanders.

A. *Culture contacts on Raroia*

Type of contact	Duration	Frequency	Period
Rumours of foreign visits to other atolls	Not known	Not known	1606–1830s
Visits of trading schooners	1–2 days	Once a year	1830s–1869
Visits of trading schooners	1–2 days	5–6 times a year	1870–1920
Visits of trading schooners	1–2 days	Once a month	1920–
Visits of missionaries	About a month	Once a year	1870–
Visits of administrators	1–2 days	Twice a year	1900–

B. *Culture contacts elsewhere*

Type of contact	Duration	Frequency	Period
Average visits by a Raroian to other atolls during the diving season	1–4 months	Every second or third year	1900–
Average visits by a Raroian to Tahiti	1–2 months	Every second or third year	1920–

CHAPTER IV · **Demography**

From the geographical, botanical and geological point of view Raroia is certainly typical of the Tuamotu group and does not in any marked respect deviate from the general pattern found, with surprisingly few variations, everywhere in the archipelago. Culturally Raroia occupies a central position between the more "conservative" Eastern atolls and the more "progressive" Western atolls, and is thus truly an "average" Tuamotuan atoll. But is the composition of the population also representative of the Tuamotus in general? As no detailed comparison has previously been made between the demographic situation in the Tuamotus on the one hand and in French Oceania as a whole on the other, such material has been brought together here in section A, in spite of the fact that it falls a little outside the general scope of this study. In section B the demographic structures and trends on Raroia are analysed separately.

A. COMPARATIVE STATISTICS

In order to discern the main patterns, I have compiled comparative tables based on the published figures from the latest census report (Teissier, 1953), to some extent supplemented with data from the original documents. All figures in this section therefore refer to the situation at the time of the census, September 17–18, 1951. My study is otherwise limited to the period January 1 to December 31, 1950, but as no significant changes took place during the time up to the census, all findings in this section are also valid for the study as a whole.

The census figures are broken down according to the following criteria: administrative unit, race, sex, age, marital status, professional situation, and church membership. No further analysis is possible on the basis of the available census data, and is, in any case, unnecessary for my limited purpose.

1. Administrative units

On September 17–18, 1951, the total population in French Oceania was 62,828, divided among the five administrative units or groups in the following way:

Tahiti and dependencies	35,423
Leeward Islands	12,920
Tuamotu group	6,733
Austral Islands	3,983
Marquesas Islands	3,257
Mangareva	512

Of the 78 atolls in the Tuamotu group, many are grouped together for administrative purposes, as, for instance, is Raroia and its neighbouring atoll, Takume. The total number of these smaller units, usually called "districts" is 35, and the frequency distribution of the population is as follows:

Population	Below 100	101–200	201–300	301–400	401–500	Above 500
No. of districts	4	19	8	1	1	2

The arithmetic mean per district is 192, which is very close to the figure for Raroia-Takume, 160, but still more significant is, of course, the frequency distribution above, in which Raroia-Takume is in the modal class. As it is impossible with available data to compute the exact population for each inhabited atoll, we have to content ourselves with these rather crude figures, which, however, clearly show that Raroia-Takume in this respect is typical of the Tuamotus as a whole.

Comparisons between the Tuamotus and the whole of French Oceania are meaningless in this case, as the other groups are completely different as to topography and general conditions.

2. Racial composition

The racial composition of the population in French Oceania is according to the official census as follows:

Race	French Oceania		Tuamotu		Raroia	
	Total	Per cent	Total	Per cent	Total	Per cent
Pure Polynesian	40,099	63.8	5,905	87.7	95	87.2
Mixed Polynesian	13,769	21.9	742	11.0	12	11.0
Chinese	6,655	10.6	68	1.0	2	1.8
Caucasian	1,860	3.0	18	0.3	0	0.0
Other	445	0.7	0	0.0	0	0.0
Total	62,828	100.0	6,733	100.0	109	100.0

The attribution of a person to the class of pure or mixed Polynesians is in the official census made simply on the basis of his own declaration, and therefore cannot be regarded as reliable. As a rule, however, the intermixture is undoubtedly slighter in the Tuamotus than in any other group in French Oceania, and the figures therefore certainly have some basis in fact. The percentages are strikingly similar for Raroia and the Tuamotu group, but how unreliable verbal declarations as to racial extraction really are will be shown in Chapter V, where a detailed analysis of the race mixture on Raroia, based on genealogical records, will be made.

3. Sex ratio

Sex	French Oceania		Tuamotu		Raroia	
	Total	Per cent	Total	Per cent	Total	Per cent
Men	32,920	52.4	3,677	54.6	51	46.8
Women	29,908	47.6	3,056	45.4	58	53.2
Total	62,828	100,0	6,733	100,0	109	100,0

The disproportion between the number of men and women is very marked, especially if they are compared with Europe and America, where in almost all countries the difference is insignificant. The most surprising thing is that there is a surplus of men in *all* the five groups in French Oceania in spite of the varying local conditions. This situation seems also to be fairly stable, or at least has been for the last 50 years for which we have reliable data (Valenziani, 1949, p. 666).

Whatever the explanation may be for this curious preponderance of men, the Tuamotus follow the general pattern. That the figures are slightly more disproportionate in this group than in French Oceania as a whole is certainly due to a greater female migration to Tahiti. The figures for Raroia are strangely enough reversed, and seem to have been so for a long period. The percentages correspond to a sex ratio of 120 men to 100 women for the whole group, and 88 men to 100 women for Raroia.

4. Age classes

The official census separates the population into only two groups, those above and those below 20 years of age. For Raroia a more complete break-down and also separation according to sex has been undertaken in the next section of this chapter, but here I simply follow the census.

Age	French Oceania		Tuamotu		Raroia	
	Total	Per cent	Total	Per cent	Total	Per cent
Below 20	33,239	53.0	3,249	49.5	49	45.0
Above 20	29,422	47.0	3,317	50.5	60	55.0
Total	62,661	100,0	6,566	100,0	109	100,0

The reversed figures for the Tuamotus when compared with French Oceania as a whole are certainly—like the similar disproportion between the sexes in the previous table—due to a migration to Tahiti. It seems to be a little more pronounced on Raroia than on the average, but on the whole it can certainly be said that Raroia in this case also is typical of the group.

5. Marital status

The figures in the table below should be compared with those in the preceding part showing the age classes, where we find that roughly half of the population is above 20 and consequently of marriageable age. (The figure is actually somewhat higher, as the natives are often physically mature long before the age of 20.) The discrepancy between the

Status	French Oceania		Tuamotu		Raroia	
	Total	Per cent	Total	Per cent	Total	Per cent
Unmarried	48,491	77.4	4,772	72.7	76	69.7
Married	14,170	22.6	1,794	27.3	33	30.3
Total	62,661	100,0	6,566	100.0	109	100.0

number of marriageable and married persons is easily explained by the fact that the majority of the natives still have a considerable reluctance to adopt foreign patterns of a complicated legal character. Co-habitation without legal marriage is therefore the rule, and these *de facto* marriages are not shown in the census. The situation is evidently the same on Raroia as in the Tuamotus and French Oceania as a whole.

6. Professional status

Status	French Oceania		Tuamotu		Raroia	
	Total	Per cent	Total	Per cent	Total	Per cent
Employer	748	1.2	10	0.2	0	0.0
Employee	3,529	5.6	21	0.3	0	0.0
Independent	58,384	93.2	6,535	99.5	109	100.0
Total	62,661	100.0	6.566	100.0	109	100.0

The few employers, usually French or Chinese, and employees in the total population almost all live in Tahiti, the only island with an embryo of industry. On Raroia as well as everywhere else in the Tuamotu group the natives are practically all independent land owners who prepare the copra themselves, or with the help of other islanders who work part-time.

7. Church membership

Church affiliation follows clearly distinguishable geographical patterns, which is easily explained if we consider historical events. (Chapter III.) The first missionaries in French Oceania were Protestants. They established themselves principally in Tahiti, Moorea, the Leeward islands of the Society group, and the Austral islands, where they soon converted all the natives. Missionaries arriving later representing other churches (Catholic and Mormon) therefore naturally concentrated on virgin fields like Mangareva, the Tuamotus and the Marquesas. There they succeeded in establishing themselves firmly before the Protestants took up the competition in earnest. It is thus not at all surprising that the religious situation is different in each group.

Denomination	French Oceania		Tuamotu		Raroia	
	Total	Per cent	Total	Per cent	Total	Per cent
Protestant	34,441	55.0	494	7.5	3	2.8
Catholic	15,096	24.1	3.443	52.4	100	91.7
Kanito[1]	2,073	3.3	1,346	20.5	4	3.7
Mormon[2]	1.218	1.9	510	7.8	1	0.9
Other	9.833	15.7	773	11.8	1	0.9
Total	62,661	100.0	6,566	100.0	109	100.0

[1] The Reorganized Church of the LDS (Independence Branch).
[2] The Church of the LDS (Salt Lake City Branch).

Whether Raroia is typical of the Tuamotu group or not, is another question which it is unfair to answer on the basis of these figures alone, as the churches are not evenly distributed throughout the group. A more important criterion is therefore the *total number* of churches represented on *each* atoll. In the following table the administrative units or districts into which the group is divided have been classified according to this criterion. "Major" is arbitrarily defined to mean a church to which above 50 % of the population belongs. If two churches exceed 35 %, both are regarded as major. Churches with less than 10 % membership have not been included.

Out of the total number of 25 single major churches, 18 are Catholic,

and out of the total number of 10 major churches sharing the dominance, 7 are Catholic. As Raroia-Takume not only belongs to the first
class (atolls with only one major church), but also is Catholic, the
district can be said to be much more representative than the figures in
the census indicate.

Total no. of districts[1]	Number of atolls with						
	1 major church	1 major+no. of smaller			2 major churches	2 major+no. of smaller	
		1	2	3		1	2
35	17	3	3	2	6	3	1

[1] Atolls or group of atolls.

8. Position of Raroia

The question of the relationship between the Tuamotu group and
French Oceania as a whole is already sufficiently illuminated by the
data presented above, and I shall therefore limit myself here to a
brief summary of the place of Raroia in the Tuamotu group. The size
of the population of Raroia is close to the mean. As to the racial
composition, the age classes, the marital and professional status, the
population on Raroia is identical with or only insignificantly different
from that of the whole group. The sex ratio shows a slight surplus of
women, whereas generally in the Tuamotus there is a small surplus of
men. Finally in the religious field, there is greater homogeneity than on
most other atolls, as more than 90 % of the population belong to the
same church. Though these two last-mentioned facts may have some
influence on the local social and economic conditions, it can certainly
be said that Raroia is typical for the demographic set-up in the Tuamotuan atolls. As other factors such as physical environment, general
culture and economy are also shared with the other atolls, the findings
of the present study can certainly to a large extent be applied to the
group as a whole.

B. POPULATION TRENDS

In the previous section a comparison of the composition of the populations in French Oceania, the Tuamotus and Raroia *at a fixed time* (cen-

sus of September 17—18, 1951) was made. The comparison was based on some *basic characteristics* selected by the census officials. Here *additional* data collected on Raroia will be presented, and where possible the *changes* over longer or shorter periods will be followed, thus showing also the *dynamic* aspect of the demography.

1. Native come-back

At the end of the last century the Polynesian race seemed doomed. Since the first contact with Western culture the decline had everywhere been rapid, and it was widely thought that the Polynesians ultimately were to become extinct. A marked change has, however, taken place since then—maybe principally due to intermarriage and to a greater immunity against epidemic diseases—and in French Oceania as everywhere else in Polynesia, the survival of the native population seems now assured. (Keesing, 1945, pp. 46—51.)

TABLE II: *Population trends in French Oceania, 1863–1951*

Group	YEAR								
	1863	1881	1892	1902	1911	1926	1936	1946	1951
E.F.O.	—	—	—	27,167	28,875	30,043	38,132	48,370	53,868
Tuamotu	6,588	5,500	4,734	4,294	4,711	4,276	4,668	6,142	6,647
Tahiti	7,642	8,500	9,500	9,634	9,128	8,335	13,182	17,456	23,812
Marquesas	12,000	5,776	4,445	3,563	3,116	2,255	2,400	2,968	3,257
Austral	2,000	1,500	1,814	2,106	2,484	3,170	3,341	3,921	3,983

In order to show this evolutionary trend and the local variations in the principal groups of French Oceania, I have prepared Table II (based on the figures published by Valenziani and Teissier and additional data in the Papeete archives), which *excludes* all other racial groups than the Polynesians, pure *and* mixed. The reason for lumping the pure and mixed Polynesians together here is simply that they are recorded in this way in most cases. For Raroia where the islanders, as on many other of the Tuamotu atolls, still preserve their genealogies, an attempt has been made in Chapter V to classify the inhabitants more accurately, but here the census figures, grouping mixed and pure natives together, will be used in order to permit comparisons.

As the figures show, the unexpected native come-back was for French
Oceania as a whole very slow until 1926, and thereafter increasingly
rapid. (The statistics permit valid comparisons for French Oceania only
from 1902, as previously the Leeward islands were not pacified and no
figures are available.)

Fig. IV: *Graph showing the differential evolution*

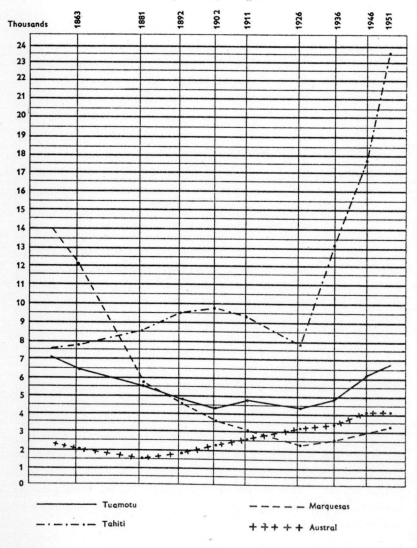

The trend for French Oceania as a whole, is, however, not followed in detail in each of the listed groups, taken separately, and this fact is brought out still more clearly in Figure IV. The most striking feature is the different times at which each group reached the bottom. In Tahiti this occurred in the 1840s (not shown in the graph), in the Austral Islands in the 1880s, in the Tuamotu group around 1900, and in the Marquesas not until the 1920s. The main reason for this differential evolution seems to be the uneven impact of epidemics in the different groups evidently related to the distance from and the means of communication with Papeete. The Spanish influenza, for instance, caused a downward trend between the 1911 and 1926 censuses in all the groups, except the most isolated, the Austral Islands.

If we now compare the trend in the Tuamotu group as a whole with that on Raroia, as is done in Figure V (based on unpublished data in the Papeete archives), the most significant difference is that the upward trend seems to have started later on Raroia than on the average in the Tuamotus. Whether this is due to prolonged epidemics or migratory

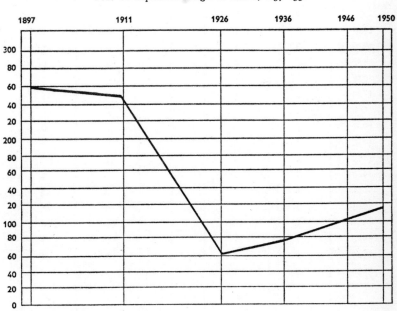

FIG. V: *Population changes on Raroia, 1897–1951*

movements is hard to say. As to the period prior to 1897 it must be noticed that no accurate census was taken. The estimate in the *Annuaire des Etablissemets Français de l'Oceanie* for 1863 gives 300 persons for Takume-Raroia, which figure certainly is too low.

2. Natural increase, 1931–50

No detailed population statistics for the individual atolls in the Tuamotu group have ever been published, but in the existing civil register on Raroia I have found complete data as to the number of births and deaths for at least the last 20 years, and they are presented here in Table III.

TABLE III: *Number of births and deaths on Raroia, 1931–1950*

Year	Births	Deaths			
		Total	Below 1 year	1–20 years	Above 20 years
1931	5	1	0	1	0
1932	5	1	1	0	0
1933	5	2	2	0	0
1934	4	1	0	0	1
1935	5	2	1	0	1
1936	5	1	0	0	1
1937	0	0	0	0	0
1938	5	3	1	0	2
1939	6	1	0	0	1
1940	2	0	0	0	0
1941	8	0	0	0	0
1942	2	2	0	0	2
1943	5	4	2	1	1
1944	2	4	2	0	2
1945	6	3	1	0	2
1946	2	2	1	0	1
1947	2	1	1	0	0
1948	2	1	0	0	1
1949	1	4	3	0	1
1950	5	3	2	0	1
Total	77	36	17	2	17

Few comments are needed. The high infant mortality is to a large extent due to ignorance on the part of the parents of even the most elementary principles of hygiene, but seems also to be a result of the lack of appropriate baby food. As the mothers usually participate in the copra work and take their young children with them to the copra sectors outside the village many of the babies also easily catch colds and develop pneumonia.

3. Composition of the population

A careful census was made on January 1, 1950. First the whole population on Raroia was counted and the exact age of each person was determined with the aid of the civil register (the difference between actual and supposed ages was in many instances as great as five years!). Then the head of each household was asked whether any persons belong-

TABLE IV: *Composition of the permanent population, January 1, 1950*

Age	Males	Females	Total
– 4	2	6	8
5– 9	3	10	13
10–14	5	9	14
15–19	8	7	15
20–24	3	2	5
25–29	3	4	7
30–34	8	2	10
35–39	2	4	6
40–44	5	5	10
45–49	5	2	7
50–54	4	2	6
55–59	3	2	5
60–64	0	1	1
65–69	2	3	5
70–74	0	1	1
75–79	0	1	1
80–84	1	0	1
85–89	1	0	1
Total	55	61	116

ing to it were temporarily absent. Those persons were added in a special column and the total is called the permanent population. The figures for this so-called permanent population, whose exactness I was able to verify subsequently during my stay on the island, are given in Table IV. Graphically the composition of the population is pictured below.

One reason for the uneven proportion between the sexes in the youngest age groups seems to be the persistence of the ancient custom of adoption (see further Chapter XII, part 4). Boys are as a rule in greater demand than girls and many Raroian boys have been adopted by couples on the neighbouring atoll of Takume, where the population is extremely small compared to the total area and practically all families therefore need reinforcements. When the children in these age groups grow up the disproportion between the sexes will obviously lead to still more frequent intermarriage with persons from other islands, thus eventually effacing all cultural differences between the various groups. The few persons who are above 60 still form a link with the past, which will be broken forever when they die, as the younger generations do not show much interest in and respect for the old native culture.

FIG. VI: *Permanent population, January 1, 1950.*

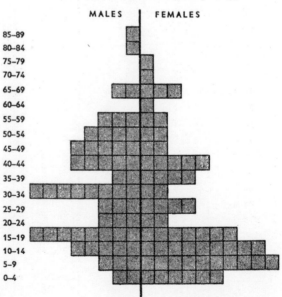

4. Inter-island mobility

When living in the village on an atoll in the Tuamotus, even for a very short time, one is immediately struck by the continuous changes in the number of persons present. One week the whole population may be there, the next only a handful, a third week only the women or the older people, and so on. As these frequent variations—which of course are not shown in any ordinary population statistics—may be of great significance for understanding the economic and social life, I have also recorded them.

These population movements are of three types:

1. Intra-atoll travelling, i.e. trips to various parts of the home atoll
2. Inter-island travelling, i.e. visits to other islands
3. Real emigration or immigration

The intra-atoll mobility (1) depends on Raroia entirely on the economic activities and will therefore be considered in a later chapter on copra production but the other two types of mobility will be dealt with here.

In order to distinguish between inter-island travelling (2) and migratory movements (3), I have repeated my censuses at certain intervals. The figures are presented in Table V.

If we compare the permanent population for each year in this table

TABLE V: *Composition of the permanent and actual population, 1950–53*

Age	¹/₁ 1950				¹/₁ 1951				¹/₇ 1952				¹/₇ 1953			
	Perm.		Actual		Perm.		Actual		Perm.		Actual		Perm.		Actual	
	M	F	M	F	M	F	M	F	M	F	M	F	M	F	M	F
0–14	10	25	9	25	11	27	10	20	15	28	9	20	17	26	15	25
15–29	14	13	13	13	14	13	12	12	14	12	14	12	15	13	12	13
30–44	15	11	15	11	15	11	13	11	15	11	16	14	14	12	14	10
45–59	12	6	10	5	11	6	9	5	10	6	7	5	9	7	8	7
60–	4	6	3	3	4	6	2	1	4	6	2	2	4	6	3	5
Total	55	61	50	57	55	63	46	49	58	63	48	53	59	64	52	60

with the natural increase during the same period, also according to my own records (see Table III), we get the following series:

Date	Perm.	Actual	Natural Increase
$^1/_1$ 1950	116	107	2
$^1/_1$ 1951	118	95	2
$^1/_7$ 1952	121	101	2
$^1/_7$ 1953	123	112	4

Some interesting conclusions can immediately be drawn:

1. There is an uninterrupted *steady increase* of the population, as shown in the column for the permanent residents. This increase would eventually be brought out even if only the number of actual residents were counted (as during the official censuses), but for shorter periods these figures may be deceptive.

2. There is *very little immigration or emigration,* as shown by a comparison between the number of permanent residents and the natural increase.

3. There is a *considerable mobility,* as shown by the discrepancy between the permanent and the actual population.

The natural increase has been discussed in part two, and the figures here simply show that the general trend noticed for the period 1931—50 continues. The true migratory movement will be dealt with in the next part, and a short explanation of the figures in Table V will therefore suffice here. During the period 1950—53 there was only one "immigrant", a young man who took up living with a Raroian woman, built a house in the village and seemed intent on staying. This explains the increase of three persons between 1/1 1951 and 1/7 1952, when the natural increase was only two persons. Between 1952 and 1953 the natural increase was four, but two girls went to live with men elsewhere in French Oceania, and the actual increase is thus only two. If we are to judge from my limited data, some migration to Tahiti is thus going on. The extent of it and the reasons for it will be discussed in the next section.

The general *mobility,* which is our main concern here, is actually much greater than the figures indicate, as they simply show the *balance* between the number of departed and returned persons at the given time. If instead we take into consideration not only these figures, but also *who* was absent at the time of the various censuses, the natives' fondness for travelling is still more evident. The difference in actual population between 1/1 1950 and 1/1 1951 is 12 persons. The number of persons absent for longer or shorter periods during the year was, however, according to my records more than double, or 29.

Some of my other data are still more eloquent. Between January 1, 1950 and July 1, 1952, for instance, the following changes took place:

Out of the 107 persons on the atoll on January 1, 1950, 22 were elsewhere in French Oceania in July 1952, and 6 were dead.

On the other hand, on July 1, 1952 there were on the atoll 14 persons (Raroians and others) who were living on or visiting other islands on January 1, 1950. The number of births during this period was 10.

If we go only by the absolute figures in the table, the difference between the figures for 1950 and 1952 is 6 persons. As a matter of fact, the total number of persons who have been away from Raroia during these two and a half years is at least 36! (A completely accurate check was not possible as several "key persons" were absent on July 1, 1952.)

Of the 29 Raroians visiting other islands in 1950, 25 had Tahiti as their destination. The main reasons for undertaking a voyage to Tahiti, which may take anything from five days to two weeks are according to their own verbal declarations in probable order of importance:

1. A desire for a change and diversion
2. Necessity of medical treatment
3. Legal matters which must be settled
4. A wish to see relatives

There seems to be a seasonal pattern for these voyages if we are to judge from the data collected during a single year and presented in Table VI. The increased number of voyages towards the end of the year is certainly due to the fact that the months of November and December are an off-season immediately preceded by copra work in the most productive sector. The Raroians then have a considerable amount of money and no imperative duties. The length of a visit to Tahiti is rarely less than one month, and often it is prolonged for several months or even half a year, but the limited data I have do not permit any far-ranging conclusions. An interesting fact, which also must be recorded, is that 18 persons, mostly children and old women, have never been to Tahiti.

The visiting between Raroia and Tahiti is pronounced but natural considering the paramount importance of Papeete. The Raroians are practically never visited in return by their relatives living in Tahiti, and Tahitians other than those employed on the schooners rarely have reason for visiting an atoll. The few Tahitians living on Raroia in 1950 were either married to Raroians or temporarily employed as workers by wealthy local landowners.

Only four of the 29 Raroians who visited other islands in 1950 had an atoll in the Tuamotus as their destination. It must be noted, however, that the frequent visits to Takume, the only atoll which can be reached by existing canoes and boats on Raroia, are not included in this figure. Neither have I recorded the great number of visits from Takume to Raroia.

It is surprising that so little visiting takes place between Raroia and the other atolls in the group (except Takume), in spite of the fact that there is a great deal of intermarriage (see next section). The explanation might simply be that Tahiti is the common meeting-ground for natives from all the atolls, and that it is always difficult to secure a passage both ways between Raroia and other atolls within reasonable time.

TABLE VI: *Number of Raroians visiting Papeete in 1950*

Age	Jan.		Feb.		March		Apr.		May		June		July		Aug.		Sept.		Oct.		Nov.		Dec
	M	F	M	F	M	F	M	F	M	F	M	F	M	F	M	F	M	F	M	F	M	F	M
0–14	1	1	0	2	0	2	0	2	1	3	1	0	1	0	1	1	0	1	1	6	1	6	1
15–29	0	0	1	0	0	0	2	1	1	0	0	0	0	1	1	1	2	2	3	2	2	2	2
30–44	1	0	1	0	1	0	1	0	1	0	0	1	0	0	0	0	1	1	4	2	4	2	4
45–59	3	3	2	1	3	3	2	2	1	1	1	1	0	2	1	0	1	1	1	0	1	0	1
60–	0	2	1	0	0	2	0	1	0	1	1	1	1	1	1	3	0	3	1	2	1	2	1
Total	5	6	5	3	4	7	5	6	4	5	3	3	2	4	4	5	4	8	10	12	9	12	9
	11		8		11		11		9		6		6		9		12		22		21		21

5. Migration and intermarriage

The figures in the previous sections indicated that some real migration occurred, although the period for which I had data was too short to permit any general conclusions as to its extent. As the only way to get any additional information and the necessary time perspective seemed to be to investigate the geographic origin of the population and to study family stories, I tried both methods. The geographic origin, defined as the permanent residence of the parents, is shown in the following table:

TABLE VII: *Geographic origin of the population, January 1, 1950*

Origin	Men	Women	Total
Raroia	34	43	77
Tuamotu	5	8	13
Tahiti	9	5	14
Moorea	0	1	1
Raiatea	2	0	2
Total	50	57	107

There are thus 16 "foreign" men and 14 "foreign" women on the atoll, all from the Tuamotus and the Society Islands, or from two out of the five groups in French Oceania. That there is no intermarrying with the Marquesas is not too surprising, as the natives of this group speak their own local dialect and have somewhat different customs, but why the Austral Islands and Mangareva are not represented it is difficult to explain.

If we now consider the marital status of these "foreigners" we find the following. Out of the total number of 16 "foreign" males, 13 are married to Raroian women, 1 is the widower of a Raroian woman, 1 is an adopted baby, and only 1 is married to a woman who is also a "foreigner". Out of the total number of 14 "foreign" women, 8 are married to Raroian men, 2 are widows of Raroian husbands, 3 are adopted young girls, and only 1 is married to a "foreign" male.

Immigration into Raroia is thus intimately linked with marriage. This intermarrying has probably been constant over the years, which is shown by the fact that of these 24 marriages between a Raroian and a "foreigner" (13 + 1 males and 8 + 2 females), 15 were contracted more than 10 years ago and 9 since then.

A corresponding *emigration* is going on all the time, too, as a perusal of the family stories and genealogies indicates, but its extent is of course impossible to ascertain with the same exactness, and I have not tried to compile any statistics.

The main reason for these frequent inter-island alliances is the continued operation of the old incest rules, which forbid marriage between all persons more closely related than third degree cousins. Most families are closely related and the common practice of adoption, which has the same force as actual blood ties, still further reduces the number of "unrelated" people. The possibilities for an individual to find a sexual mate and marriage partner on the home island are thus considerably limited. The great difference between counting according to the French system legally in force and the Polynesian system is best shown by means of some figures. According to the French point of view seven of the nine young Raroian women considered to be of marriageable age should be able to find mates among the eleven "mature" youths on the island. According to the islanders' own opinions, however, only two of the seven women may marry Raroian youths. The same conditions are prevalent on the other islands in French Oceania, and there is therefore every reason to suppose that in the long run the emigration *from* Raroia is compensated by an equally extensive immigration *to* the atoll.

The residence rule is bilocal and neolocal, and the actual choice of dwelling place seems to a large extent to be determined by economic considerations, i.e. the home atoll of the partner who possesses most land is usually preferred. In all probability both sexes are therefore represented in approximately the same number among the emigrants. This is rendered still more likely by the fact that the number of male and female immigrants for the period covered by Table VII is roughly the same.

CHAPTER V · **Race mixture**

An inevitable result of the frequent intermarriages between Raroians and other islanders is of course a progressive race mixture. The number of mixed Polynesians on Raroia was, according to the census of 17–18 September 1951 (see Chapter IV), only 12, while the remaining 95 natives were listed as pure-blooded, and the number of Chinese was 2.

These figures were based solely on the verbal declaration of each person, and thus of doubtful reliability. I tried therefore to determine the number of mixed persons on a more exact basis, viz. the pedigree of each individual. In addition I have measured almost the whole adult population.

1. Extent of race mixture

Contrary to the situation in other parts of French Oceania, the islanders in the Tuamotus (especially in the eastern half) still possess genealogies going back *at least to the time of the first contact* with other racial groups. I have gone over each individual's pedigree on Raroia and marked off all persons of non-Polynesian extraction, and, depending on the nearness to these ancestors, the degree of intermixture has been fixed for every islander present on January 1, 1950.

Persons who did not know their genealogies (mostly Tahitians) and Tahitians found in the pedigrees have arbitrarily been counted as having $\frac{1}{8}$ foreign admixture. Persons with less than $\frac{1}{8}$ foreign admixture have been counted as pure Polynesians. There may still be some hidden intermixture, but as the islanders seem to keep track of all adulterous children and usually without hesitation indicate the real father, this source of error is negligible.

The result of the classification of the Raroians according to this considerably more rigorous, although of course not completely satisfactory, definition of racial purity is shown below.

TABLE VIII: *Racial composition of the population, January 1, 1950*

Race	Males	Females	Total
Pure Polynesian	34	39	73
Pure White	0	0	0
Pure Chinese	1	0	1
Mixed Polynesian-White	14	15	29
Mixed Polynesian-Chinese	1	1	2
Mixed Pol.-White-Chinese	0	2	2
Total	50	57	107

The number of mixed persons is thus altogether 33, or almost three times greater than the figure based on the verbal declarations, which was 12 (Chapter IV, section A 2). That the mixed persons are justified to a large extent in identifying themselves with the group of pure Polynesians is, however, proved by the fact that the admixture is very slight in most cases, as shown in the following table.

TABLE IX: *Extent to which the mixed persons are Polynesian, January 1, 1950*

Degree Polynesian	Males	Females	Total
$7/8$	5	5	10
$3/4$	2	7	9
$1/2$	5	4	9
$1/4$	3	2	5

The many varying degrees of intermixture show that the intermarrying between the various racial groups has gone on for a considerable time. A still better way to follow the trend backwards is simply to classify all the mixed persons according to age, which has been done in Table X.

The distribution of mixed bloods over all three age groups in a number roughly proportionate to the total number of persons in each age group (Cf. Table IV), definitely shows that racial mixture first appeared several generations ago, and that it still occurs to a large extent. It is very likely that this process will eventually lead to the same marked changes of the islanders' physical characters as those which have taken place in so many other Polynesian groups.

TABLE X: *Age of the mixed persons, January 1, 1950*

Sex	Age			Total
	0–14	15–44	45–	
Male	2	10	3	15
Female	9	6	3	18
Total	11	16	6	33

2. Physical characteristics

During my various stays on Raroia I have succeeded in measuring almost the whole adult population. As shown by previous statistics (Table V) the total population on 1st January 1950 was 107 persons, of which 37 men and 29 women were above 18 years of age. An examination of their genealogies revealed a certain foreign admixture, the extent of which has been indicated in the previous section of this chapter. (It must also be remembered that one of the adult men was a pure Chinese.) The number of persons measured compared to the total number of persons over 18 years was:

Racial group	Males		Females	
	Total	Measured	Total	Measured
Pure	24	23	23	20
Mixed	12	10	6	4
Total	36	33	29	24

My measurements are limited to twelve, which are the same as those usually taken during the Bishop Museum surveys in Polynesia. (See

Shapiro, 1942, pp. 141–69, and 1943, pp. 3–8 and Marshall.) The results are shown in the following table.

TABLE XI: *Physical characteristics of 57 adult Raroians*

Measurement	Males (33)				Females (24)			
	Pure (23)		Mixed (10)		Pure (20)		Mixed (4)	
	Range	Mean	Range	Mean	Range	Mean	Range	Mean
Stature	1565–1810	1697	1648–1846	1727	1481–1675	1595	1584–1662	1620
Shoulder	1309–1527	1425	1382–1550	1444	1224–1404	1327	1313–1388	1344
Middle finger	570–698	641	596–707	644	536–661	602	570–636	613
Sitting height	1250–1384	1337	1304–1394	1348	1238–1343	1292	1262–1323	1295
Head length	176–198	186	177–199	188	168–187	178	175–188	181
Head width	145–167	154	150–167	155	142–159	151	146–156	152
Face height	114–134	122	112–131	119	105–123	115	109–117	111
Face width	133–150	143	128–148	139	127–144	137	134–141	138
Frontal width	100–119	105	98–123	108	95–112	103	102–108	104
Bigonial diam.	99–118	109	103–125	110	92–120	103	99–113	107
Nose height	47–60	53	46–54	51	46–60	51	48–54	51
Nose width	36–49	42	35–44	41	34–44	39	38–43	39

The only indices which have been computed here are the cephalic, and they are for the various sub-classes:

Racial group	Mean	σ	Range
Pure men (23)	82.7 ± 0.9	4.1 ± 0.6	$75.0 - 89.3$
Mixed men (10)	82.8 ± 1.0	2.9 ± 0.7	$78.9 - 86.3$
Pure women (20)	84.5 ± 0.7	3.3 ± 0.5	$79.7 - 89.7$
Mixed women (4)	84.1 —	—	$80.2 - 87.4$

The slight difference between the pure and mixed groups is what could be expected with such a limited foreign admixture, but the difference between the male and female indices is unusually great.

No attempt will be made here to compare my data with those collected from other Polynesian groups, and such comparisons must in my opinion be made with great caution. The samples from most groups are not representative and usually too small moreover. Important local variations exist in the Tuamotu group, and the natives from certain islands like Reao, Takoto and Napuka are easily recognized at a glance. Shapiro's caution (1943, p. 3) is therefore well warranted: "The belief that the Polynesians are not only a composite population racially but a heterogeneous one geographically has grown widespread and firmly established. Although these concepts are not necessarily corollary, they have tended to become so and to acquire the status of an equation in an anthropological cliché. If space permitted, it would be instructive to trace the genesis of the one and its influence upon the other. But whatever the origin of this conjunction may be, it is necessary to bear in mind that both the racial composition and the local differentiation of the Polynesians remain problems which have not yet received their final solution." More light will be shed on the problem of the Tuamotuan islanders' racial complexity when the results of the Bishop Museum surveys in the 1930s are eventually published.

CHAPTER VI · **Annual cycle of events**

1. General events

The following table shows in chronological order all events of general interest and importance in 1950:

JANUARY	1	Sunday. Whole population in village.
	2–10	Repair work on the wharf and preparations for an expected visit by the governor. Rains and calm.
	13	The administrator of the Tuamotu group visits Raroia.
	middle	Some of the islanders begin to prepare copra in the Raro sector on the southwest side of the atoll.
	16	Schooner loads copra.
	21	Schooner loads copra.
	end	Half of the population works in Raro.
FEBRUARY	beginning	Strong wind. Between half and three quarters of the population works in Raro.
	middle	Heavy rains.
	16	Schooner loads copra.
	22	Schooner loads copra.
MARCH	beginning	The work in Raro continues.
	19–21	Schooner loads 18 tons in Raro, the whole population back in village for several days. Many persons drunk.
	end	Work continued in Raro.
APRIL	1	Whole population back in village for Easter.
	2–7	Complete calm.
	6	Two schooners load copra.
	7	Good Friday.
	10–11	Three schooners load copra.
	end	First shoals of *Selar crumenophtholmnus* appear, and many postpone their departure to Raro.

MAY	beginning	About a quarter of the population works in a new copra sector, Gake.
	7–8	Schooner loads copra.
	15	Schooner loads copra.
	14	Jeanne d'Arc celebration. The whole population in village.
	middle	Numerous shoals of *Selar crumenophtholmnus*. Heavy rains and winds.
	18	Ascension Day. The whole population still in village.
	end	Most people back in Gake.
JUNE	whole month	Shell diving by a small number of men.
	beginning	A few families continue the work in Gake.
	3–6	Three schooners load copra.
	13	The missionary arrives. The whole population in village.
	16	Schooner loads copra.
	18	De Gaulle Day celebrated. Restaurants and wheel of fortune. The celebrations continue a week.
	second half	The turtles begin to appear. Strong wind.
	27–30	Schooner loads copra in Gake.
	30	Communion for the children. The whole population in village.
JULY	whole month	Shell diving by a small number of men.
	beginning	Strong wind. The whole population stays in village waiting for better weather and provisions. Turtles frequently caught.
	middle	No food and very little water left. Most people live on fish and coconuts. Strong wind.
	14	French National Day celebrated. Restaurants and wheel of fortune continue a week.
	23–24	Schooner arrives with provisions.
AUGUST	beginning	Some families return to work in Raro. Many men chase turtles.
	15	Assumption celebrated. The whole population in village.
	18	The missionary leaves.
	end	Calm. Impossible to return to Raro. The men on turtle hunt.
SEPTEMBER	whole month	Three quarters of the population works in Raro.
	1	Schooner loads copra. Visit by the deputy.
	12	The administrator of the Tuamotu group visits Raroia. The whole population in village.
	middle	The turtle season over.

OCTOBER	beginning	Three quarters of the population still in Raro.
	15–19	Two schooners load copra. Everybody plays card. Many drunk.
	end	Most islanders work again in Raro.
NOVEMBER	whole month	The lands around the village worked. Everybody permanently returned to the village.
	8–10	Schooner loads copra. Complete calm.
	middle	Bird catching and egg collecting begin and last until the end of the year.
	11	Armistice Day celebrated. Wheels of fortune and restaurants. The celebration continues two weeks.
	end	Strong wind.
DECEMBER	whole month	Everybody in village making copra on the adjacent lands.
	beginning	Bad weather.
	middle	Rest period.
	20	Christmas celebrations begin and last until the end of the year.

2. Schooners calling at Raroia

The schooner calls are such important events in the annual cycle and play so vital a part in the islanders' lives, that I have decided to present here separately the complete data on the frequency of the schooner communications with Papeete.

There is no boat or schooner on Raroia seaworthy enough to carry people or freight to Papeete, and the few canoes or boats in existence cannot even be used for visiting other atolls in the Tuamotu group with the exception of the neighbouring atoll of Takume. The Raroians therefore depend for travelling and transport exclusively on the trading schooners belonging to private owners or (in one case) to the Tuamotu Co-operative Society.

The total number of boats calling at Raroia in 1950 was 38. Of these three were administration schooners and one a naval hydrographic ship. The Raroians thus had 34 opportunities to sell copra and to buy merchandise. (Which was more than enough from the commercial point of view as the islanders had copra to sell to only 24 of the schooners.)

All the trading schooners have their base in Papeete and return there after each cruise to unload the copra and take aboard a new stock of merchandise. This does not necessarily mean that the islanders had 34 opportunities to go to Papeete during the year. Practical and economic considerations greatly reduce this number. A trading voyage to the Tuamotus usually lasts from four to six weeks, and in some instances when the schooner also visits the Marquesas or Mangareva, it takes at least two months. Since the passengers pay so much per day for their transportation, the itinerary of the schooner *after* it leaves Raroia is of considerable importance. Thus it can be seen that all the schooner calls cannot be regarded as being of the same value to the islanders, and I have therefore in Table XII classified them according to the *real* opportunities to travel which they offer.

TABLE XII: *Number of trading schooners calling at Raroia in 1950*

Month	Total	Coming from Papeete		Returning to Papeete	
		Announced	Unannounced	Announced	Unannounced
January	4	1	2	—	1
February	3	1	1	1	—
March	2	—	1	—	1
April	6	2	2	—	2
May	3	—	—	1	2
June	5	3	—	—	2
July	1	—	1	—	—
August	1	—	—	1	—
September	4	2	1	1	—
October	2	1	—	1	—
November	2	1	—	—	1
December	1	1	—	—	—
Total	34	12	8	5	9

Let us first consider the opportunities to travel *from Raroia to Tahiti*. The important factor here is of course the length of the voyage, and I have therefore separated the 34 schooners calling at Raroia into two groups: those which call at Raroia at the beginning, and those which call at Raroia towards the end of their cruise. (Called respectively "Coming" and "Returning".) If we disregard all the schooners in the first category, as the Raroians do themselves, the number of opportunities to go to Papete is immediately reduced to 14. (Whether the call of

133

the schooner is announced beforehand over the radio is of no importance in this case, as the islanders are ready to leave at very short notice.)

The number of occasions to travel in the opposite direction, *from Papeete to Raroia,* must also be reduced. None of the schooners follows a regular schedule or a fixed itinerary, but the atolls where the schooner is to call are announced for each voyage over the French broadcasting system in Tahiti. Depending on the circumstances and information gathered during the cruise the itinerary may, however, be changed, some atolls by-passed and additional ones visited. For Raroians who want to travel from Papeete the only communications on which they can depend are of course the schooners which have announced that they have included Raroia in their itinerary, and the fact that other schooners may call there eventually does not help them in the slightest. When the announced schooners coming from Papeete are separated from the un-announced ones, the number of practical opportunities for transportation is reduced from 20 to 12.

For Raroians who wanted to go to Tahiti in 1950 there was thus at least one schooner a month, except during the months of July and December, and the mean number of opportunities per month was 1.2. For Raroians who wanted to return to their home island from Papeete, there were no schooners during the months of March, May, July and August, and the monthly mean was only 1.0.

These relatively rare and irregular communications with Papeete are certainly to a large extent the cause of the retarded development of certain aspects of the economic and social life on Raroia.

CHAPTER VII · **Land ownership**

The problems of land ownership are serious and extremely complex on Raroia as everywhere else in the Tuamotus, and a special study would be required in order to throw full light on them. I have lacked the time for this, and the following is therefore only a rapid survey of the situation with some general observations.

1. Origin of difficulties

At the root of all difficulties is undoubtedly the rapid change in the economic system without corresponding necessary adjustments in land usage and ownership. Before the rise of the copra trade, each atoll was divided into districts, which belonged to the various kindreds (see Chapter II), and even if there was some rivalry over the food resources, certainly no disputes occurred within each district concerning the land itself.

When, however, during the second half of the last century (see Chapter III), the natives began to realize the value and advantage of making plantations of coconut palms, they also gradually became "land-conscious" and wanted to secure the exclusive rights to the profits from the lands they had planted. This created considerable friction, and the situation soon became very confused. After 1880 an attempt was immediately made to create order and to introduce legal procedures. Committees of prominent natives were created on all the atolls—on Raroia in 1883—which were thoroughly to examine the question of land ownership.

The basic principle governing the work of these committees was that legal title to land should be given only to the individual who could prove by reciting his genealogy that he belonged to the descent group *(gāti)*, which owned the land in common in ancient times. When there were rival claims, the ownership was to be attributed to the person with the closest genealogical affiliation with the ancestor who first occupied the disputed land. This principle was generally respected by the natives, and the genealogies for each *gāti* were officially recorded in public books, which henceforth were to be the basis of all land settlements.

The committees were furthermore charged with the task of making accurate surveys and determining the boundaries of each plot. (A work for which they were poorly equipped and which they therefore could not perform properly.) In each case the documents were sent to the Land Bureau in Tahiti, and once confirmed by publication in the official journal and registered at the bureau they had legal validity.

This arrangement seems at first glance adequate, but a basic injustice was inherent in it. Many epidemics and diseases had already ravaged the group, and a great number of people had died on Raroia as elsewhere in the Tuamotus. The decrease in population was naturally not proportionate in all the different districts into which the atoll was divided. Thus while in one district only some few persons had survived, in another of approximately the same size, there were perhaps ten times as many survivors. As assignment of land titles was based on genealogical affiliation with the *gāti* traditionally occupying the district, in the former case each individual got a considerable piece of land, whereas in the latter, the allotment for each individual was diminutive.[1]

Leaving the question of equitable distribution aside, the problem seemed nevertheless to be satisfactorily resolved. New difficulties soon arose, however, and they were principally of two kinds:

1. Due to the instability of the marriages, the complexity of the relationships and the uncertain status of the various children (legitimate, illegitimate and adopted), the inheritors preferred in many cases to cultivate the land in common in accordance with old native custom. In

---

[1] The appearance of these difficulties as soon as the old lineal kindreds (nonunilinear descent groups) broke up confirms Goodenough's hypothesis about their land-regulating character (see Chapter II, pp. 63–64).

this way the clear titles established in 1883 were already confused after one or two generations.

2. In other cases the existing land was too pedantically divided up among all inheritors, which meant that the parcels of land, continuously increasing in number, grew smaller and became more widely scattered. A family which in one generation applied this principle, might in the next adhere to the first, which of course did not make the situation any better.

The only possible remedies would have been: in the first place to settle the inheritance questions after each death, and in the second place continuously to redistribute and concentrate the land holdings through buying and selling. These solutions, which are applied regularly in countries with Western economic and legal systems, have *not* been tried by the natives. The reasons for this are probably:

a. The natives have still not adopted a commercial attitude towards land, but regard it as inalienable, as did their ancestors.

b. Most of the land surveys made by the committees in 1883 were faulty and could never be used as a basis for commercial transactions.

c. Many of the titles established in 1883 were never registered for one reason or another, and others were lost at the Land Bureau in Papeete during the cyclones of 1903 and 1906. Therefore no one any longer knows who is the owner of these lands, and they cannot be traded.

d. The natives are completely ignorant and even suspicious of Western legal procedures. Furthermore, they have to go to Papeete each time they want any legal settlement, which makes them still less inclined to have recourse to the law.

The situation has gradually deteriorated, and to-day the atoll is split up into innumerable plots of ridiculously small size, each owner's land holdings are extremely scattered and very few Raroians have clear titles or any titles at all to the land they use. As a result there are many disputes, much time is lost in traveling between the scattered lands, and long stretches of land are not planted, as nobody knows who the owners are. Therefore, when I subsequently speak of ownership, *de facto* occupancy is thereby meant.

2. Number of plots

The total number of parcels of land outside the central village, where the conditions are different, is on Raroia approximately 1,000 for a total vegetated area of 921 hectares. Theoretically the barren parts of the atoll rim have owners, too, but as nobody is interested in these portions and no reliable information concerning ownership could be obtained, they are not included in this number.

Thanks to the detailed map of Raroia prepared on the basis of aerial photographs taken by our Pacific Science Board team on June 20, 1952 (Newell, 1954 a, p. 3), it has been possible to determine the vegetated area with sufficient accuracy. (The map is included in Newell, 1954 c.) Together with Dr. Maxwell Doty of the Department of Botany of the University of Hawaii I later tried to determine how much of the vegetated area was taken up by palm plantations. The conclusion arrived at in this way is that of the 921 hectares of vegetated area, 587 hectares are covered with coconut palms. (The remaining 334 hectares probably indicate the approximate proportion of disputed lands or lands without known owners). The average size of each plot is thus less than one hectare, and few seem to surpass or fall below this figure. There may be 20 or 30 land holdings bigger than 2 hectares, but on the other hand, even many of the 75 islets with a vegetated area smaller than one hectare are divided up between two or more owners.

The biggest land holdings are on the five big islets with the notable exception of the islet where the village is situated. I have surveyed two of these islets, Tetou on the east side of the atoll, Teputaiti, south of the village, on the west side, and the whole stretch of land north of the village. The figures for these parts of the atoll are:

Tetou	18 hect.	19 parcels
Teputaiti	63 hect.	52 parcels
North of the village	26 hect.	63 parcels

How much land, measured in hectares, each individual owns unfortunately cannot be computed with any exactness, as no map indicating the land holdings exists and titles are lacking for a great number of lands as mentioned above. In order to get at least a rough idea of the distribution of the land, I have chosen to use as a basis for my estimate the total amount of copra produced by each Raroian land owner on his own lands during 1950 (see Table XIII). As these figures are complete and reliable, I think that they give a better picture of the situation than simply a list of the *number* of plots owned by each person.

TABLE XIII: *Land holdings on Raroia as judged from production figures*

Annual production in tons	Number of producing		Total number of persons	Total number of tons
	Men	Women		
0	16	13	29	0
1	2	1	3	3
2	3	2	5	10
3	2	4	6	18
4	2	3	5	20
5	2	2	4	20
6	2	2	4	24
7	3	0	3	21
8	1	2	3	24
9	3	0	3	27
10	0	0	0	0
11	0	0	0	0
12	0	0	0	0
13	1	0	1	13
Total	37	29	66	180

The difference between the total annual production of copra, 187 tons (see p. 165), and the figure above, 180 tons, is due to the fact that some few individuals who own land on Raroia live elsewhere in French Oceania. But as a person who migrates to another island as a rule, cannot depend on his remaining relatives to send him money from the produce of his lands, the actual number of absent land owners is probably somewhat higher than the statistics indicate.

The group of landless persons is principally made up of the "foreigners", i.e. natives from other islands in French Oceania, married to Raroians. The only exceptions are two "foreigners" who were adopted young and given land. A young Raroian man or woman customarily

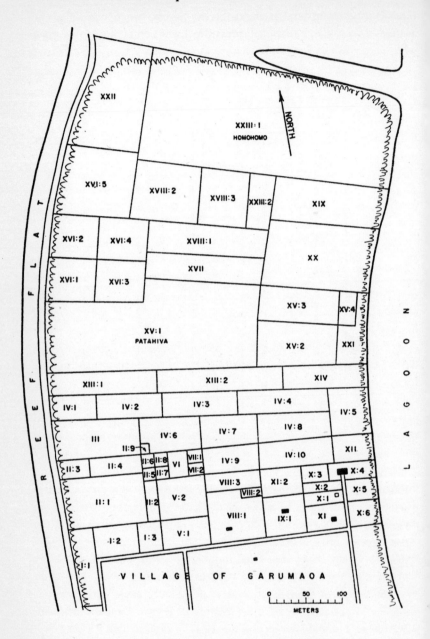

Map C. *How the land north of the village is divided*

receives a parcel of land from his or her parents when marrying, and as the Raroians marry young, all individuals who can do an adult's work, with one or two exceptions, also have their own lands.

3. Concrete examples

Finally, in order to give concrete examples of how confused the land question is in all its aspects, I include here more detailed data for one section of the atoll. The section is the northern part of the islet on which the village is situated, and it measures roughly 400 × 650 metres. I surveyed it simply by pacing it out in company with the members of the village council who indicated the boundaries of the land holdings. The result is shown on map C.

The total number of plots for this section, measuring 26 hectares, is 63. Many of the parcels of land have identical names, and altogether there are only 23 names for these 63 parcels. This fact seems to indicate that larger land units have been divided fairly recently. This is also the opinion of the natives, who claim that the splitting into smaller units has occurred since the official survey in 1883.

In order to verify this and to study in more detail the changes which have taken place since 1883, I have searched through the entire register for Raroia at the Land Bureau in Tahiti. That the register is incomplete was immediately shown by the fact that titles for only 19 land parcels in the chosen section were found. These 19 parcels totalled roughly *10 hectares,* whereas the section actually measures *26 hectares!* For almost two thirds of the land there are thus no titles at all.

Of the 23 land names in use today 8 were found in the register, and the number of plots with identical names was much greater in 1950 than in 1883.

That a considerable fragmentation has actually taken place during the last 70 years is thus amply demonstrated in these cases, and everything seems to indicate that this is the general trend on Raroia, and probably also in the Tuamotus as a whole. Subdivision of lands had, however, in all possibility already occurred in post-contact time previous to 1883, as the situation was then already at variance with the old Polynesian principle: one land—one name.

Out of the 17 parcels of land for which titles were found in the register,

16 had single owners, and one had three brothers as owners in 1883. The situation was thus surprisingly clear at the outset, but during the intervening 70 years it has become so confused that it is now almost impossible to trace the history of many of these parcels with certainty. How rapidly the changes have taken place is best shown by this comparison between the number of plots with identical names in 1883 and 1950:

Land on the map no.	Number of parcels	
	1883	1950
IV	3	10
V	1	2
X	3	6
XV	1	4
XVI	3	5
XIX	2	1
XX	3	1
XXIII	1	2
Total	17	31

I have interrogated all the individuals at present regarded as owners of the 63 parcels into which the section (map C) is divided. They are at least 150 in number—I gave up at this point from sheer exhaustion—but many of them are, of course, identical, as the same person frequently claims more than one parcel. It would be useless to repeat the explanations of each individual as to how he establishes his claims, as they are too conflicting and fragmentary, and I shall therefore only give a few examples.

Let us for instance take land no. IV (map C) and cite the histories of a few parcels:

Parcel 1 is owned by person "A" and his sister who lives in Takume. Their right is, however, violently contested by three second degree cousins. "A" makes the copra, but does not send any money to his sister. He has no title to the land.

Parcel 2 is owned by a woman who received it in the following way: Three generations ago there lived on Raroia a couple who possessed a great number of lands. The two daughters "B" and "C" inherited all the lands, but did not divide them up between themselves. "B" died first and left four children, but her sister "C" took control of all the lands. "C" had no children and before she died she distributed the lands among her nieces, the four daughters of "B". The first received 30 parcels (among them the one in question), the second 27, the third 6 and the fourth 5. The reason for this unequal distribution is said to have been that the two first nieces were the favourites of "C". The husband of "C" received nothing. He is still alive but does not seem to have any objection to the arrangement. No title exists.

Parcel 3 is owned by a single person. There is a title to the land, or at least a title, which with some benevolence could be interpreted as describing this parcel, but the owner is not able to prove his relationship with the original owner, in whose name the title was issued.

Parcel 4 is disputed by half a dozen persons with conflicting versions of the legal and genealogical facts.

And so on *ad absurdum*.

It is of course outside the scope of the present study to try to indicate definite solutions to the problem, but it must be mentioned that a prescription law, granting title to a person after 30 years of uninterrupted and uncontested occupancy of land, has been applied elsewhere in French Oceania in troublesome cases. Such a solution, however, first requires a detailed land survey and careful examination of the situation.

CHAPTER VIII · **Surplus production**

The main feature of the economic system on Raroia is the startling degree to which the islanders have abandoned the old direct subsistence activities in favour of a surplus economy. It is therefore only logical to begin the description of production on Raroia with the activities directed at the creating of a surplus.

Due to the infertile soil and the limited natural resources there are few products of an atoll like Raroia on which a surplus economy dependent on the world market could be based, and the only ones which have been tried so far are mother-of-pearl shells, sea slugs, and copra. Of these copra has gradually become of paramount importance as previously described in Chapter III.

A. COPRA PRODUCTION

As the basis of the economy and the only *regular* source of income copra production has profoundly influenced all aspects of the natives' lives. I have therefore judged it more appropriate and convenient to treat here in its functional context not only the purely economic activities related to copra growing, but also the interrelation and interdependence between these and other activities.

1. Sectors and seasons

For the purpose of making copra, the atoll is divided into several sectors (Map D), which are visited in turn by all land owners simultaneously, according to a rotation system previously agreed upon. The main reason for this system is the scattered distribution of land holdings which makes it virtually impossible for the owner to watch his parcels from the village where he lives, and to prevent the theft of nuts. The system has an ancient taboo practice at its basis, and the same word, *rāhui*, which formerly was used for trees periodically set aside, is now used for the sectors.

A certain sector is declared open for copra work for a well defined period by the chief after close consultation with the village council (and frequently the whole population). The owners who have land in this sector—and usually all have at least one parcel—sail over from the village and establish themselves somewhere in the sector until the work is done, whereafter they return to the village and await the opening of the next sector.

The sectors are open for work 2, 3 or 4 months depending on the prospects for the harvest. The round of all sectors is usually made in eight months, and some adjustments have therefore to be made to the annual weather seasons.

The number and boundaries of sectors vary somewhat, but at the beginning of 1950 there were three, called Raro, Village and Gake. Raro (I) comprised all the land south of the islet on which the village is situated. The village lands (II) stretched from there to the pass. The rest (III) which thus included both Tokerau, Gake and Kereteki, formed the remaining sector, which took the name Gake (see Map D).

In November and December 1949, the islanders worked in Gake. According to their previous agreement, they should therefore have continued to work the sectors in the following order in 1950:

> I. Raro   4 months (January–April)
> II. Village   2 months (May–June)
> III. Gake   2 months (July–August)

And beginning the cycle anew:

> I. Raro   4 months (September–December)

According to the schedule the islanders worked the Raro sector during the first 4 months of the year, but already by April it was decided to change the sequence and work sector III before the village lands (II). The next change in the schedule was made in June, when the Raroians

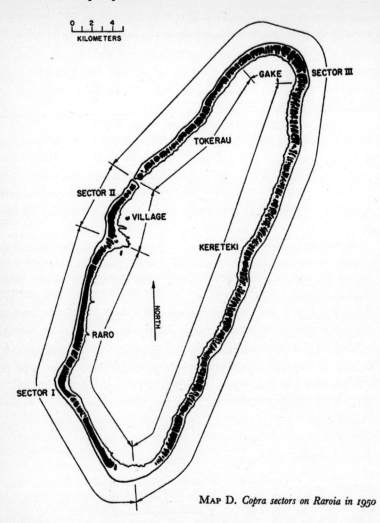

MAP D. *Copra sectors on Raroia in 1950*

discovered that there was an unusual abundance of nuts in Raro. They decided immediately to return there in July instead of working sector III. The period was eventually extended to the end of October. After the termination of the work in the Raro sector, the population decided suddenly to change the schedule completely. The atoll was now divided into only two sectors, Raro and the rest, and work was to be done 4 months at a time in each sector.

146

Not even these modified schedules were adhered to, and the time was actually divided between the sectors in the following way in 1950:

January	Sector I
February	,,
March	,,
April	,,
May	Sector III
June	,,
July	Sector I
August	,,
September	,,
October	,,
November	Sector II
December	,,

When I revisited Raroia in 1952 the islanders had changed their work schedule again, and the island was now divided into five sectors: Village, Tokerau, Gake, Kereteki and Raro. The diving for mother-of-pearl shell on Takume that year, however, completely upset the copra work and eventually forced the Raroians once more to improvise a new schedule.

That rigid working programs are not and cannot be followed is only natural, as they do not leave room for other activities, religious and civil celebrations, seasonal fishing, bad weather and so on. How closely the copra work actually depends on other activities and events will be shown in the next part.

2. Interdependence of activities

Some important interrelationships are immediately brought out by the plotting of the main activities in the accompanying chart (Fig. VII). In order to determine the influence of the weather, all periods of heavy rains, complete calm and strong wind lasting longer than five days have been indicated. The stress here is on the interdependence of the activities, and for more detailed information on the various events during the year of 1950, Chapter VI, Annual cycle of events, must be consulted.

The Raro sector was opened on January 1, but the first workers did not leave the village until the middle of January mainly because of complete calm. As there was only one motor-boat on the atoll and the majority of the natives therefore had to depend on their sailing canoes, calm or stormy weather of course completely prevented all intra-island travelling. From the middle of January to the end of March most of the islanders worked in Raro. The two spells of calm and the strong winds in February resulted in fewer visits back to the village, and thus more time spent on work.

The first gap in the work schedule occurred in April. It corresponded to the Easter week, which is elaborately celebrated on Raroia, and was prolonged a couple of days by the unique event of three schooners simultaneously loading copra. In May, only a short time after the opening of sector III, the population again returned to the village for Jeanne d'Arc Day (May 14) and Ascension Day (May 18). The stay in the village was prolonged about ten days this time, as the wind was too strong and large shoals of fish appeared along the village shore.

This fish, *Selar crumenophtholmnus,* is caught with long palm leaf sweeps, both the preparation and handling of which require a great number of men and women. The result is, however, always splendid, and many of the Raroians were so tempted by this easy way to procure

Fig. VII: *Interdependence of activities in 1950*

	Jan.	Feb.	March	April	May	June	July	Aug.	Sept.	Oct.	Nov.	Dec.
Work outside the village	▬	▬	▬	▬	▬			▬	▬	▬		
Shell-diving						▬	▬	▬				
Turtle season						▬	▬	▬				
Fish shoals				▬								
Birds and eggs											▬	
Celebrations				▬	▬	▬					▬	▬
Missionary						▬	▬					
Heavy rains	▬	▬		▬								▬
Complete calm	▬	▬		▬				▬			▬	
Strong wind		▬			▬	▬	▬					▬

NOTE: The heavy lines indicate the most important activities of the islanders and the approximate duration of these activities. The exact degree of participation in copra work is shown in part 5, Table XIV, and the relative importance of the other activities is indicated in Chapter IX. See also: Annual cycle of events, Chapter VI.

delicious food, that they stayed on in the village from Easter, when the shoals first appeared, until their disappearance at the end of May. This can be seen clearly in the production records. (Part 7 of this chapter.)

The long work interval from the middle of June to the middle of August was partly due to the weather. June and July are the winter months with relatively cold and strong winds, which often prevent canoe voyages. Still more important is that it is also the turtle season. The turtle is an eagerly sought food and each time a turtle is caught the whole population gathers. Two national holidays also fall in these months, the anniversary of General de Gaulle's rallying speech on June 18, and Bastille Day on July 14. Both celebrations, which include speeches, games, and markets with wheels of fortune, were prolonged about a week.

The work stoppage—which was never complete (see Table XIV in this chapter)—would certainly not have been of such a long duration, if some additional reasons for staying in the village had not existed that year. The first one was the visit of the missionary, who came in the middle of June and remained on the atoll until the middle of August. Although it is certainly a coincidence that the gap in the work schedule exactly corresponds to the time of the missionary's stay, the importance attached to this visit by the islanders must not be underrated.

Diving for mother-of-pearl shell was allowed during June and July, and though the number of men who actually dived was only about a dozen, this meant at least double that number of persons absent from copra work, as the divers' families stayed in the village.

In spite of all these events and activities, the Raroians would probably have begun work in Raro, which sector was opened July 1, much earlier if an unexpected and rather unfortunate circumstance had not prevented them from doing so. Due to the capricious schedules of the schooners (see Chapter VI), none appeared in time to replenish the stocks of the store-keepers, and during the first three weeks of July there was a severe food shortage. As the islanders depend to a great extent on flour, canned food, cigarettes, coffee and other imported goods when making copra, they naturally hesitated to go to work before they had been able to buy new supplies.

From the middle of August to the end of October there were no additional activities going on, except turtle catching until mid-Septem-

ber, and the uninterrupted concentration on the copra work is therefore easily explained. During all this time the sector worked was Raro.

During the final months of the year, the whole population resided in
the village. A certain amount of copra was prepared on adjacent lands,
but much time was also devoted to bird catching and egg collecting in
Tokerau. The weather which was very capricious, as always during this
time of the year, usually determined whether the islanders prepared
copra or sailed over to the northern islets on food gathering expeditions.
The last week of December was of course dominated by the Christmas
celebration and no work whatsoever was done.

It is thus evident that it is a combination of factors rather than isolated events which influence the working cycle. Probably still other
factors than those listed above are influential in determining the decisions of the islanders and could be discovered through deeper probing,
but we have to content ourselves here with these main indications and
clues.

3. Working conditions and techniques

Raroia is an atoll of considerable size, 44 km long and 14 km broad.
The total area is about 400 km² and the circumference of the reef 90 km
(Chapter I). With the scattered distribution of land holdings and the
concentration of the whole population in one village the islanders have
to make many long canoe voyages in order to work the copra.

All these trips are made in sailing canoes with outriggers or in small
boats, and as the wind is fairly strong as a rule and the surface of the
lagoon rather rough for such small craft, the voyages to and from copra
sectors are far from comfortable. The travellers are frequently drenched
and during bad weather suffer a great deal from cold. The result is an
almost continuous prevalence of coughs and bronchitis, as the Raroians
have no water-proofed or warm clothing.

Under most favourable conditions, a canoe voyage from the village to
the southern sector (Raro) or the northern (Gake) takes a little more
than two hours. Heavy seas or contrary winds can, however, easily prolong the voyage to five or six hours. Only one person had an outboard
motor and boat of European type in 1950, but it was little more seaworthy than the outrigger canoes, and could not be used at all when
the sea was rough.

It must be noticed, incidentally, that for easy canoe communications, the village is not ideally situated, as it lies on the western side of the atoll, along the lagoon shore, exposed to the continuous easterly trade winds. The nearness to the pass and the good anchorage seem, however, in the opinion of the islanders, to compensate for this disadvantage.

Only one sector, Raro, can be reached on foot from the village, and even then only with considerable difficulty as there are many intervening channels with waist-deep water. If the easterly trade winds are exceptionally strong over a prolonged period, the men may drag their canoes across the land rim and travel outside the reef along the west coast of the atoll, keeping close to the shore. Both Raro and Tokerau can be reached in this way from the village.

If possible, most of the Raroians prefer to band together when working in the copra sectors. There is a total of four small villages or hamlets: two in Raro (Teputaiti and Oneroa), one in Kereteki (Tetou) and one in Gake (Tikaheru). The houses are rather primitive and invariably made of plaited palm fronds. No furniture whatsoever is used, and the family members sleep either on the earth floor or on elevated platforms. The food is cooked over open fires. No good fresh water wells exist anywhere, and the most serious inconvenience of life in the copra sectors is, according to the islanders themselves, the inability over extended periods to wash in fresh water. Most of the sectors are infested with mosquitoes, and in some places fires are necessary to keep them away. The prevalent attitude towards work in the sectors is that it is trying and uncomfortable, and everybody always expresses great satisfaction upon return to the permanent village.

It should be noted in passing that the mosquitoes principally breed in the holes made by the numerous land-crabs (*Cardisoma carnifex Herbst*) and in broken coconut shells. "The brackish (or sometimes fresh?) groundwater of enclosed ponds on the lower areas of some of these islands, and the groundwater exposed in the burrows of these 'Papaka Tupa' [land-crabs] are one of the sources of a considerable population of bird mosquitoes (*Culex* spp.). Another source of this mosquito population is the ever-present large number of rain-filled broken or half coconut shells lying around on both high and low ground, on and around the coconut groves. This secondary coconut shell habitat of the mosquito larvae dates only from the time the coconut palm was brought to Raroia

151

by the Polynesian natives." (Morrison, 1954 a, pp. 2–3.) As the Raroians formerly used to eat land-crabs and no copra plantations existed there were fewer breeding places for the mosquitoes. In addition to the breeding places mentioned by Morrison there are also numerous abandoned taro ditches, which always contain groundwater. The appearance of mosquitoes—which did not exist in former times according to the old inhabitants—is thus a secondary result of the changed economy.

The preparation of copra follows the general pattern found everywhere in the Tuamotus. The ripe nuts which fall are gathered into heaps in open clearings. They are cleft into halves by a single, well-directed blow of the axe. The halves are piled one upon the other in wall-like rows with the convex outside upwards and the hollow inside downwards. This protects the flesh against rain and provides good air circulation.

In Tahiti and other mountain islands with high humidity, drying boards which can be covered at night are required, but on Raroia, where the air is comparatively dry, this is unnecessary. The simple method just described is very well suited to the local conditions with scattered land holdings and great mobility of population, but it takes more time to pile the coconut halves than immediately to take out the flesh and lay it on a drying board.

When the copra kernel has dried—in 4 to 8 days, depending on the weather—it is separated from the husk and put into sacks holding about 50 kgs each. The husk, together with uprooted plants and weeds, is burned. The clearing of the land may continue, but as a general rule very little time is spent in the copra sectors above the minimum required for the copra preparation.

The only implements used are a stick with a hook for gathering nuts, an axe for cleaving them and an S-formed knife for separating the flesh from the husk. A long bush-knife, similar to the South American machete, is used for clearing the bush. These implements are the same as those originally introduced when the islanders were first taught copra preparation about seventy-five years ago. The only technological improvement during this time which I have been able to discover is the method of drying the nut halves. Until the early 1930s the islanders suspended the nut-halves on fiber cords from the trees, as still is done for instance in the Leeward Is. But after having been persuaded by a missionary of the time gain and work economy of the method of piling the nuts in rows, they all changed over to that method.

4. Agricultural methods

The islander's attitude towards his plantation is very different from, for instance, that of a modern farmer. As a rule he regards the trees as able to take care of themselves and never seems to think that the yield could be increased by better agricultural methods. This is not really surprising, as it certainly was the prevailing attitude towards the coconut tree as well as the pandanus palm in pre-European times.

The change-over to a modern surplus economy has in this case as in so many others been partial. The islanders were taught to plant trees, and did so out of profit motives, but no pertinent knowledge about new or better plantation methods ever reached them. This can be seen in innumerable instances.

To begin with, the palms are rarely planted with enough space between the trees, and there is today hardly a single plantation on Raroia planned so as to give a maximum yield. A condition which undoubtedly has contributed greatly to over-planting is the small size of the land holdings. In order to make maximum use of his diminutive plots, each owner has planted his trees right up to the border line. The result is of course double lines of palms along nearly all the borders.

The necessity of replacing old trees hardly seems to be understood either. Most of the palms are too old and the yield greatly reduced, but due to the work it requires to cut down the palms with hand axes and to the temporary loss that ensues, few owners are inclined to replant their lands.

Instead of controlled replanting, a spontaneous planting occurs all the time, as in many cases nuts which have fallen are left on the ground so long (especially when lost in the brush) that they finally grow into new palm trees. The islanders rarely want to cut down these trees under the false conviction that they mean additional nuts. 300 to 400 trees per hectare is therefore not an unusual average.

Even if the nuts are not allowed to grow into trees, they lose their value for copra preparation if they are left on the ground too long. Ordinarily a nut begins to sprout after three or four months, after which time the flesh is unsuitable for copra. Therefore the time between the visits to a sector should not be longer than about three months. Actually the sectors are often unworked for periods greatly exceeding this limit, as in 1950 in the case of the village lands which were first revisited after eight months, and the lands in Gake which were not visited for six months.

Very few lands are cleared, which can to some extent obviously be explained by the fact that the labour force (almost exclusively the landowners themselves) on Raroia is not sufficient, but also probably due in part to the system of joint ownership. If a plot is owned by several persons, none of course is inclined to clear and improve it, as he does not know whether he will eventually inherit it and reap the fruit of his work or not.

No fertilizers are used, and no trees are circled with rat-protecting bands of aluminum. How many nuts are eaten by the rats is of course impossible to compute with exactness. Judging from the number of pierced nuts found on the ground, the natives estimate that the rats eat between one third and one half of the crop. Morrison (1954 a, pp. 3–4) writes: "There are two species of rats on the islands of Raroia Atoll. One, *Rattus exulans,* the small reddish species commonly known as the Polynesian Rat, has no fear of man or his flashlights, lives on various seeds, and has been seen feeding on the flowers of *Guettarda*. This species probably arrived at Raroia with the coming of the Polynesian people ... *Rattus exulans* is not known to affect the crop of coconuts or copra. The second species *(Rattus rattus alexandrinus),* larger and grayish, runs away and hides when discovered at night, and actively feeds on the coconuts. It gnaws a hole in the side of small green coconuts on the trees to eat out their contents, causing them to drop off later and be lost; it also gnaws a hole into ripe coconuts on the ground, and eats the coconut meat out of them. Crop production figures have been gathered on Tahiti, in the Society Islands, that show that this species of rat may destroy up to 40 % of the copra crop from those coconut trees that are not protected by a sheet metal band of sufficient height and smoothness to prevent the rats from climbing the tree trunks, and reaching the green coconuts. Also, this gray rat species travels from tree to tree across the touching and/or overlapping coconut leaves where the trees are crowded and not isolated. This larger grayish rat has apparently completely displaced the small reddish Polynesian Rat on those islands of Raroia Atoll the gray rat now inhabits. According to the people of Raroia this gray rat appeared on Raroia Atoll only after the development of the commercial copra trade began about a century ago."

The annual output is still further reduced by insects of which *Aspidiotus destructor*[1] is the worst. This insect first appeared on Raroia after the cyclone of 1906 and has since then gradually spread over the atoll. The insect attaches itself to the leaves and sucks out the sap, which seriously impedes the growth of the nuts and in extreme cases eventually kills the tree. On the seaward plots, where the soil is poor, a great number of palm trees are actually unproductive. The natives are not fully aware of the menace, and the only action they have so far taken to exterminate the insects is to burn husk and refuse at the root of the palm trees, which of course is a completely inefficient measure and furthermore is harmful to the trees.

The general outlook on Raroia is far from bright, in spite of the fact that the present annual production of coconuts is more than enough for the islanders' needs. The greatest impediment to greater agricultural efficiency is simply the ignorance of the islanders. The Raroians have taken over the idea of planting and producing a surplus, but are still unaware of the necessary requirements for such large scale enterprise. As in so many other cases, they have adopted only *one* element of a cultural complex, and they now suffer from the consequences of partial lags.

5. Work participation and organization

As I considered it of the greatest importance and interest to have complete and detailed data on the work participation and organization, I took exceptional pains to record during the whole year of 1950 exactly *who* participated in the copra preparation, to *what extent* and for *how long*. As I lived most of the time in the village, which is the permanent dwelling place of all the islanders and the point of departure in each case, and thus could easily keep track of the movements of every individual, the errors and omissions are at a minimum.

[1] This insect was identified during a visit to Raroia in 1953 by Dr W. V. D. Pieris from the South Pacific Commission. I am also indebted to him for other valuable information concerning agricultural methods.

TABLE XIV: *Number of persons per month working outside the village, January–October 1950*

	AGE	MALES			FEMALES		
		Total	Working		Total	Working	
			Persons	Days		Persons	Days
JANUARY	0–14	9	6	55	24	8	94
	15–29	14	9	127	13	9	94
	30–44	14	8	113	11	6	95
	45–59	9	3	18	3	0	0
	60–	4	2	22	4	0	0
	Total	50	28	335	55	23	283
FEBRUARY	0–14	10	6	182	23	11	207
	15–29	13	12	246	13	10	124
	30–44	14	10	248	11	6	164
	45–59	10	4	46	5	2	21
	60–	3	2	39	4	0	0
	Total	50	34	761	56	29	516
MARCH	0–14	10	6	165	23	11	261
	15–29	14	12	240	13	7	193
	30–44	14	6	188	11	6	133
	45–59	9	4	33	3	0	0
	60–	4	2	27	4	0	0
	Total	51	30	653	54	24	587
APRIL	0–14	10	2	8	23	9	62
	15–29	12	9	88	12	7	55
	30–44	14	7	63	11	5	51
	45–59	10	5	21	4	2	12
	60–	4	1	8	5	0	0
	Total	50	24	188	55	23	180
MAY	0–14	9	3	40	22	11	108
	15–29	13	11	98	13	8	76
	30–44	14	8	81	11	6	52
	45–59	11	4	44	5	2	15
	60–	4	0	0	5	0	0
	Total	51	26	263	56	27	251

| | AGE | MALES | | | FEMALES | | |
| | | Total | Working | | Total | Working | |
			Persons	Days		Persons	Days
JUNE	0–14	9	2	18	25	7	30
	15–29	14	12	88	13	4	35
	30–44	15	5	40	11	5	45
	45–59	11	5	33	5	2	18
	60–	3	0	0	5	0	0
	Total	52	24	179	59	18	128
JULY	0–14	9	0	0	25	3	14
	15–29	14	5	27	12	2	18
	30–44	15	5	16	11	2	9
	45–59	12	4	24	4	3	14
	60–	3	0	0	5	0	0
	Total	53	14	67	57	10	55
AUGUST	0–14	9	4	24	24	11	92
	15–29	13	13	106	12	10	96
	30–44	15	15	119	11	6	65
	45–59	11	7	72	6	5	54
	60–	3	1	2	3	1	7
	Total	51	40	323	56	33	314
SEPTEMBER	0–14	10	4	77	24	11	209
	15–29	12	11	241	11	8	168
	30–44	14	14	273	10	6	139
	45–59	11	9	108	5	4	89
	60–	4	1	30	3	1	28
	Total	51	39	729	53	30	633
OCTOBER	0–14	8	3	52	21	3	13
	15–29	10	7	73	8	4	31
	30–44	12	11	93	9	5	72
	45–59	11	5	51	6	3	53
	60–	4	1	2	5	0	0
	Total	45	27	271	49	15	169

The work participation broken down according to sex and age is shown in Table XIV, and the percentages and means are given in Table XV. These tables cover the first ten months of 1950, when the Raroians worked exclusively in the sectors outside the village. For the remaining two months, November and December, the whole population lived in the village and worked the lands adjacent to it alternately with performing all sorts of minor tasks.

The continual coming and going during these last months of the year made it of course impossible to record the number of persons working the copra each day with the same exactness as during the previous months. Therefore I abstained completely from collecting data during November and December. A fairly accurate estimate of the number of working days during these months could, however, be made on the basis of the amount of copra produced.

If we study Tables XIV and XV closely, some general patterns are immediately discernable. The *total number* of persons going away to the sectors outside the village each month does not seem very impressive and rarely amounts to more than approximately half of the population. The figures may give the impression that many islanders never work, and this is of course the case with many of the children and old people, but all those of the most productive ages spend at least some months a year working in the various copra sectors. Due to the unequal distribution of the lands a Raroian may, however, work for a prolonged period in one sector and very little in another one. Hence a rotation of the working personnel every month.

The difference between male and female participation is not great, as seen from the figures of the percentages and the mean number of working days, which are 57.0 % and 12.4 days, respectively 42.2 % and 12.6 days. The high female participation is not surprising, as most women are land owners. It must, however, be noted that their husbands usually do the copra preparation while the women take care of clearing and household duties.

As so many women participate, a natural consequence is that many of the children also spend prolonged periods in the working sectors outside the village. The proportion of children in the working population varies considerably from month to month as seen in Table XIV, but is on the average between 1/4 and 1/5. Older people usually stay behind in the village, and as could be expected, the bulk of the copra workers are the males and females in the most productive ages, 15—44, who account for 62.3 % of the total number of working days for the period January—October. (2,568 out of 3,769 days for the males and 1,715 out of 3,116 days for the females.)

The participation or non-participation cannot, however, be explained solely on the basis of such isolated criteria as sex and age. The total *family situation* of each individual must be taken into consideration, which has been done in Table XVI. Whereas Table XIV on pages 156—157 simply shows *how many* persons participated in the copra work in 1950, Table XVI on page 161 shows *who* they were as determined by family status (or relationship to the other members of the household, as I have here equated family with household). Those who usually participated in the work have been indicated by the letter *c* (copra work), and those who as a rule stayed behind in the village by the letter *v* (village). Only the *structure* of the various families or households is shown in Table XVI, and those who also want to know the *number* of persons in each family are referred to Table XXVII, Chapter XII.

TABLE XV: *Number of persons and days spent in work outside the village in 1950*

Month	MALES					FEMALES				
	Total population	Working	Per cent working	Days of work	Mean no. of work days	Total population	Working	Per cent working	Days of work	Mean no. of work days
January	50	28	56.0	335	12.0	55	23	41.8	283	12.3
February	50	34	68.0	761	22.4	56	29	51.8	516	17.8
March	51	30	58.8	653	21.8	54	24	44.4	587	24.5
April	50	24	48.0	188	7.8	55	23	41.8	180	7.8
May	51	26	51.0	263	10.1	56	27	48.2	251	9.3
June	52	24	46.2	179	7.5	59	18	30.5	128	7.1
July	53	14	26.4	67	4.8	57	10	17.5	55	5.5
August	51	40	78.4	323	8.1	56	33	58.9	314	9.5
September	51	39	76.5	729	18.7	53	30	56.6	633	21.1
October	45	27	60.0	271	10.0	49	15	30.6	169	11.3
Mean	50.4	28.6	57.0	376.9	12.4	55.0	23.2	42.2	311.6	12.6

Only in two families out of the total number of 27 did both husband and wife regularly stay in the village all year. The exceptions are number 21 and 25. The husband in family 21 was ill and his wife therefore stayed home in order to take care of him. The copra was made by the grown-up children. Family 25 is made up of the part-native storekeeper and his wife, who both attened to the business, while the grown-up children made the copra.

In the remaining 25 families, both husband and wife went to work in 21 cases (two widowers and one single man are included in this figure), only the husband in three cases and only the wife in one case. The husband staying behind in the village and letting his wife go to work alone was the chief.

As a rule it can therefore be said that *all* men who can possibly do so participate in work, which undoubtedly shows the importance of the economic motive. That the women accompany their husbands in almost all cases is somewhat surprising as their participation in the work is very limited. A possible explanation which the islanders themselves frequently give is that the women are jealous and do not want to let their husbands go away alone to a copra sector where young girls are always present.

As the women accompany their husbands, the arrangements concerning the young children depend on the existence of old relatives in the families. Eleven of the 27 parents have *small children* below school age. Seven of these parents take the children with them and the remaining four leave them in the village with a parent or old relative. Four of the seven parents who take their children with them have old relatives in the village.

Out of the 14 parents with *children of school age* (6—14 years), eight leave their children in the village. Six of these eight parents have an old relative in the village who takes care of the children, whereas in the remaining two cases one or both parents stay in the village. The remaining six parents usually take their children of school age with them to the copra sectors. Significantly *none* of these parents has an old relative in the village.

The *grown-up children* work regularly in eleven cases out of twelve.

The dependence on older relatives for the care of the young children is thus amply proved by the figures. In the case of the children below school age there is no problem, as they can travel with the parents, if

TABLE XVI: *Family composition and work participation*

Family composition		Participation by family member					
		Hus-band	Wife	Small child	School child	Grown-up child	Old relative
Single:	Family 1	c	—	—	—	—	—
Husband, wife:	Family 2	c	c	—	—	—	—
,,	3	c	c	—	—	—	—
,,	4	c	c	—	—	—	—
,,	5	c	c	—	—	—	—
,,	6	c	c	—	—	—	—
Husband, wife, small child:							
	Family 7	c	c	c	—	—	—
Husband, wife, small child, old relative:	Family 8	c	c	c	—	—	v
Husband, wife, small child, school age, old relative:	Family 9	c	c	c	v	—	v
,,	10	c	—	v	v	—	v
,,	11	c	v	v	v	—	c
Husband, wife, small child, school age, grown-up child:	Family 12	c	—	c	c	c	—
Husband, wife, small child, school age, grown-up child, old relative:							
	Family 13	v	c	v	v	c	v
,,	14	c	c	c	v	c	v
Husband, wife, small child, grown-up child:	Family 15	c	v	v	—	v	—
,,	16	c	c	c	—	c	—
,,	17	c	c	c	—	c	—
Husband, wife, school age child:							
	Family 18	c	c	—	c	—	—
,,	19	c	c	—	c	—	—
Husband, wife: school age child, old relative:	Family 20	c	v	—	v	—	v
Husband, wife, school age child, grown-up child:	Family 21	v	v	—	v	c	—
,,	22	c	c	—	c	c	—
,,	23	c	c	—	c	c	—
,,	24	c	c	—	c	c	—
Husband, wife, grown-up child:	Family 25	v	v	—	—	c	—
,,	26	c	c	—	—	c	—
Husband, wife, grown-up child, old relative:	Family 27	c	c	—	v	—	v

no old relatives exist. The children of school age, however, create a conflict when there is no old relative living with the family. All parents affirm that they want their children to go to school and seem to have a firm belief in the advantages of acquiring a European education. Yet, in spite of this, each time when this desire conflicts with the work, the latter is given precedence, as seen in the six cases above.

A simple solution would of course be to leave the wife behind in the village with the children. Another would be to co-ordinate better the annual working cycle with the school terms. As the women seem to have a strong inclination—due to jealousy or whatever it may be—to accompany their husbands to the work outside the village, the second solution would certainly be the most acceptable. No attempt has yet been made, however, to achieve such a co-ordination, which shows once more how erratic the islanders' efforts are to adjust themselves to new situations and how unsatisfactory the integration of the various cultural elements sometimes is.

6. Weekly variations

The predominance of economic considerations in the case of the conflict between work and school duty of the children is evident. It may therefore be of interest to examine also the relationship between economic and religious activities.

From the very beginning of my stay I noticed a marked tendency among the islanders to return every Sunday to the permanent village, where the only church on the atoll is situated. That this is a regular habit is confirmed by my data for the whole year, but in order to avoid unnecessary repetitions, I have here limited my analysis to a sample month, September.

In Table XVII are shown the number of persons in the village on Sundays (September 3, 10, 17 and 24) and Thursdays (September 7, 14, 21 and 28). In addition, another table, XVIII, has been prepared, showing the variations according to sex and age classes. This differential treatment of the data brings out some unsuspected facts.

The extent to which the islanders return to the village on Sundays— even if it requires a long canoe trip and the loss of at least one working day—is surprisingly great, as shown by the *differences* between the village population on weekdays and Sundays, which are respectively: +44, −50, +17, −19, +35, −36, +30, −26! The high figures are, however, less surprising if we take into consideration that Sunday in any event is sacred, and that no islander works on this day, even if he is alone on an isolated islet far from the village.

TABLE XVII: *Number of persons in village on weekdays and Sundays during September, 1950*

Sex	Age	Total	Number of persons in village on September								
			1	3	7	10	14	17	21	24	28
MALES	0–14	10	6	9	7	6	5	7	4	6	4
	15–29	12	2	12	3	8	3	11	2	10	3
	30–44	14	4	13	4	8	2	11	3	10	3
	45–59	11	8	11	6	5	3	6	4	5	6
	60–	4	3	2	2	2	2	2	2	2	2
	Total	51	23	47	22	29	15	37	15	33	18
FEMALES	0–14	24	15	22	13	15	14	18	13	14	14
	15–29	11	3	11	2	7	5	9	4	11	3
	30–44	10	4	10	4	6	5	8	6	7	5
	45–59	5	4	4	3	4	3	5	3	5	5
	60–	3	3	2	2	2	2	2	2	3	2
	Total	53	29	49	24	34	29	42	28	40	29
Males & females		104	52	96	46	63	44	79	43	73	47

Fig. VIII: *The same data presented in graphical form*

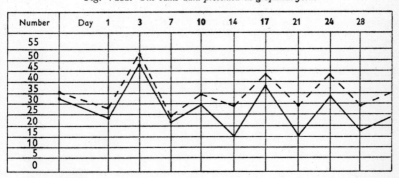

———— males
– – – – females

On the basis of the data presented hitherto, it seems natural to conclude that the islanders return solely for the purpose of attending the church service. If, however, we take the *age* factor into consideration, as done in the following table, we shall find that evidently there is an additional motive present.

TABLE XVIII: *Mean number of persons in village on weekdays and Sundays*

Sex	Age	Total	Weekdays	Per cent	Sundays	Per cent
MALES	0–14	10	5.2	52.0	7.0	70.0
	15–29	12	2.6	21.7	10.2	85.0
	30–44	14	3.2	22.9	10.5	75.0
	45–59	11	5.4	49.1	6.7	60.9
	60–	4	2.2	55.0	2.0	50.0
FEMALES	0–14	24	13.8	57.5	17.2	71.7
	15–29	11	3.4	30.9	9.5	86.4
	30–44	10	4.8	48.0	7.7	77.0
	45–59	5	3.6	72.0	4.5	90.0
	60–	3	2.2	73.3	2.2	73.3

This table is based on the preceding one, and the percentage shown is the per cent of persons present on Thursdays and Sundays as compared with the total number of individuals in each age class during September. The significant factor is thus the *increase* of the percentages on Sundays.

One is immediately struck by the fact that this increase is considerably less for the youngest and oldest age groups than for individuals of the most active ages. In age group 0–14 the increase is only from 52.0 % to 70.0 % for the males and from 57.5 % to 71.7 % for the females. For the age groups above 45 it is still less, and in one case, males above 60, even replaced by a decrease. On the other hand, for the age groups 15–29 and 30–44 there is a big jump from the percentage figures for weekdays to those for Sundays, doubling or tripling them.

If the motive to return to the village were exclusively religious, it should be expected to operate with equal force for *all* age groups, (as it obviously does when the whole population lives in the village, for church attendance during these periods is regularly 95–100 %), but this is clearly not the case. The only possible explanation is therefore, that the *social* and *recreational* motives are as important as the religious one. These motives are of course more dominant in the ages 15—44, and most men and women of these ages evidently return to the village seeking diversion, whereas the older people stay behind with the children in the working sector. At important church festivals, religious considerations are, however, paramount, as *all* the workers irrespective of age return to the village.

This tendency to return to the village regularly on Sundays, of course, greatly reduces the time actually spent on copra work, as the sectors are situated at a great distance and bad weather frequently prolongs the canoe trips. The influence of this habit on the annual output of copra is therefore considerable.

7. Actual and potential production

According to the chief, the total copra production in 1948 was 221 tons and in 1949 as much as 253 tons. How reliable these figures are is difficult to say, but for 1950 I kept record of all copra produced, and the total amount was 187 tons. If the figures for the preceding years are correct, the average output per year should be around 200 tons.

For producing about 200 tons of copra a year on the soil found on Raroia, 200 hectares should suffice. The total area planted with coconut palms is according to my estimate, based on a study of the aerial map, 587 hectares (Chapter VII, 2). Almost three times as much copra could therefore be produced on the atoll, if my estimate is correct. The great discrepancy between the actual and potential output must be due to such factors as dense planting, old trees, abundant underbrush, ravages by rats, insect pests, lack of fertilizers, picking of drinking nuts, and so on. Some of these aspects have been discussed in previous chapters, but the problem as a whole must of course be left to a specialist.

The tonnages of copra produced each month of 1950 were as follows:

January	7.5	July	2
February	30	August	14
March	24	September	40
April	11	October	14
May	12.5	November	8
June	10	December	14

The variations are principally due to the amount of time the islanders devoted to other activities and will be clearly understood only by a comparison with the facts presented in part 2 of this chapter which deals with the interdependence of activities.

Divided between the various sectors (see Map D) the copra production for 1950 was as follows:

I.	Raro (January–April, July–October)	142.5 tons
II.	Village (November–December)	22.0 tons
III.	Rest of the atoll (May–June)	22.5 tons

Of the output in 1950, 76.2 % of the copra came thus from Raro, 11.8 % from lands around the village and 12.0 % from the rest of the atoll. The relative size of the planted area in the three sectors is approximately, in the same order, as 7 to 2 to 3, or expressed in percentages:

Raro	58 $^1/_3$ %
Village	16 $^2/_3$ %
Rest	25 %

This comparison between the relative percentages of output and of planted area brings out some interesting facts. For the village lands the output was only slightly below what could be expected judging from the size of the planted area, and the figures are almost identical if we do not count the village itself, where few palm trees are planted. A disproportion between the production and the area in the two other sectors undoubtedly exists, however, and the figures only confirm my personal impressions during the year.

The discrepancy of the figures seems to indicate that the third sector (comprising all the land on the eastern, northern and northwestern side of the atoll) was not worked to full capacity. This neglect is easily explained by the fact that it is more difficult to reach these parts of the atoll and much more time-consuming to make copra on the numerous small islets there than on the connected lands in the two remaining sectors.

A comparison between the size of the planted area in each sector and the time during which the sectors were open is also illuminating. The sectors were open respectively 8, 2 and 2 months, which expressed in percentages and compared to the proportional size of each sector gives us the following table:

Sector	Area	Time
Raro	58 $^1/_3$ %	66 $^2/_3$ %
Village	16 $^2/_3$ %	16 $^2/_3$ %
Rest	25 %	16 $^2/_3$ %

The length of time during which each sector is open is thus not completely proportional either to its size or to the output and the total time actually spent in each sector, which once more shows the lack of integration of the various activities.

8. Working efficiency

Finally, in this section I shall try to ascertain the working efficiency, or the mean time needed for producing one ton of copra, in order to see whether the relatively low annual output can be explained in these terms. The figures presented here are based on the complete records of work participation in part 5 of this chapter (Table XIV).

Before I can proceed to a computation of the mean working time and output, some adjustments have to be made. In the first place it should be noted that the time spent in sectors outside the village is counted from the departure to the return. As distances are great and some preparation necessary each time, usually no work is done on travel days. Another factor which frequently reduces the time spent in effective work is bad weather or calms. These often prevent the islanders from fulfilling their work schedules. Moreover, each worker as a rule spends some days fishing or gathering other foods. All this considerably reduces the time actually devoted to copra production, and if we estimate the effective working time as $\frac{2}{3}$ of the total time, our figure is certainly not too high.

The contributions of the different age classes also varies. Children below 14 years of age may help a great deal at the camp with food-preparation and also often go fishing, but their contribution to copra production must otherwise be disregarded. The same is true for the few individuals above 60, who occasionally accompany the working parties.

The output of the age group 45—59 is doubtless much less than that of the younger men, and I have therefore estimated their efficiency as 50 % of the latter group.

The contribution to the copra works of the women who accompany their husbands is as a rule very slight, and even the women who are land owners themselves, usually let their husbands or a male helper do the collecting and cutting. This does not mean, however, that the women are without occupation. They tend the children, take care of household duties, clear lands and assist their husbands in minor ways. This limited role of the women is, however, impossible to confirm statistically. The population was always widespread and I lived in the main village most of the time, but repeated visits to the different sectors throughout the year led me to believe it to be the general pattern. In the following estimate of the working tempo I have therefore preferred to disregard the female participation completely.

The total number of working days for the men during January—October thus was, as seen in Table XIX, 2,568 for the age class 15—44,

TABLE XIX: *Working days of the productive males compared to copra production*

Month[1]	Working days		Tons of copra
	15—44	45—59	
January	240	18	7.5
February	494	46	30.0
March	428	33	24.0
April	151	21	11.0
May	179	44	12.5
June	128	33	10.0
July	43	24	2.0
August	225	72	14.0
September	514	108	40.0
October	166	51	14.0
Total	2,568	450	165.0

[1] The figures are for the first ten months of the year during which the sectors outside the village were worked. For the remaining two months, when the lands around the village were worked, only the amount of copra produced was recorded. These figures were 8 tons in November and 14 in December.

and 450 for the age class 45–59. If we first reduce these figures by ⅓ for lost time, and then discount 50 % for the latter class for lost efficiency, we get the following figures:

$$
\begin{array}{lrll}
\text{15–44 years old} & 2,568 & \text{working days} \\
\text{Less } ^1/_3 & \underline{856} & \text{,,} & \text{,,} \\
& 1,712 \\
\text{45–59 years old} & 450 & \text{,,} & \text{,,} \\
\text{Less } ^1/_3 & \underline{150} & \text{,,} & \text{,,} \\
& 300 & \text{,,} & \text{,,} \\
\text{Less } ^1/_2 & \underline{150} & \text{,,} & \text{,,} \\
& 150 & \text{,,} & \text{,,}
\end{array}
$$

The total is thus 1,712 plus 150 = 1,862 effective working days. 165 tons of copra were produced, making a mean of 11.3 days per ton, which seems reasonable. In Tahiti a good worker prepares one ton a week, but working conditions are very different there, as no time-consuming piling of the nuts is necessary, the undergrowth is kept at a minimum, the plantations are much bigger and the existence of covered platforms makes the work more independent of the weather.

If only men between 15–44 are counted (the total number was 29 according to Table IV), the mean output per individual for these ten months is 5.69 tons, which is very little, but easily explained if we take all the previously mentioned factors into consideration.

B. MOTHER-OF-PEARL SHELL DIVING

As the shells grow only under specific conditions they are not found everywhere in the group, and where they are found they have greatly decreased in number. (Ranson, 1952 a, p. 2.) The actual number of highly productive lagoons (above 100 tons per season) is therefore not more than five. The number of lagoons of secondary importance (among them Raroia) is seven. On Raroia diving is, however, difficult as the lagoon is rather deep, 20–50 metres, and only the most skilled divers can share in this source of income.

Owing to the danger of exhausting the lagoons strict measures have been taken to preserve the remaining beds and diving is permitted now only at certain atolls during limited periods in well defined sectors. Certain years a limited number of natives from other atolls come to Raroia in order to participate in the diving, and the last time this happened in 1947 the total amount of shell gathered was 11.7 tons. (Ranson, 1952 b, p. 3.) The Raroians contribute, however, only a small proportion of this amount. The number of Raroians diving during the two months the season lasted in 1950, when no natives from other atolls participated, was only eleven. The total amount of shells collected was 2,742 kgs, or just below 250 kgs per diver. Since the sums earned in this way are insignificant (in spite of the high 1950 price of 30 francs a kilo) compared with their copra earnings, the men do not take this diving on the home atoll seriously, but combine it with fishing or do it mostly for fun.

Like all other natives in French Oceania, the Raroians may participate in the diving permitted seasonally every year on certain of the other atolls in the Tuamotu group. As a rule few of them find it worthwhile, in spite of the huge sums a good diver can earn. When the neighbouring atoll of Takume is open for diving, however, almost the whole population migrates there. The reasons for this preference for Takume are very simple. The atoll is so close to Raroia that it can be reached with outrigger canoes, and the lagoon is so shallow that even inexperienced divers and women can participate. Furthermore it is enclosed, which means that there are no dangerous sharks.

No diving took place on Takume during 1950, when most of the data for the present study were collected, but in 1951 and 1952 when I revisited the atoll, diving was going on, and I gathered some additional information. (Danielsson, 1953 a, pp. 262–289.)

The tendency to migrate to Takume in whole family groups seems very pronounced, as seen by the following table showing the number of Raroians living on Takume during the middle of the diving season, on September 8, 1952:

Age	Males	Females	Total
0–14	5	14	19
15–29	9	8	17
30–44	13	9	22
45–59	5	3	8
60–	2	1	3
Total	34	35	69

Thus about two thirds of the total population of Raroia lived at this time on Takume, and all except the children under 14 were more or less actively engaged in the diving. Those left behind on Raroia were mainly small children and old people.

The income derived from diving is good by any standard. An adult male can collect between 50 and 100 kgs of shells per day, and a woman or younger man at least half that amount. I have no exact figures for the total income of the Raroians, as I visited Takume only briefly. Diving was still going on when I left, but I have tried to make a rough estimate based on information volunteered by the divers themselves.

As a rule the divers do not stay the full season of four months on Takume, but relax from time to time and return to Raroia. Between 45 and 60 days of actual diving per individual per season is therefore a fair guess. Since the price paid for the shells varies between 30 and 45 francs a kg, a good diver should be able to earn about 200,000 francs ($3,125) and a woman or young man half that sum during a season.

It must, however, once more be stressed that the diving is a strictly seasonal activity, that prices fluctuate greatly and that most of the money earned is immediately spent. In spite of the big occasional income a Raroian may derive from shell diving, it nevertheless plays a subordinate part to copra growing in the economic life of the islanders.

A special study of the diving is highly needed, not only from the economic point of view but also for clarifying certain social processes, as a great deal of acculturation occurs during these visits to other atolls. The limited time and the concentration of my work on one atoll has hitherto prevented me from studying more thoroughly this interesting problem.

CHAPTER IX · **Subsistence activities**

With the year-round work on the plantations and the good earnings from copra and mother-of-pearl shell sales, the islanders neither have time nor find it necessary to carry on any extensive planting or food-gathering, as they did in pre-European times. The taro fields were abandoned after the cyclone in 1903 and nobody has planted any taro since then. The pandanus palm still grows wild in many places, but is no longer used for food.

Few domesticated animals are kept, and these consist almost exclusively of hens, pigs and dogs, which as in ancient times are still eaten. Fishing is practised to a considerable extent, especially during the working periods away from the village, but shell fish, of which there has never been any abundance on Raroia, are rarely gathered. Turtles are caught and sea birds and eggs collected, but these are strictly seasonal activities and more practised as a sport than as regular food-gathering activities.

Instead of these traditional foods the islanders now buy imported provisions like canned beef, flour, rice and biscuits, which make up a diet much inferior to the ancient one. The main aim is, however, achieved from the islanders' point of view: no working time is lost on prolonged food-gathering and tedious preparations and all efforts can be concentrated on the production of a surplus, the income from which permits the acquisition of all sorts of luxury articles.

A. PLANT CULTIVATION

The poor soil and high salinity of the ground water (Chapter I) are serious obstacles to the cultivation of varied and abundant crops, and the rare attempts the islanders have made to introduce new and useful plants in addition to those existing in pre-European times have practically all failed miserably. The only exception is the papaya tree which seems to thrive well in the atoll sand, and it is possible that a few other foreign plants could also be grown on Raroia. To find suitable new plants would, however, require prolonged agricultural experiments and preliminary studies, and no such methodical efforts have yet been made.

1. Coconut palms

Of all the plants and trees that existed on the atoll in pre-European times only the coconut palm is still an important food resource, but strangely enough no separate plantations of palm trees with nuts especially suited for food are made, in spite of the fact that several such varieties exist. The nuts used in each household (usually one or two green drinking nuts and one mature nut for preparing sauce per person and day) are collected on the copra plantations, and therefore the distances the Raroians have to walk when living in the village are frequently considerable.

The importance of the coconut palm to the natives—in the subsistence as well as the surplus economy—is reflected by the detailed terminology. Every part of the tree is given a specific name, and the different stages of development of the nut are distinguished with an almost scientific accuracy. At least a dozen varieties are known to the islanders and used according to their special properties.

The usual word for the palm tree is *hakāri*, but *niu*, the older word of pan-Polynesian distribution, is also known. Only a full-grown tree is called *hakāri*, however, and before it reaches this stage three distinct name are used. *Nana* is a very young plant with sprouts not yet split into leaflets. The roots are short and the mesocarp or husk is still attached to the sprout. At the next stage, *tikovae*, the leaves are fully developed, 6–10 feet high, and emerge like a fan from the ground. Gradually the trunk is formed, and from the moment it can properly be called a tree, it is termed *hoka*. At the age of six or seven years the tree reaches maturity and is a *hakāri*.

The terms for the different parts of the full-grown tree are very numerous. To begin with the roots, these are called *aka*, which simply is the generic name for root. The lower, thicker part of the trunk is called *tūrei*, and the rest of it *tumu*. The upper part of the stem, the vegetative bud, which is edible, is named *muko*.

A young undeveloped leaf still folded against the midrib has a special name, *mote*, in contrast to the fully developed leaf for which two words are used, *rauniu* or *gāofe*. The first word is the pan-Polynesian term and the second the local term. Both are also used for the smaller leaflets attached to the central midrib, the *katakata*. The term for the midrib of the leaflet is *koitika*.

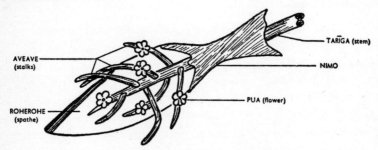

FIG. IX. *Flower stem and spathe*

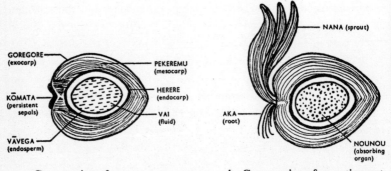

a. Cross section of mature nut   b. Cross section of sprouting nut

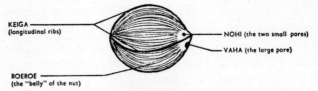

c. Husked nut

FIG. X. *The different parts of a coconut*

The parts of the fully developed flower and their names are shown in Fig. IX. A flower bud is called *kumoa,* but there is no word for the fully developed flower cluster *as a whole.*

All features of the nut, even the smallest and most insignificant from a Western point of view, are recognized and named by the natives. They are shown in Fig. X.

As everywhere in Polynesia several well defined stages in the growth of the nut are distinguished and on Raroia their number is five. No generic term for "nut" exists, which is another example of the strictly utilitarian attitude of the islanders. Each type of nut has its own properties, useful in different ways and accordingly each has a special name. A "nut in general", on the other hand, combining in an abstract way the qualities of several types of nuts, is of no use whatsoever, and no such term has therefore been created.

The names and principal characteristics of the nut at the different stages are as follows:

Stage of growth	Characteristics
pūriri	Recently formed nut, no cavity inside.
rehi	Almost full size but still green nut. Cavity filled with bitter water. No or very little flesh formed.
viavia	Full size but still green nut. Thin slimy flesh. Water slightly sweet.
kōmoto	Full size nut with spots of darker colour. Flesh thick and firm. Water effervescent and bitter.
gora	Maximum size, brown nut. Flesh of maximum thickness. Water sour.

The natives distinguish at least a dozen varieties of coconut palms, but it is doubtful whether the distinctions are all justified from the point of view of scientific botany. The distinctions are based on the following classificatory principles: colour of nuts, arrangement of nuts, and special properties of nuts.

Varieties based on the colour of the nuts:

māmāgu	dark green nuts
motea	pale green nuts
fateka	light yellow-green nuts
koheko	reddish-brown nuts
heheko	

kurakura	reddish nuts
heru	nuts of which the upper part is scarlet-coloured

Varieties based on the arrangement of nuts:

takaveatīka	the nuts lack stalks and are attached directly to the stem
makire	abundant, small nuts in thick grape-like clusters

Varieties based on special properties of nuts:

kaipoa	nut with edible, sweet husk or mesocarp
pururoa	nuts with thick husk and small nuts
karava	oval nuts with long husk fibres

The following miscellaneous terms were recorded:

nounou	absorbing organ (haustorium) in a *gora* or fullgrown nut
kōkā	oily substance on the *nounou*
puha	*gora* with dry detached meat
vavako	*gora* without water or *nounou*
kōvari	prematurely fallen nut
kererau	cluster of nuts
popōga	flesh attacked by insects, or deteriorated in other ways

2. Other plants and trees

Few other Polynesian fruit trees and food plants are grown. One of the islanders tries to grow bananas in a ditch filled with refuse but this must be regarded chiefly as a luxury hobby, as the yield is not more than five or six bunches a year. There are 73 breadfruit trees altogether, but only 23 bear any fruit. The total number of fruits on these trees each season does not exceed 300, and therefore their role in the diet is insignificant.

The only introduced plant cultivated to any extent is the papaya (*Carica papaya*), of which there are 87 trees; only one third of these are fruit-bearing, however. According to Doty (p. 25) "the variety seems to be a poor one and could not compete with those grown in Hawaii". Most of these have been planted by the Chinese storekeeper, who gives away the fruits as goodwill service. In spite of the fact that the papayas,

Copra preparation. When the kernel is dry it is scooped out of the coconut halves with a curved knife, a tedious and monotonous task.

The copra, as the dry kernels are now called, is put into bags, which are weighed by primitive methods. Each bag holds about 50 kgs.

PLATE 5 None of the outrigger canoes can be used today in the open sea more than a couple of miles from shore. When the wind is strong, they cannot even be used on the lagoons.

The small paddle canoes for two or three men are principally used for fishing and turtle catching expeditions in both the lagoon and the sea.

like the breadfruits, are highly appreciated by the islanders, very few of them have planted any, and only half of the 27 families have trees of their own. Some species of melons seem also to thrive well, but the islanders neglect the few plantations of them that exist.

This lack of interest in plant growing is probably a result of the islanders' ignorance of modern agricultural methods and of the relative nutritive value of the various kinds of food. Nobody suspects for instance that the fruits contain vitamins which are not found in the imported food, and these valuable food resources are therefore completely overlooked.

In addition to the plants already mentioned, Doty lists (pp. 36—41) more than eighty species of flower plants and other exotic curiosities which are restricted to the village. With the exception of a sort of panax used for hedges along the new boundary lines these plants are very few in number and very little valued. Doty (p. 36) very appropriately sums up the islanders' attitude towards these recent introductions thus: "Successful horticultural practice is generally so lacking as to disincline one to even refer to it as primitive. People pull up a growing plant and stick it in the ground in a new place, usually not even watering it once. If it seems to show signs of surviving that makes it desirable for some other place and the plant is moved again. Thus many of the plants listed here ... must be dead now."

B. ANIMAL HUSBANDRY

The number of pigs, hens, ducks and dogs per family on July 1, 1950 is shown in Table XX.

The total number of domesticated animals is not very impressive, and the islanders often say that they would like to keep more, if only they were able to feed them. But this is difficult for the Raroians for two reasons: there is little food for animals besides nut kernels, which are too valuable, and the nomadic character of the islanders' existence does not go very well with animal husbandry.

This applies especially to pigs, which explains their comparatively small number. Significantly enough, pigs are also kept only by families who always leave someone, usually an old relative who takes care of the school children, behind in the village during the working periods in the sectors. (Cf. Table XVI.) But even some of these families hesitate to have a pig owing to the fact that it has to be fed with coconuts.

Contrary to the pigs, which because of the feeding, are always kept in enclosures of palm logs, the hens and ducks roam about in complete

TABLE XX. *Number of domesticated animals*

Family[1]	Pigs	Hens	Ducks	Dogs
1	—	—	—	2
2	1	5	—	2
3	—	—	—	1
4	—	—	2	1
5	—	—	—	—
6	—	—	1	1
7	—	3	—	3
8	1	4	—	2
9	2	—	3	1
10	1	—	—	2
11	—	3	3	2
12	—	—	—	1
13	2	6	2	2
14	2	2	—	—
15	—	7	2	2
16	—	—	4	2
17	—	6	—	1
18	—	12	4	4
19	—	—	—	—
20	1	—	—	—
21	1	10	7	3
22	—	3	2	4
23	—	—	—	2
24	—	—	—	1
25	—	9	7	2
26	—	—	—	1
27	1	6	4	2
Total	12	76	41	44

[1] For composition, see Table XVI and XXVII.

freedom, as they are supposed to be able to take care of themselves. A greater number of families can therefore keep hens and ducks without interference with their work. The number is nevertheless very limited, which is certainly due to the fact that the hens and ducks under these conditions are of little value. The eggs are never found, or they are eaten by rats, and the hens and ducks so meagre that they are hardly palatable.

Of all the domesticated animals the dogs alone can accompany the islanders on their trips to other parts of the atoll, which is certainly the main reason for their continued popularity. Dogs seem primarily to be appreciated for their food value and only in a very secondary way for their companionship. As no dogs are regularly fed, only young dogs are tender enough to be eaten. Many dogs are, however, saved for reproductive reasons, and most of the 44 dogs found at the time of my survey were of a fairly advanced age, many of them actually too old, which is not so surprising as the Raroians never kill a dog except when they intend to eat him. There is a tax imposed in order to keep down the number of dogs, but as it is extremely small it does not have the desired effect.

C. BIRD CATCHING AND EGG COLLECTING

I have elsewhere published a list of the birds found on Raroia (Danielsson, 1954 b). In order to determine the importance of birds and eggs as food resources for the islanders a mere list is not enough, however. Both their habitat zones, their number and their migratory habits, if any, must be taken into consideration. Morrison (1954 b, p. 19), has made a useful ecological classification of the birds on Raroia, which I shall follow here.

The first group comprises sea birds that feed out at sea and roost on the atoll and numbers six species: the brown booby *(Sula leucogastra plotus)*, *karīga*, the redfooted booby *(Sula sula rubripes)*, *karīga hopetea*, two species of frigate birds or man-o-war birds *(Fregata ariel* and *Fregata minor)*, *kōtaha*, and two species of tropic birds *(Phaethon lepturus dorotheae* and *Phaethon rubricaudra)*, *tavake*.

Of these the migratory tropic birds are extremely rare, and it is regarded as a great event when one is found at infrequent intervals varying from one to several years. The boobies are almost exterminated, and only the frigate birds are still numerous. The probable reason is that their meat is regarded as a very poor food.

Smaller sea birds that feed on the atoll in the shallow waters make up the second group, and the number of such species is seven, all resident terns. Of these the formerly most common and appreciated species, the sooty tern *(Sterna fuscata oahuensis)*, *kāveka*, is almost exterminated and no nesting places were discovered in 1952. The blue ternlet *(Procelsterna cerulea teretirostris)*, *gāgā*, and the spectacled tern *(Sterna lunata)*, *oreore*, are rare. The four remaining species, the crested tern *(Thalasseus bergii cristatus)*, *tara*, the fairy or white tern *(Gygis alba candida)*, *kīrarahu* or *kītaketake*, the white-capped noddy *(Anous minutus minutus)*, *kīkiriri* and the brown noddy *(Anous stolidus pileatus)*, *goio*, are all very common.

In the third group, shore birds which feed on exposed reefs and shores, we find two resident birds, the reef heron *(Demigretta sacra sacra)*, *kōtuku*, and the wandering tattler *(Heteroscelus incanus)*, *kuriri*, which exist in considerable numbers but are not eaten. There are also two highly appreciated migrant birds in this group, the Pacific golden plover *(Pluvialis dominica fulva)*, *torēa*, and the bristle—thighed curlew *(Numenius tahitiensis)*, *kivi* or *keufēa*, which both roost in the northern part of the Pacific during the dry season and return to Raroia in October—November.

Finally, there is the class of land birds which feed on the vegetated areas of the atoll. They are two, the migrant long-tailed cuckoo *(Urodynamis taitensis)*, *kūrevareva*, which leaves when the other migratory birds return, and the resident Tuamotuan warbler *(Conopoderas atypha atypha)*, *kokīkokīko*, *kotīotīo* or *makomako*. The warbler is fairly common whereas few cuckoos exist. At least three other species which formerly lived on the atoll have disappeared. Old natives still remember them and they can be identified as the Polynesian sandpiper, the little rail and the fruit dove.

That so many valuable food birds have been exterminated or nearly so is probably a result of the breakdown of the old taboo system. In ancient times the chiefs and priests were able to enforce restrictions and decide when bird catching might take place. The new elected chiefs and councillors do not have the same authority (for the simple reason that they not are religiously sanctioned like the old leaders) and the islanders therefore kill birds indiscriminately.

Egg collecting is naturally a strictly seasonal activity and takes place during the last months of the year, October–December, when the terns –the only birds of which there is any large number–roost on the northern part of the atoll (Tokerau and Gake).

As the terns lay their eggs in nests on the ground or in the branches and hollows of bushes and low trees, they can be collected without any difficulty. The birds caught are young noddies which are simply taken by hand. This roosting season for the terns coincides with the return of the migrant Pacific plover and bristle-thighed curlew. In addition to the roosting terns and young terns some of these returning migrants may therefore also be caught.

Once or twice a week during this season small groups of young people sail over to the northern part of the atoll and spend a day at a time there. Each person brings back at least four or five dozen eggs and half a dozen young birds from such a trip. The eggs are all eaten irrespective of the stage of development of the embryo. Some of the birds may be kept in captivity and fed for some time before being killed, but most of them are eaten immediately.

D. FISHING AND TURTLE CATCHING

The absence of land animals and the infertility of the soil have always obliged the Raroians to rely on fish and sea food to a large extent, which of course has led to highly developed and specialized fishing methods. Although the sea and the lagoon as sources of food no longer play the same dominant roles as in pre-European times before the rise of the copra trade and the introduction of canned food, the natives still fish regularly and have a thorough knowledge of the fishing waters. Except for the inevitable replacement of old material like mother-of-pearl shell and bone by iron, the fishing methods have generally preserved their Polynesian character. (For comparative material see Anell.) As a matter of fact no other elements of the old culture, either spiritual or material, have survived so well. As the present study deals primarily with present conditions, no effort has been made here to reconstruct the fishing methods which have been lost, but only those still in use will be described.[1]

Of the between 400—500 different species of fish found in the lagoon and sea around Raroia the islanders have names for roughly 150 (for classification and descriptions see Harry, 1953, and for an alphabetical list of the native names see Danielsson, 1954 b), and this indicates the approximate number of food fishes, for only in exceptional cases have they bothered to give other fishes names. The islanders' strictly utilitarian point of view is still more clearly shown by the fact that the most appreciated food fishes have not only one but several names, indicating different sizes. Of the 150 named species only one third, however, are commonly used for food, and the natives are rather selective even among these preferred species. This is very understandable, as there is a great abundance of fish everywhere in the lagoon. Only some ocean species like dolphin, swordfish and flying fish, which were frequently caught in ancient times, are not fished for any more, because the present-day inferior canoes do not permit extended sea voyages. Eels, octopuses and one species of shark (*Triaenodon obesus*) are occasionally caught and eaten.

1. Fishing methods

The general term for fishing is *tautai,* but as for so many other highly specialized activities the natives have also in this case numerous specific names. I have indicated the terms where necessary and grouped my data under four main headings: spear fishing, hook and line fishing, net fishing and miscellaneous methods.

Spear fishing

The greatest bulk of fish by volume is caught with spears in the inter-islet channels, along the shore and around lagoon reef patches. The species caught are parrot fishes, goat fishes, surgeon and unicorn fishes and certain wrasses, jacks and sea basses. The spears are usually made of *mikimiki (Pemphis acidula)* wood fitted with an iron point. This point is mostly made by the islanders themselves out of scrap-iron over a primitive forge. The spears have either a single barbless tip or four barbed prongs. The single, barbless spears are of two sizes, one 1—2

[1] A more detailed paper on pre-European fishing techniques will be published separately.

metres and the other about 3 metres long, whereas the four-pronged spears are all 3—4 metres long.

Of the barbless spears, the short ones are used for poking under stones in shallow water, the long ones for under-water fishing, during which the fisherman dives down and transfixes his quarry. The barbed, four-pronged spears are thrown from a standing position on the shore or the edge of the reef. The spear is held by the right hand at the extreme end with the index finger on the butt and supported in the middle by the left hand. The spear is cast with an overhand throw and the precision is amazingly good.

The word *pātia* is used both for the spear and the method in general. The names for the varieties are: *pākeke*, poking out the fish from holes with the short, barbless spear and transfixing them; *tūpoa*, under-water spearing with the help of tridacna shells which attract the fish; and *fautau*, throwing the four-pronged spear.

Hook and line fishing

The general word for hook and line fishing is *kānehu*, but specific names exist for every variety of it. A very common method in ancient times, called *tōpepu*, was to swim slowly about in the lagoon or open sea, supported by a log while holding the line in one hand. This method is very rare to-day and as a rule hook and line fishing is practised less than spear fishing. Stationary hook and line fishing is generally done from canoes anchored in the ship pass or from the shore. On Raroia, as in the rest of Polynesia, the islanders practically never use floats and rarely rods. A special sinker is usually deemed unnecessary, and when fishing at great depths the hook is simply lowered with the help of a coral stone tied to the line with a slip knot. As soon as the hook reaches the desired depth, the stone is released by giving the line a sharp jerk. Fishes caught in this way comprise several species of trigger fishes, jacks and sea basses.

In pre-European time most hooks were made of mother-of-pearl and turtle shell and were of the circular, barbless, Polynesian type, which is ideally suited for the marine environment as it does not get entangled in branching corals. (For details see Seurat, pp. 295—302.) Unfortunately in the Tuamotus they are now everywhere replaced by European iron hooks of the ordinary U-shape, which are far inferior. The excellent commercially made iron hooks of Polynesian design used in Hawaii and previously unknown in French Oceania were introduced by me on Raroia in 1952.

Trolling with hook and line from canoes, *tāvere,* in the pass and along the outer reef is principally done for catching tuna and bonitos. The ancient mother-of-pearl shell hook, *kāviti,* is still in use. It is vaguely shaped like a fish and trimmed at its distal end with cattle hair or pig's bristle forming a sort of brush. The point, bound on the lure, was formerly made of bone but is now often of brass or iron. All shells are not equally suitable for hooks of this type, and the natives claim that only a certain kind of yellowish shells are attractive to the predatory fishes. I have often been able to verify the correctness of this statement.

Net fishing

Net fishing is very little practised, even less so than in pre-European times, in spite of the fact that ready-made nets and seines can now be bought in Papeete or aboard the schooners. The reasons for this decline are probably the improvement of other types of fishing gear like hooks and spears by the introduction of iron, and the cumbersome character of a net. A man can always take a spear and a couple of hooks with him during his trips to his copra plantation, and invariably does so, whereas a net is heavy and usually cannot be handled by one man alone. Another fact, which certainly limited the use of nets even in pre-European times, is the unfavourable environment and the existence of sharks. Nets are easily entangled in sharp and branching corals and sharks destroy both fish and nets alike.

The only nets in common use to-day are small seines attached between poles and handled by two men who encircle the fish with the net. The net is called *kōpe,* and used principally in shallow water along the lagoon shore or in the channels between the islets. Fishes caught in this way are goat fishes, parrot fishes and mullets.

Miscellaneous methods

The only other methods worth mentioning are:

Fakakopa. The fishes, usually parrot fishes, are chased when they appear in the shallow water on the outer reef until beached or enclosed in an embayment. They are then speared or taken by hand.

Rena. This is the garland fishing with palm leaves called *hukilau* in Hawaii. The garland may be up to 200 yards long and is made of palm leaves cut in halves lengthwise, twisted and joined together. The garland is handled by a great number of people and this is actually the only community fishing undertaken to-day. Seasonal fishes like *Selar crumenophtholmnus* and small parrot fishes are caught in this way. The catch is always shared equally among all the participants irrespective of age, sex or role during the fishing.

Rama. Night fishing on the outer reef flat. The fish is blinded by light, usually from a Coleman kerosene lantern, and stunned by a blow over the back with a long bush knife. Fishes caught are principally squirrel fishes and certain wrasses.

One obsolete fishing method is finally worth mentioning, since the reason why it was abandoned is a good example of the many secondary effects of the acculturation process. Here and there along the shore of the lagoon and in the channels huge stone traps are still encountered. "These traps—often with arms several hundred yards long and a labyrinth of compartments in which the fish easily lose their way—provided the islanders with quantities of food in old times. Although they could be put into working order with comparative ease, no one lifts a finger to repair them. The reason is quite simple: the old communal spirit and solidarity have disappeared since there is no longer any strong temporal or religious authority to compel the Raroians to collaborate.

'There's no point in trying to repair the stone traps,' Tupuhoe explained to us one day. 'It would only mean trouble and quarreling. The stone traps belong to everyone. Suppose we repair them and decide that the catch shall be divided in equal shares on certain days. That's easy enough. But how are we going to prevent people from sneaking off at night and stealing the fish? We can't keep watch all day and all night. In the old days one of the priests used to declare the stone traps taboo, and then no one dared touch the fish. That was a good simple way of doing it. But no one believes in a taboo nowadays." (Danielsson, 1953 a, p. 216.) As previously shown (part C) the disintegration of the old social order has similarly prevented necessary checks on the islanders' wilful bird catching and egg collecting methods.

2. Survival of magic

Fish-magic was very common in ancient times, but only once during my various stays on the atoll have I seen the islanders resort to it. Significantly enough it was one of the oldest men who practised it, and as a rule the younger generations know very little or nothing about magic. The occurrence I witnessed was the following.

One morning a large school of trigger fishes was sighted a little way out to sea. Every year at the beginning of the rainy season these schools enter the lagoon through the ship pass, and the Raroians are in the habit of going up to the pass in their canoes in order to meet the fishes. On this occasion, however, the school showed no signs of approaching. When two days had passed without a single fish having entered the lagoon, it was finally decided, not without a certain hesitation, to fetch Hono, the former sorcerer. Hono immediately sent out the men to collect hermit crabs and when he had got a fine heap, he retired and did not turn up again until several hours later. He had then crushed the crabs and concocted a thick mixture, the additional ingredients of which were his trade secret. Carrying the crab-mixture in a wooden bowl he was conducted to the pass in the chief's canoe. He got out on a large coral head in the middle of the pass and ordered the fleet of canoes to withdraw. In a loud voice he began to intone magic incantations, all the time making violent movements with his arms. After a while he stopped, filled his mouth with crab-mixture and spat it out in the direction of the open sea. Thereupon he once more began with his incantations.

While the rest of us watched the scene in silence from our canoes, the old man continued for more than an hour to make his spells and spit crab-mixture into the water. We had almost given up hope, when there was a sudden gleam in the entrance to the pass. Wonder of wonders, it was the school approaching! Slowly the immense mass of living fish glided through the waters towards the spot where Hono sat. The latter now began to sing, first softly, then louder and louder. When the school was only a few yards from where he sat, he suddenly poured the rest of the crab-mixture into the sea, getting up at the same time and motioning us to approach. We paddled up to the coral head as fast as we could and threw out our hooks. The fish bit like mad, and hardly had a hook had time to sink below the surface before a pull was felt. For half an hour we literally scooped up fish, and the final catch was so large that the whole population had enough to eat for many days.

Similar cases of fish-magic on Hikueru and Vahitahi have been described by Anne Hervé (p. 53).

3. Fishing calendar

In ancient times the Rarorians had names for all the nights of the moon[1] and knew the right time for catching any particular sort of fish. To-day only half a dozen men above 40 years of age know all these names, but most Raroians know the principal ones and still have a fairly good knowledge of the movements of the fishes. The calendar below shows the interdependence between the phases of the moon and the relative abundance of fish, regardless of species.

Night	*Name*	*Fishing prospects*
1	Hīro	There is plenty of fish during the first five days after
2	Hōata	the new moon.
3	Hanīa tahi	
4	Hanīa roto	
5	Hanīa fakaoti	
6	Korekore tahi	On Korekore tahi the fish begin to disappear and dur-
7	Korekore roto	ing the following six days they hide.
8	Korekore fakaoti	
9	Tamatēa	On the day Tamatēa there are, however, good chances
10	Huna	of catching parrot fishes.
11	Rapu	
12	Maharu	
13	Hua	From Hua and until two days after Hotu (full moon)
14	Māitu	there is plenty of fat fish.
15	Hotu	
16	Māragi	Crabs should be taken on Māragi when they are soft-
17	Penu	shelled.
18	Rākau tahi	The fish begin to disappear on Rākau tahi. All Rākau
19	Rākau roto	nights are moreover dangerous, as ghosts roam about.
20	Rākau fakaoti	
21	Korekore tahi	On all three Korekore days fish are scarce.
22	Korekore roto	
23	Korekore fakaoti	

[1] With the word "night" (*po*) is meant the period from the rising of the moon in one phase to its rising in the next. This period thus includes part day and part night.

24	Tāiva tahi	On Tāiva tahi the fish return in great numbers and
25	Tāiva roto	can easily be caught until Rogomauri.
26	Tāiva fakaoti	
27	Tikatika	
28	Rogo nūi	
29	Rogo mauri	Both the moon and the fish go to sleep.
30	Mauri kero	

Similar lists with somewhat different names and internal order between them have been recorded from all Polynesian groups (see e.g. Handy, 1932, pp. 76—81 and Williams, pp. 338—356). On Raroia, as elsewhere, the natives were able to supply much additional information concerning the separate movements of many species, but unfortunately I did not find time for recording and checking this wealth of material. That general variations on the whole occur according to the calendar above, however, I had many occasions to verify.[1]

4. Relative importance of fishing

Since pre-European days, when probably every adult spent several hours a day fishing or gathering shells and clams, the time devoted to these activities has gradually decreased with the emergence of a money-economy.

In order to get some measure of the relative importance of fishing to the present-day economy I recorded the number of persons going out

[1] Handy (1932, pp. 76—77) says about the fishing in Tahiti: "The subject of times, places, and seasons of fishery is one that calls for long and painstaking collecting of information ... For a comprehensive study of these matters, information from many different localities, and gathered over a period extending over a number of years, will be required. Should such a study ever be made the information collected will constitute an exceedingly useful record for natural science. There are five factors that enter into the subject under discussion. In the first place there is the annual round of the seasons, during which the amount of rainfall, winds, currents, and temperatures all combine to affect fishing conditions and the habits of certain varieties of fish. Then there is the smaller round of the lunar month, during which the run of certain varieties of fish would appear to be definitely controlled by the phase of the moon. Locality is obviously an important factor: fishing grounds, and also the peculiarities of different islands and different parts of the coasts of larger islands. Winds and the currents that are directly affected by them, are likewise directly related to favorable and unfavorable conditions and to the run of particular fish in particular localities. And finally, the native fisherman is equipped with a wast knowledge concerning the habits peculiar to each kind of fish."

on fishing trips during a sample week, December 4–10, 1950, when the whole population was in the village. Another similar sample taken in a more summary way in June the same year under identical conditions, gave approximately the same results, and it therefore seems reasonable to regard the following sample week as fairly typical of the fishing activities of the islanders *during their stays in the village.*

TABLE XXI: *Number of persons fishing, December 4–10, 1950*

Age	Total in village		Monday		Tuesday		Wednesday		Thursday		Friday		Saturday	
	M	F	M	F	M	F	M	F	M	F	M	F	M	F
0–14	9	21	4	0	6	2	5	0	6	1	3	2	9	6
15–59	35	27	9	4	7	3	11	3	6	0	10	3	21	7
60–	3	2	1	0	0	1	0	0	0	1	0	0	1	1
Total	47	50	14	4	13	6	16	3	12	2	13	5	31	14

The number of persons fishing on week-days is rather low, especially if we discount the boys under 14 years who often roam about or play instead of making serious efforts. The increase in the number of fisher-men on Saturday is in accordance with the Raroians' general working cycle. No work whatever is done on Sunday, which is a real holiday with absolute rest and copious meals. The preceding day is therefore devoted to food gathering and preparations of all kinds.

Another thing clearly shown in the table is the insignificant partici-pation of the women. The explanation of this is simple. In ancient times there was a sharp division of labour according to sex in this case as in so many others, and the men did the actual fishing with hook and line, spear or net, while the women only gathered shells, clams, crustacea and similar sea foods. The islanders still cling to this labour division, but the supply is not the same as in old times, owing to the new habitation pattern.

There is still plenty of fish around the village, but the supply of other sea foods is exhausted and insignificant as a source of food for the great number of persons living on this limited part of the atoll. With the scattered dwellings in pre-European days, each family had long stretches of reef at its disposal, but this is no longer the case. Therefore the women cannot continue their traditional activities, and as they consider it unthinkable to take over the men's activities, it is not much use for them to go out collecting.

If this is true, the women should devote more time to the collecting of sea food, when they are away from the village working in the various copra sectors, where clams and shells are more plentiful. I have not been able to gather any quantitative data on this, but if I am to judge from my own subjective impressions during repeated visits and stays in the copra sectors, this seems actually to be the case. Even the men seem to fish more frequently when they work in the copra sectors, and I have gained the definite impression that almost all of them spend an hour or so a day fishing. This is only logical as the supply is more abundant in the less-frequented waters far away from the village, and as the amount of other food which can be brought in the canoes is always limited.

5. Turtle catching

The season lasts from June to September during which months a small number of turtles appear in the sea immediately west of Raroia fairly close to the shore. At the beginning of the season both male and female turtles are caught when they breed in the water. At the end of the season, however, most of the turtles caught are females overtaken when they crawl up on the sand beaches to lay their eggs.

The Raroians have names for eight different species of turtles, but it has unfortunately not yet been possible for me to identify them scientifically. Beginning with the egg there are different terms for the various stages in the growth of a turtle: the egg is called *tōuo vaki,* the new born turtle *karēa* and the following three successive stages respectively *torēarēa, kōpue* and *mākui.* A full-grown turtle is called *tīfai,* but the pan-Polynesian word *honu* is also known. Only a really fat turtle should, however, be called a *tīfai,* and if it has less than the maximum quantity of fat it is called *kāveka, takōmo,* and *tuēga,* each term indicating that the turtle thus named has a successively thinner layer of fat.

A turtle catch undertaken in the open sea is a *kauhoka,* in the lagoon a *tūagēra.* The following methods of catching a turtle are known:

Here or snaring. A man dives into the sea with a loop of a rope around his body and passes it over the head or one of the flippers of the turtle. The rope is pulled in by the helpers in the canoe, while the diver sees to it that the animal does not escape.

Haru or seizing. A man dives into the sea and seizes the turtle with his hands. Three different grips are used: *koaro, tui* or *fakarei*. In all three cases the diver approaches the turtle from above, but in the first case he passes both arms under the fore flippers and seizes hold of the head of the animal, in the second case he passes his right hand under the right fore flipper and seizes the left fore flipper while he clutches the head of the turtle with his left arm, and in the third case he seizes the carapace with one hand on the fore part and the other hand on the rear part.

Pātia or spearing. The turtle catcher simply tries to spear the turtle in the neck or in one of the flippers. This method can rarely be used as the turtle dives as soon as it is approached.

Tākatu or hooking. This is by far the most commonly used method to-day, as the natives now possess iron hooks. The hunter, equipped with a long rope, to the end of which a huge iron hook is attached, paddles together with assistants to the spot where a turtle has been seen. He dives into the sea when the turtle appears and tries to place a hook in its throat, the only vulnerable spot of the animal. If he succeeds, his companions in the canoe, who have held fast to the other end of the rope all the time, slowly haul up the turtle. It is turned over and towed ashore.

Fakatīraga or overturning. When a cache of turtle eggs is discovered (usually with the help of the traces) the Raroians watch the spot until the female turtle returns a second time, rush upon the animal and turn it over. All firmly believe that the day when the female turtle returns can be predicted by counting the number of eggs. If a turtle has laid let us say 84 eggs the first time, she will return in 4 days, if there are 85 eggs in 5 days, and so on.

The Raroians show a great appreciation for turtles as food and during the season men, women and children are continuously on the lookout, ready to abandon all other occupation when a turtle is sighted. This is understandable, as turtles constitute the only first class fresh meat obtainable on the atoll. A turtle catch and feast are also still surrounded by some of the old ceremonies. When the animal is brought ashore for instance the following song is sung by the person who caught it:

191

> *Toinoino eeeeee!*
> *Tiriri, tiriri!*
> *Tararā, tararā!*
> *Ko te maro teie*
> *i hūakīa mai ai,*
> *takīna mai ai*
> *te Tumu o Togareva.*
> *Ei puga nūi, ei puga iti,*
> *ei kau marahi!*
> *Pakīa te manu i ruga nei,*
> *te manu kapīri.*
> *E tagāta haru ai taua ika nei,*
> *e ika nūi, e ika iti,*
> *i rau ki te matau na Ruahatu!*
> *Tākai, tākai, tākai te maro no Tu.*
> *Fatīa te pēkau o Matarīki! (or Tākero)*

Translation:

> Toinoino eeeeee!
> Tiriri, tiriri!
> Tarara, tarara!
> This is the girdle
> through which was uncovered
> and fetched
> the bottom of Togareva,
> (which was) as a big coral stone, as a small coral stone,
> as a swimming coral head.
> The bird beats its wings above,
> the crying bird.
> By so-and-so was this fish caught,
> a big fish, a small fish,
> taken on the hook of Ruahatu!
> Wrap round, wrap round, wrap round the girdle of Tu!
> Broken is the flipper of Matariki (or Takero)!

It is not without some hesitation that I have ventured into the difficult field of Polynesian mythology and linguistics and tried to translate this song with the help of Te Iho. The literal meaning was not too difficult to establish, but, to tell the truth, the mythological allusions and poetical metaphors baffled even this learned scholar in some instances. The following interpretation seems the most likely. Togareva is the abyssal depth in the open sea where the turtle is caught, and the

A wooden spear with an iron point, a cotton loin-cloth and a pair of tight-fitting eye-glasses are the standard equipment of a Raroian fisherman. Many species of eels and fish are caught only by the spear.

PLATE 7   Turtle feast. The chief has cut up the turtle into the thirty-two traditionally recognize parts and spread them out on palm leaves.

The meat and intestines wrapped in green leaves, are baked in an earth-oven, on top which the carapace is placed.

turtle itself is compared to the bottom, to a stone and to a swimming coral head brought up to the surface by the hunter, symbolically called a girdle as this is his principal attire. The bird above that beats its wings and cries, is also the turtle hunter, and this is even more clearly brought out in a somewhat different version from another atoll published by Emory (1947, pp. 60—61) in which the hunter is called *torea huru kore,* a plover bird without feathers. Ruahatu is one of the sea gods, patron of the fishermen, and Tu belongs to the pan-Polynesian pantheon. Matariki is the native name for the Pleiades, which stands for a female turtle, whereas Takero (the Belt of Orion) stands for a male turtle. The connection between the turtles and these star constellations is explained by Emory (1947, pp. 61—62).

In ancient times the turtle was an animal eaten only after appropriate religious ceremonies and only by men. (See Chapter II.) On Raroia the women are now allowed their share of the turtle meat, but it was only about 20 years ago that this old taboo was broken. Since a turtle usually weighs about 200 pounds, one is enough for a real meal for the whole population. The turtle is cut up, cooked in an earth oven (the only occasion when it is still in use), and the meat divided up among all the persons present. All the intestines are named and eaten. The men who have caught the turtle are paid between ten and twenty francs by each of the persons partaking of the meal (usually the whole population). The individual who first sights the turtle receives a big chunk free of charge.

In 1950 the total number of turtles caught was 17, and the average number per season seems to have been between 15 and 20 both the preceding and following years. The successful turtle hunts are matched by an approximately equal number of unsuccessful ones, which means that between 30 and 40 days a year are devoted to this activity. About a dozen men are engaged in the hunt and food preparation each time. The number of lookouts and assistants is of course much higher. The turtle catching therefore to a certain extent limits the time which can be devoted to other occupations during these months.

CHAPTER X · **Organization of work**

Certain forms of work organization have already been described in Chapter VIII dealing with surplus production. What I intend here to treat is therefore only the organization of other types of work and the emergence of individualism, professional specialization and new forms of labour division.

1. Disappearance of co-operation

Work, which in pre-European times was characterized by a high degree of co-operation, has now become almost wholly individual as a result of the introduction of a competitive money economy and the breakdown of the old social system with hierarchial authority. When, for instance, to-day a man wants to build a house or needs help for other big enterprises, he has to pay the workers, and the wages are almost as high as in Tahiti, i.e. 100 francs a man per day.

The only instances of extensive co-operation among the islanders during my various stays, in addition to the previously described garland fishing and turtle catching (Chapter IX, D), were the launching of a boat and repair work on the quay.

The boat-launching I witnessed was undertaken by practically the whole population, who pushed and pulled a newly constructed cutter from the work shed down to the beach 300 metres away. The old work-songs, which otherwise are never heard, were sung, probably to a large extent because the islanders knew that I was interested in ancient customs. After the launching the owner of the boat distributed two cases of corned beef (48 cans) and one sack of flour (50 kgs) to the population, and the day ended with a community feast.

The repair work on the quay lasted about a week. It was not a voluntary co-operation like the previous one but actually an imposed chore, organized by the chief by orders from his superiors.

2. Specialization and professionalism

In pre-European times there existed on Raroia specialists in the sense that certain individuals were more skilled in the generally known crafts and therefore in addition to their everyday activities also performed work for other members of the community. (See Chapter II). In several other Polynesian groups many of these specialists were *professionals,* who supported themselves completely on what they received for their work (e.g. Gifford, pp. 143—146, for Tonga and Handy, 1923, pp. 143—161, for the Marquesas), but not so in the Tuamotus, where the difficult living conditions and small number of individuals on each atoll evidently ruled out such full time work. During the last seventy-five years professional specialists have, however, gradually emerged on Raroia as well as on other atolls in the group, and I can say without exaggeration that to-day *all* the Raroians are professional specialists, but of only two kinds: copra-growers and traders. The proportion is uneven, with 64 adult (above the age of 20) copra growers as compared with two traders, but what is significant is that the persons in both categories can all be regarded as full time professionals.

An incipient but rapidly growing tendency towards a more varied specialization is noticeable and seems intimately connected with the more and more uneven land distribution. As shown in Chapters VII and XI certain individuals have for various reasons very little land, and it is especially these landless persons who have tried to find other ways of earning money.

The most common source of income for these individuals is the transportation of copra sacks from the distant sectors to the central village, where most of the schooners have to load the copra because of the lack of good anchorages in most of the other parts of the lagoon. There are often opportunities for those who want to take on such work, as many of the Raroians lack adequate canoes and the wealthy land owners usually find it an unnecessary loss of time to do the transporting themselves. The payment is fixed at 25 francs per 50 kgs sack, and most of the islanders who engage in this business have canoes which can take 8 sacks each trip. Some of these canoe owners also transport the workers and their families. Six men regularly undertake transporting of this kind and they all belong to the group of small landholders. Their employers are all among the richest land owners. Here the boundary line between "primitive" and industrial specialization as defined by Herskovits (1952, p. 125) is transgressed. "The worker becomes specialized not in the production of a certain good, but of only a portion of that good."

Another means resorted to in three cases is to make a sort of coarse doughnuts which are sold at 5 francs apiece. The demand for them is great and the supply never enough as the production limit is usually about 40 doughnuts a person/a day. Usually a married couple acts as bakers, and they may carry on for as long a time as the whole population is gathered in the village. As this was the case only during the months of July and November—December in 1950, baking could not form a very important extra source of income. All the three couples establishing themselves as bakers during these periods also belong to the class of small landholders.

Some men belonging to this class set out at rare intervals to specialize in manufacturing diving goggles or doing repair-work of various kinds; but strangely enough nobody has yet seen fit to try out the most natural expedient, often resorted to in Tahiti, of specializing in fishing. It happens that some of the young men go fishing when they are in special need of money, and the fish they bring back are always eagerly bought at good prices by the other islanders. The reason nobody tries in earnest to become a professional fisherman, at least during the months when the whole population is in the village, seems to be the persistence of an old pre-European attitude that fishes are to be distributed as gifts and the resulting feeling of shame for asking to be paid. Significantly it is never the landless or land-poor individuals who occasionally practise commercial fishing but young men or boys driven by occasional need.

3. Division according to sex

The division of labour according to sex, prevalent in pre-European days, is still adhered to, when traditional chores are performed, and new activities are divided in a similar manner within this general framework. In the following table I have included not only the activities within the framework of the surplus and subsistence economy dealt with in preceding chapters, but also most of the other common occupations of the islanders.

Men's work	Women's work	Joint work
Copra cutting	Piling the nuts	
Clearing of lands		
Separating the copra from the husk		
Fishing with line and hook, spear and net	Gathering shells and crustacea	Torch fishing
Turtle catching		Egg collecting and bird catching
Canoe building		
House building	Plaiting of palm leaves	
Cooking in earth oven	Other cooking and household duties	Water carrying
		Training and care of children

This division of labour is certainly a result of various factors, such as the biological difference between the two sexes, the peculiar environment and the traditions. No attempt will, however, be made to solve this intricate historical problem, which is often over-simplified in certain anthropological studies.

CHAPTER XI · **Income and expenditures**

A study of this type would not be complete without some information about the differential income and the use the islanders make of their money. In spite of the great difficulties in obtaining exact information of this kind for persons who rarely or never keep any books, I have nevertheless tried to gather enough data to be able to discern at least some basic patterns.

The data I have been able to collect are:

1. The approximate total income during 1950 for each family, with sources of income indicated.

2. Expenditures for a sample group comprising about one third of the total population.

3. The property holdings of each family.

For data on total income I have relied on existing records of sales of copra and mother-of-pearl shell supplemented by the interrogation of all the family heads. The expenditures for the sample group are taken from the books of one of the storekeepers, and also in this case I have checked with the islanders themselves as much as possible. The list of property holdings, finally, is based on my own systematic survey. The least reliable figures are thus those for the expenditures, but the errors are probably kept at a minimum and the sampling is fairly representative, as will be shown subsequently.

1. Total income

The income for each family is shown in Table XXII. From the total sum of 1,923,060 francs, 35,000 + 104,800 under the headings

"Transport" and "Other activities" must be deducted, as these sums come out of the money earned on copra and mother-of-pearl shell diving. The actual income was therefore 1,783,260 francs for the whole population in 1950, or 15,373 francs per capita. With an exchange rate of 64 Pacific francs[1] to 1 U.S. dollar, this corresponds to 27,863 U.S. dollars for the year and 240 U.S. dollars per capita.

The main source of income is, of course, copra. The price varied during the year between 8.35 francs and 11.35 francs a kg, but in order to simplify the calculations I have used the average price of 10 francs a kg as a basis. The income from copra is divided into two categories: that coming from copra grown on their own lands and that from preparation of copra for others. The persons employed in making copra are namely as a rule not full time wage earners but simply small land owners who occasionally work for the richer islanders, usually one of their distant relatives. The income from the sale of copra thus produced is always equally divided between the worker and the land owner.

If we are to judge solely from the table, there are three families completely without land, but actually only No. 5, a couple of "foreigners" working for the part-native storekeeper, is really landless. Families No. 6 and 8 both work together with other related families and always prepare copra on certain lands. As they are technically not regarded as the owners of the land by their older relatives, from whom they will eventually inherit, they are not here classified as such.

As the families in Table XXII are arranged according to the gradual increase of their income, the relation between the income from own lands and that from other activities is clearly brought out. Evidently only the families with an income below 60,000 from copra plantations find it necessary to earn money in other ways. The apparent exceptions to this, the incomes of the heads of families No. 17 (8,000 francs) and No. 25 (60,000 francs), are respectively the annual salary of the chief and the supposed annual income of the part-native trader.

The estimate of the trader's annual income is based on the fixed legal percentage of 10 % on an annual turnover of 600,000 francs. As he also acts as a money lender, his actual income is probably much higher. The

[1] All prices in the present study are in Pacific francs. The rate of exchange is 5.50 metropolitan francs to 1 Pacific franc.

other trader, a Chinese, was not willing to give any details of his activities, and he is therefore not included in the table.

The means of finding additional sources of income—besides the preparation of copra for wealthy land owners discussed above—are, as men-

TABLE XXII: *Total income per family during 1950*

Family	Copra from own lands	Pearl-shell diving	Making copra for others	Transport	Other activities	Total
6	—	—	20,000	4,100	—	24,100
8 [1]	—	—	20,000	8,600	—	28,600
5	—	—	22,000	7,100	6,000	35,100
4 [1]	20,000	—	10,000	—	7,000	37,000
9 [1]	40,000	12,390	—	—	—	52,390
12	50 000	3,360	—	—	—	53,360
11	20,000	—	20,000	8,300	6,000	54,300
3	40,000	9,330	5,000	—	—	54,330
20	20,000	9,540	20,000	—	4,800	54,340
22	40,000	6,120	10,000	—	—	56,120
24	60,000	—	—	—	—	60,000
26	60,000	—	—	—	—	60,000
2	30,000	5,370	20,000	6,200	—	61,570
15 [1]	35,000	—	15,000	700	13,000	63,700
13 [1]	70,000	—	—	—	—	70,000
7	70,000	—	—	—	—	70,000
1 [1]	65,000	7,590	—	—	—	72,590
10	60,000	14,460	—	—	—	74,460
14	75,000	2,490	—	—	—	77,490
21	90,000	—	—	—	—	90,000
27	90,000	—	—	—	—	90,000
18	90,000	1,560	—	—	—	91,560
19 [1]	100,000	—	—	—	—	100,000
17	110,000	—	—	—	8,000	118,000
25	60,000	—	—	—	60,000	120,000
23 [1]	120,000	4,050	—	—	—	124,050
16	130,000	—	—	—	—	130,000
Total	1,545,000	76,260	162,000	35,000	104,800	1,923,060

Families marked[1] make up the sample in the next part

tioned in the preceding chapter, the transport of copra sacks from other parts of the atoll to the central village and the setting up of a bakery. The only exceptions are the head of family No. 20, who earned most of his money classified as coming from "Other activities" as a wage worker, and the head of family No. 11, who earned additional money from the sale of ice cubes from a refrigerator.

Whereas all these activities are limited to the families with small land holdings, the diving for mother-of-pearl shell is undertaken by members of families in all income classes. The reason for the even distribution of this income is simply that diving on Raroia, where the lagoon is very deep, requires special skill, which of course is not limited to the lower classes. Considering the small returns (2,742 kg, worth 76,260 francs), the diving on Raroia must be regarded more as a sport than a professional activity. The situation is different during the diving seasons on other atolls as shown in Chapter VIII, B.

2. Expenditures of sample families

None of the islanders keep any record of their expenses, and the only way to get this information was, as I soon realized, to consult the store-keepers' books. At least I could in this way find out what the islanders' expenses were for such things as they themselves regarded as essential—food (canned food, flour and rice), household items (soap, kerosene and gasoline), clothing, cigarettes and a few other miscellaneous items—as the islanders always buy these at the local stores.

Even if I had wanted to, it would have been impossible to gather data of this kind for the whole population as one of the two storekeepers, the Chinese, was not co-operative and besides his books were kept in Chinese. The part-native storekeeper on the contrary did not hesitate to give me permission to copy the accounts, and I used this opportunity to select representative sample families.

The sample thus obtained comprises 8 families, who regularly made their purchases at the part-native trader's store, and the accounts included cover two whole months, June, when most of the islanders lived in the village, and August, when they almost all worked in a copra sector. As these families only on rare occasions bought anything from the Chinese storekeeper—who, by the way, carries exactly the same goods as the part-native trader—we can be fairly sure the figures represent the total purchases of these families during the selected months.

The eight families in my sample population came from the following income classes:

Income class	I Below 37,000	II 37–60,000	III 61–90,000	IV Above 90,000
Total number	3	9	9	6
Number in sample	1	2	3	2

They can thus be said to reflect possible variations in spending habits between the economic classes, if any such variations exist. The composition of these eight sample families in respect of relationship, sex and age is as follows:

Family no. 8:	Hu 31, Wi 41, HuMo 65, Da 5
Family no. 4:	Hu 32, Wi 26,
Family no. 9:	Hu 32, Wi 21, WiGrMo 58, So 7, Da 1
Family no. 15:	Hu 40, Wi 41, Da 17, Da 3
Family no. 13:	Hu 42, Wi 37, HuFa 81, So 19, Da 18, So 14, Da 10, Da 8
Family no. 1:	Single male 45
Family no. 19:	Hu 46, Wi 35, So 11, So 9
Family no. 23:	Hu 57, Wi 49, So 24, SoWi 16, So 9, GrDa 1

Compared to the total permanent population of 116 persons (Table IV, Chapter IV), the sample shows the following characteristics:

Sex	Age			
	Under 15		Above 15	
	Total	Sample	Total	Sample
Males	10	5	45	11
Females	25	6	36	12
Total	35	11	81	23

The sample can therefore be regarded as fairly representative of the total population. The expenditures for the sample group are presented in Table XXIII, and in addition a comparison between income and essential expenses for the same families is made in Table XXIV.

TABLE XXIII: *Expenditures for the sample families during June and August, 1950*

Family	Month	Food	Household	Clothing	Cigarettes	Misc.	Total
8	June	682	947	40	549	—	2,218
	Aug.	1,633	46	—	317	491	2,487
4	June	1,350	24	180	105	—	1,659
	Aug.	965	170	200	1,030	389	2,754
9	June	705	130	2,367	917	1,177	5,296
	Aug.	574	—	—	484	543	1,601
15	June	1,276	125	505	330	47	2,283
	Aug.	2,361	55	475	603	315	3,809
13	June	1,199	—	400	970	177	2,746
	Aug.	2,497	66	488	1,441	418	4,910
1	June	403	85	557	331	467	1,843
	Aug.	303	105	—	471	147	1,026
19	June	2,097	181	559	644	508	3,989
	Aug.	1,229	199	60	1,077	120	2,685
23	June	1,482	105	4,755	818	1,053	8,213
	Aug.	2,901	200	1,678	1,614	343	6,736
Total	2 months	21,657	2,438	12,264	11,701	6,195	54,255

TABLE XXIV: *Income, expenses and surplus of sample families*

Family	Income class	Annual income	Expenses 2 months	Estimated annual expenses	Estimated annual surplus
8	I	28,600	4,705	28,230	370
4	II	37,000	4,413	26,478	10,522
9	II	52,390	6,897	41,382	11,008
15	III	63,700	6,092	36,552	27,148
13	III	70,000	7,656	45,936	24,064
1	III	72,590	2,869	17,214	55,376
19	IV	100,000	6,674	40,044	59,956
23	IV	124,050	14,949	89,694	34,356
Total for all families		548,330	54,255	325,530	222,800

Another important item of expenditure is liquor, which is smuggled and sold by many crew members on the various schooners calling at Raroia. The price of a litre of rum—the most popular drink—usually varies between 600 and 1,000 francs. Some islanders obviously spend huge sums on liquor, but exactly how much it was impossible to find out.

The 54,255 francs spent by the sample group on essential items during two months correspond to an annual expenditure of 325,530 francs. Expressed in percentages the income is spent thus:

Food	24 %
Clothing	13 %
Cigarettes	13 %
Miscellaneous	7 %
Household	3 %
Surplus	40 %
Total	100 %

The slight variation among the families as to the expenses for essential items is a little surprising (especially if we remember the different composition of each family), but shows that practically all the islanders have the same idea about what constitutes the minimum necessities of good living. It is important to note at the same time that all families, even those in the lowest income category, are evidently able to attain this standard. The difference between the families with a small money surplus and those with a big surplus is most clearly seen in the amount of money spent on *prestige* property as will be shown in the next section.

3. Property holdings of each family

Completely lacking any accurate figures on how the islanders' considerable surplus of money is spent, I have chosen the best possible substitute, namely to make a survey of the property holdings of each family (Table XXV) which gives us a fairly good idea of what the Raroians buy in addition to the articles regarded as essential. I have divided the property holdings into two categories: useful and prestige property. The classifications are evident, except perhaps in the case of the inclusion of bed, chair, table, bureau and bicycle under the heading "Prestige property". As, however, the furniture is not used—all Raroians still prefer, according to ancient custom, to sleep on pandanus mats on the floor—and there are no roads outside the village for bicycles, I think it is correct to designate also these items as primarily intended for the enhancement of the family prestige.

TABLE XXV: *Property holdings of each family in 1950*

Family no.	Useful property								Prestige property					
	plank-house	canoe	outboard motor	stove	lamp	sewing machine	refrigerator	radio	bed	chair	table	bureau	wall clock	bicycle
6	1	—	—	—	1	—	—	—	—	—	—	—	1	1
8	—	1	—	—	1	—	—	—	—	—	—	—	—	1
5	—	—	—	1	1	—	—	—	—	—	—	—	—	—
4	—	1	—	—	1	—	—	—	1	1	—	—	—	—
9	—	1	—	1	1	—	—	—	1	—	—	—	—	1
12	1	1	—	—	2	—	—	—	—	—	—	—	—	—
11	1	1	—	2	2	1	1	—	2	4	1	—	1	1
3	1	1	—	—	1	—	—	—	1	—	—	—	—	—
20	—	—	—	—	2	—	—	—	1	—	—	—	—	—
22	1	1	—	1	1	—	—	—	1	1	1	1	1	1
24	1	1	—	1	2	—	—	—	—	—	—	—	—	—
26	1	—	—	—	1	—	—	—	1	—	—	—	—	—
2	—	1	—	1	2	1	—	—	2	2	1	—	—	1
15	1	1	—	1	2	1	—	—	2	4	2	1	1	1
13	1	1	—	—	2	—	—	—	2	—	1	—	1	1
7	1	1	—	2	2	1	—	—	2	6	2	1	1	—
1	1	1	—	2	2	—	—	—	1	3	1	—	—	1
10	1	1	—	2	3	—	—	—	2	2	1	—	1	1
14	2	2	—	2	3	1	—	—	3	6	3	1	1	2
21	2	1	—	3	2	1	—	—	4	8	5	2	2	—
27	1	1	—	2	3	1	—	—	3	7	2	2	1	1
18	1	1	—	2	3	1	—	—	3	7	3	2	2	—
19	—	1	—	2	3	—	—	—	1	—	—	1	—	1
17	1	1	—	3	3	1	—	—	2	6	3	2	1	1
25	2	2	1	4	3	1	1	1	4	14	5	2	3	2
23	1	1	—	2	2	1	—	—	3	2	4	1	1	1
16	1	1	—	2	3	1	—	—	2	6	2	1	1	2

4. Food consumption

In order to give completely reliable results, an investigation of the islanders' food habits and average consumption had necessitated prolonged and repeated observations of several sample groups during both the work and the rest periods. Unfortunately I did not find time for such a study. The only way to give an indication of what the islanders eat is therefore once more to use the family accounts, and try to extract additional information on this aspect. Even if we do not get complete data on the total food consumption in this way, we at least get an idea of the consumption of *imported* foods, which by the way is usually a good measure of the degree of acculturation of a non-literate people.

Among the data on essential items which I found in the storekeeper's account books, those dealing with the purchase of food were complete. As the imported food comes in standard cans or the quantity sold is indicated in each customer's account, I have without difficulty been able to determine the amount of imported food consumed by the sample population of 34 persons during two months.

The monthly and daily consumption per person, based on these figures, together with the corresponding means for the daily consumption

TABLE XXVI: *Consumption of imported food in grams for the sample population*

Food item	Raroia 1950			French Oceania 1947
	Sample population 2 months	Per month per person	Daily per person	Daily per person
Flour	840,000	12,353	411.8	273
Sugar	157,500	2,316	77.2	95
Corned beef	79,000	1,162	38.7	48
Rice	63,000	926	30.9	65
Coffee	45,000	662	22.1	—
Biscuits	21,000	309	10.3	—
Peanut oil	17,600	259	8.6	9
Canned milk	15,880	234	7.8	17
Canned fruit	14,175	208	6.9	—
Canned fish	11,350	167	5.6	10
Starch	8,000	118	3.9	—
Canned butter	5,902	87	2.9	8

in French Oceania as a whole for 1947 (Jacquier, p. 601), are presented in Table XXVI.

Other imported foods, such as canned vegetables, tomato sauce, pork and beans, onions and jam can also be bought in the stores, but the islanders consume such negligible quantities of these few items that I have not found it worth-while including them in the table. As the only additional food available on the atoll and eaten regularly in such quantities that it can be regarded as constituting a part of the staple diet is fish and coconuts, the islanders' menu is evidently very poorly balanced.[1]

[1] Our knowledge of the nutrition problems will be considerably increased when the results of Miss S. Malcolm's studies in the Tuamotus are available. Miss Malcolm, who is the nutrition specialist of the South Pacific Commission, visited the group in 1953.

CHAPTER XII · **Changes in social structure**

The transformation from a simple subsistence economy to a specialized surplus economy has naturally involved numerous changes in the social structure. Many of these have already been touched upon in the previous chapters, but here I shall group all pertinent data together in order to give a more comprehensible picture. In addition to the description of these changes I shall analyse the probable causes for the widespread persistence of one old custom, viz. adoption.

1. Change of settlement pattern

In pre-European times the population was fairly evenly spread out over all the inhabitable land, and each kindred *(matakeinaga)*, composed of related extended families, had its own section of the land and lagoon. Land ownership was thus invested in the kindred as a group. The use of the products was decided by the heads of the extended families after fairly democratic deliberations. (Chapter II.) To-day all the inhabitants have their permanent residence in the village of Garumaoa on the western side of the atoll and do not spend more time in the other parts of the atoll than strictly necessary for copra preparation.

This important change in settlement pattern was initiated in the 1870s after the conversion of the inhabitants to the Catholic faith, and according to Te Iho it was Father Montiton and Father Fierens who laid out the new village on the present spot. The letters by these missionaries that I have frequently quoted in previous chapters do not mention the founding of Garumaoa village, but we learn of the construction of new villages on other atolls. Father Montiton writes, for instance, in 1872 that on the neighbouring island of Fakahina "we traced two roads, as on Fangatau and Takoto, which the schoolchildren cleared, smoothed and planted with coconut palms. All along and on either side of these roads a suitable parcel of land was then assigned to the head of each family, as well as to each young bachelor, who there erected a little hut and planted coconut palms."[1] Father Fierens (1879, p. 440) tells about the founding of a similar village on Napuka.

The reasons that actuated the missionaries to try to bring about this change of the settlement pattern are obvious. That the habitations were widely scattered had not been an obstacle to the ancient religion, as each family head was his own priest and there was a "high priest" in each section occupied by a kindred. But after conversion, with only one missionary priest for the whole eastern part of the archipelago and one single church building on each atoll, the concentration of the populations became a necessity. The need for this was made still more imperative by the fact that the missionaries wanted not only to change the natives' religious beliefs but also to transform completely their outlook and way of life.

The traders, too, preferred to have the natives gathered in one place, and that trading facilities were deemed important is shown by the fact that on Raroia, as on many other atolls, the new village was built near the only pass or opening in the atoll rim deep enough to let through trading schooners. The selection of this place was the more natural as the most important kindred, Varoa, to which all the overlords *(ariki nūi)* had belonged, occupied this sector of the atoll. (Cf. Map B, Chapter II.)

Not all the inhabitants, however, moved immediately to Garumaoa in the 1870s when the modern village was founded. Te Iho and other old men and women affirm that up to the 1903 cyclone there were still many families living in Teputaiti, Oneroa, Opakea, Kereteki and Tokerau. (See end map.) As the more primitive dwellings of native material in these parts of the atoll were destroyed by the cyclone, whereas the

---

[1] "Nous traçâmes, comme à Fangatau et à Takoto, deux chemins que les enfants de l'école défrichèrent, nivelèrent et plantèrent de cocotiers. Puis, sur le parcours et des deux côtés de ces chemins, on assigna un terrain convenable à chaque chef de famille, et même à chaque jeune homme célibataire, qui y édifia une petite case et y planta des cocotiers." (Montiton, 1873, p. 376.)

wooden buildings with cement foundations in Garumaoa resisted fairly well, the refractory families were eventually induced to move over to Garumaoa. It must also be remembered that the copra trade had by then attained considerable proportions, and that the only good anchorage for schooners was in front of the new village.

Another fact which certainly also helped to accelerate the change was the decrease in the population due to the ravages of newly introduced diseases. (Chapter IV.) It was only natural for the surviving islanders to seek one anothers' company, especially as with the advent of the new order many old hostilities and suspicions between the various kindreds had disappeared.

The main reason for the scattered distribution of the inhabitants' dwellings all over the atoll in pre-European times had, of course, been economic: the food-resources were more easily exploited in this way. The switch to a new type of economy was therefore an important prerequisite for a change of the settlement pattern. In this respect, too, the missionaries and traders could readily offer something new and attractive, since the surplus copra crop soon provided the natives with money to buy food on the schooners and thus made them independent of the local supply of food. So interrelated in my opinion was the type of settlement pattern with the economic system that certainly no re-grouping of the population would have been possible, if it not had been correlated with a transformation of the economy.

2. Decreased size of kinship groups

Owing to the general migration to the central village the different kindreds intermingled and soon ceased to function as social units. In 1883, when the land was reapportioned (Chapter VII), the number of recognized kindreds was as follows, according to the report then made by the native council:

Varoa i te po	Hopuariki	Mahuruariki
Tapuhoe	Moenau	Marere
Maruake	Havaiki	Tagihia
Mahinui	Tanetefauaitu	Hoga
Tefau	Keha	Mahaga
Kaoko	Matarau	Tahuka

If we compare the district names on this list to those on map B in Chapter II we shall find that it contains three additional names: Tanete-fauaitu, Mahuruariki and Tahuka. According to Te Iho these districts were formed by setting apart portions of the Tefau and Tapuhoe sectors in such recent times that they had not acquired the same status and prestige as the other, ancient districts and therefore were usually

TABLE XXVII: *Family or household membership*

Family	MEMBERS											
	Hu	Wi	YoSo	YoDa	AdSo	AdSoWi	AdDa	AdDaHu	GrCh	HuPa	WiPa	Total
1	1	†	—	—	—	—	—	—	—	—	—	1
2	1	1	—	—	—	—	—	—	—	—	—	2
3	1	1	—	—	—	—	—	—	—	—	—	2
4	1	1	—	—	—	—	—	—	—	—	—	2
5	1	1	—	—	—	—	—	—	—	—	—	2
6	1	1	—	—	—	—	—	—	—	—	—	2
7	1	1	—	1	—	—	—	—	—	—	—	3
8	1	1	—	1	—	—	—	—	—	1	—	4
9	1	1	1	1	—	—	—	—	—	—	1	5
10	1	†	—	2	—	—	—	—	—	—	1	4
11	1	1	1	1	—	—	—	—	—	—	2	6
12	1	†	—	3	1	—	—	—	—	—	—	5
13	1	1	1	2	1	—	1	—	—	1	—	8
14	1	1	2	1	—	—	1	1	—	1	—	8
15	1	1	1	—	—	—	1	—	—	—	—	4
16	1	1	—	1	1	—	—	—	—	—	—	4
17	1	1	—	1	1	—	2	—	—	—	—	6
18	1	1	—	1	—	—	—	—	—	—	—	3
19	1	1	2	—	—	—	—	—	—	—	—	4
20	1	1	—	2	—	—	—	—	—	1	—	5
21	1	1	—	3	1	—	1	1	—	—	—	8
22	1	1	—	1	—	—	1	—	—	—	—	4
23	1	1	1	—	1	1	—	—	1	—	—	6
24	1	1	1	—	—	—	1	1	1	—	—	6
25	1	1	—	—	1	—	1	—	—	—	—	4
26	1	†	—	—	1	—	1	—	—	—	—	3
27	1	1	—	2	—	—	—	—	—	—	1	5

included in these. On the other hand, one of the old sectors on Map B, called Tane, has completely disappeared.

To-day only Te Iho and a few old men know the exact boundaries for each old district *(makateinaga)*, and only three families whose land-holdings are concentrated on certain parts of the atoll rim, and thus have a sure indication, know from which district they came themselves. A survival of the high esteem in which certain descent groups *(gāti)* formerly were held is noticeable, however, for all islanders try to find at least one branch of their pedigree leading back to the most distin-guished eponymous ancestor, Varoa. As a rule this meets with no great difficulty as numerous intermarriages between the different kindreds have taken place during the last 75 years. The present Raroians also regard themselves as a homogeneous group.

Another change that has taken place is that the size of the extended families has decreased considerably, which is no doubt due to the new economy and individual land ownership. Since work co-operation is no longer necessary, as it was in the days of a direct subsistence economy, and since adult children are no longer dependent on their fathers or other relatives, they often immediately form their own families. In the same way brothers or cousins who were formerly bound by economic ties have often preferred to separate for various reasons. The composition of the various families or households is shown in Table XXVII.

The biggest families in the table are significantly enough such in which the members still work together collectively according to the old system. As appears from the table the residence rule for one of the children is patrilocal and for three matrilocal, whereas it is neolocal in six cases, according to my investigations. The mean number of persons per family was 4.3 at the time the table was drawn up (January 1950) but towards the end of the year it was 4.8, owing to the fusion of families 4, 8 and 20 in one case and 6 and 11 in another.

Ernest and Pearl Beaglehole have compared the average size of the household in different Polynesian groups and have pointed out that this is a good measure of the degree of acculturation. In their study of the conditions in the Tongan village of Pangai (1941, p. 69) they present a comparative table and make the following comments:

"Household Membership.

Place	Pukapuka	Hawaii	Futuna	Uvea	Tonga
Average Membership	6.5	6.9	8.0	8.77	6.5

These figures suggest that the Polynesian household ranges between six and eight persons. For comparison it may be noted that the average size of the American urban family is about 3.43 persons. The Polynesian household, therefore, is much larger that the white family and manages to hold its size despite years of contact with the ways of the white man. The size of the househould group may in fact be taken as a rough index of the degree to which the Polynesian in general has assimilated patterns of white behaviour in contradistinction to the tenacity with which he holds on to native patterns of household-organization and the social values which are implied by this type of large household-grouping."

The figure 4.3 for Raroia shows that the acculturation is fairly far advanced. The families are also frequently dissolved, as the old socio-religious and economic ties that used to bind the members of the same family together have been replaced by a formal marriage ceremony of a type inconsistent with ancient customs and therefore unwillingly adopted and little respected. Knowing that a Catholic marriage cannot be annulled and that legal divorce after a civil marriage is a troublesome and expensive business, most people prefer to live together without any formal ties, especially since no social stigma is attached to this type of union. Of the 23 couples living together at the beginning of 1950 nine were united neither by a religious nor by a civil ceremony. Of course, the stability of such marriages cannot be very great.

Another interesting fact which finally must be noted is the general adoption since three or four generations of *family* names in accordance with the French pattern. No such patronyms existed in pre-European times and their introduction is certainly a result of the deliberate pressure from the authorities, who for obvious reasons prefer to have to do with identifiable individuals. As the old kindreds have disappeared and no bigger kinship groups than the families exist, it is, however, from the natives' point of view only logical that these latter should now be named. On the other hand they see no reason why a person should not, in accordance with ancient custom, change his *first* name as often as he wishes.

3. Kinship terms and ties

Owing to the break-down of the old social groups the kinship ties determine the natives' behaviour to a very small degree. In pre-European times the status and role of an individual in the social system was certainly, as elsewhere in Polynesia, fixed by his genealogical affiliation to the founder and head of the kindred to which he belonged. Supposing that the kinship ties still were important determinants of the behaviour pattern I began my researches on Raroia in accordance with accepted practice by recording the kinship terms, but I gradually found that the interaction between the individuals was as a rule determined by other factors. This is the main reason why I have waited until this chapter to present the tables of kinship terms.

Fig. XI. *Consanguinal kinship terms*

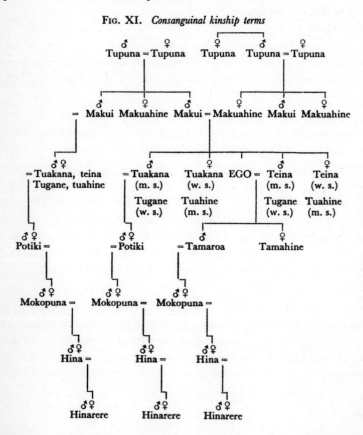

FIG. XII. *Affinal kinship terms*

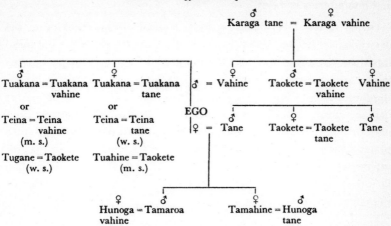

The following list contains all the terms in Figs. XI and XII properly defined and marked together with some additional terms:

mākui (kaefa)	father, father's brother, mother's brother, male cousin of parent
mākui vahīne, mākuahīne	mother, mother's sister, father's sister, female cousin of a parent
mākui tumu or *fānau*	consanguinal parent as distinct from parent's siblings and cousins
mākui fāgai	foster parent
mākui hōu	step parent
tama, tamariki	child
matahīapo	first-born child
murīga	last-born child
tamarōa, mākaro	son
tamahīne	daughter
kōpūtahi	sibling
maehaga	twin
tupuna	grandparent on either father's or mother's side and their siblings. Also used for all generations above grandparents'
tuakana	elder brother, man speaking; elder sister, woman speaking; cousin who is the child of an elder sibling of a parent
teīna	younger brother, man speaking; younger sister, woman speaking; cousin who is a child of a younger sibling of a parent
tugāne	brother of female
tūahīne	sister of male

pōtiki	sibling's child, cousin's child
mokopuna	grandchild, sibling's grandchild, cousin's grandchild
hina	great-grandchild, great-grandchild of a sibling or cousin
hinarere	great-great-grandchild, great-great-grandchild of a sibling or cousin
huāgāi	progeny, off-spring
tāne, kaefa, tikatika	husband, man
vahīne, rire	wife, woman
taokete	sister's husband, man speaking; brother's wife, woman speaking; wife's brother; husband's sister
karaga	father- or mother-in-law
hunōga	son- or daughter-in-law
tuakana vahīne	elder brother's wife, man speaking;
tuakana tāne	elder sister's man, woman speaking
teīna vahīne	younger brother's wife, man speaking
teīna tāne	younger sister's man, woman speaking
taokete vahīne	wife's brother's wife
taokete tāne	husband's sister's husband

All the terms given are referential, i.e. describe only the relationship. The only terms I heard also used in a vocative sense, i.e. when addressing a person, were *tupuna, tuakana* and *teīna*.

The existence of words like *tamarōa* (son), *tāne* (man, husband) and *vahīne* (woman, wife) besides the local Tuamotuan words *mākaro* (son), *kaefa, tikatika* (man, husband) and *rire* (woman, wife) seems at a first glance to indicate recent introductions from Tahiti, but it is very likely that these words were already used by the discoverers and first settlers of the islands. To a surprisingly large extent duplicate terms are found in the Tuamotus: one of old pan-Polynesian distribution, the other evolved later locally in the group. Great care must therefore be taken to distinguish recent introductions from old words when the Tuamotus share a word with the surrounding groups (principally the Society and Marquesas Islands). Of undeniable recent introduction are only the two French words *papa* and *mama(n)*, which now are widely used instead of the old words *mākui* and *mākuahīne*.

The ancient kinship system still completely determines the islanders' behaviour when selecting a mate, as has been shown in a previous chapter (p. 124), and cousins, for instance, feel the same responsibilities towards each others as towards siblings. Otherwise, however, few interrelationships can be discovered. The older generations have astonishingly little authority, and if a household head wants to enlist more distant relatives for canoe-building or housebuilding he has often even to pay them. That kinship ties have so little importance to-day is easily understood if we remember that with the changing social structure all power has been transferred from the heads of extended families and kindreds to completely new leaders, such as the democratically elected chief, the wealthy traders and the catechists nominated by the bishop in Tahiti.

I should like to recall here Firth's words in the final chapter of his study of the economic and social life of the Maori people (p. 483): "The need for cohesion in the economic affairs of a primitive people is met by reinforcing the economic chain of interests by some other of these powerful cultural forces, such as the socially-inspired recognition of the claims of kinship. The native is often induced to comply with his economic responsibilities because of other social ties which he is unwilling to break. To illustrate concretely what is meant—the co-operation which is essential to a working party is secured so much more easily when the members of it are already members of the same kinship group. Their economic relationship is strengthened through their reciprocal duties and common interests in other fields. Therein lies the strength of primitive society in that it enlists the binding forces from one aspect of life to support those of another." It is this binding force which has disappeared on Raroia.

4. Persistence of adoption

A fact that immediately strikes one when looking at Table XXVII, Family membership, in part 2 of this chapter is the limited range of the number of persons in the households. With the exception of the first six households, which are childless presumably because of the woman's syphilitic sterility, there are only three households with as few as three members and only three with as many as eight. All the rest have between four and seven members. This even distribution is no matter of chance, but a result of the persistence of the ancient custom of adoption. Of the 51 sons and daughters in Table XXVII 20 are for instance adopted. The extensive prevalence of this custom is, however, still better shown by Table XXIII, where the households have been broken down into nuclear families (*a* of the Hu-Wi, *b* of the HuPa-WiPa stratum) and the total number of children given away and adopted by each couple or individual *during their whole life-time* is stated.

The wide-spread existence of adoption in Polynesia in pre-European times seems to have been caused mainly by the following factors (see e.g. Beaglehole, 1940, p. 54):

1. Political: it cemented the alliances between the different kindreds or tribes.
2. Social: a childless man could in this way ensure the continuance of his line.
3. Economic: the adoption of children provided the family with an adequate labour supply.

The first motive must, of course, be completely discounted to-day, since the different islands no longer form independent political units.

TABLE XXVIII: *Number of children adopted and given away.*

Couple	Children				Couple	Children			
	Born	Dead in infancy	Given away	Adopted		Born	Dead in infancy	Given away	Adopted
1	—	—	—	—	14 a	4	—	1	1
2	—	—	—	—	14 b	4	—	1	—
3	—	—	—	—	15	1	—	—	1
4	1	1	—	—	16	1	—	—	2
5	—	—	—	—	17	5	2	—	1
6	—	—	—	—	18	—	—	—	3
7	—	—	—	1	19	3	1	—	1
8 a	—	—	—	1	20 a	5	2	1	—
8 b	4	2	—	—	20 b	—	—	—	—
9 a	5	—	3	—	21	8	2	2	1
9 b	1	1	—	2	22	—	—	—	2
10 a	2	1	—	1	23	3	—	1	1
10 b	4	—	2	—	24	3	1	—	—
11 a	2	1	—	1	25	5	3	1	1
11 b	—	—	—	3	26	—	—	—	2
12	13	5	2	—	27 a	4	1	1	—
13 a	14	5	3	—	27 b	6	—	1	—
13 b	—	—	—	2					

The second certainly has some relevance, as most Raroian men still have strong family feelings and all wish to have descendants. But the principal reason why adoption is practised to such a large extent is certainly an economic one. As is shown in previous chapters, the cultivable area is limited and no source of income other than copra exists. Such a static economy naturally makes it difficult for parents with many children to provide for them, and the natural way out is to give them away to couples with few children and plenty of land. (Cf. Table XXII with Table XXVIII.) On the other hand childless couples are pleased to adopt other people's children, for, since there is neither social assistance nor a savings bank on Raroia, the older generations are dependent on the younger. It is therefore no exaggeration to say that adoption is the Raroians' special form of life insurance. Owing to the fact that the new economy and the old subsistence economy have *the principal trait of being static* in common the custom of adoption has been preserved and still has a function to fulfil. It is perhaps needless to say that adoption always is an informal arrangement without legal validity.

In four cases (family 14 *a*, 21, 23 and 25) the gift of a child to one family is compensated by the adoption of a child from another family. The explanation is probably that we here have to do with a sort of "social climbing", as in all these cases the child given away has been placed in a more wealthy family and the child adopted has come from a less wealthy family. By raising their child's status in this way the parents also get some benefits, for an adopted child will always feel some obligations towards its blood parents, especially on an island like Raroia, where they all live in the same village and meet almost daily.

Conclusions

As far as we know, the Raroians seemed to have achieved a cultural equilibrium in pre-European times, i.e. the same values were accepted by all and the various parts of the culture were integrated in a smoothly functioning whole. About a hundred years ago the islanders first established more intimate contact with Western culture, and since then the acculturation process has continued with increasing intensity. This raises three questions of a more general, theoretical interest:

1. *What has been the result of this prolonged contact?*
2. *Which are the processes that have preceded the changes?*
3. *Can any universally valid regularities be discovered?*

In a way the entire description in the previous chapters forms an answer to the first question, and I shall therefore here confine myself to making a general survey of my findings. In their classical *Outline for the Study of Acculturation* Redfield—Linton—Herskovits distinguish the following three final results of culture contacts (Herskovits, 1938, pp. 135—136):

"A. *Acceptance:* where the process of acculturation eventuates in the taking over of the greater portion of another culture and the loss of the most of the older cultural heritage; with acquiescence on the part of the members of the accepting group, and, as a result, assimilation of them not only to the behavior patterns but to the inner values of the culture with which they have come into contact.

B. *Adaptation:* where both original and foreign traits are combined so as to produce a smoothly functioning cultural whole which is actually an historic mosaic; with either a reworking of the patterns of the two cultures into a harmonious meaningful whole to the individuals concerned, or the retention of a series of more or less conflicting attitudes and points of view which are reconciled in everyday life as specific occasions arise.

C. *Reaction:* where because of oppression, or because of the unforeseen results of the acceptance of foreign traits, contra-acculturative movements arise; these maintaining their psychological force *a)* as compensations for an imposed or assumed inferiority, or *b)* through the prestige which a return to older pre-acculturative conditions may bring to those participating in such a movement."

Beals, who has recently reviewed the works on acculturation that have appeared since the publication of this outline, concludes (p. 636) that the scheme has won general acceptance and adds some pertinent observations concerning the modes of adaptation: "In very broad terms there are agreements among students of culture contact as to some of the possible results. Virtually all discussions point out acceptance, syncretism, and reaction as being possible results of culture contact, with the recognition that in most cases all three effects may occur, with emphasis varying according to the conditions of contact as well as through time as the contact situation continues. Acceptance, without modification by other attitudes, ultimately leads to complete assimilation to the contact culture. Even if other responses intervene, assimilation may in some cases ultimately result. Syncretism is a frequent result of contact and has been well documented, especially in the studies of Latin-American Indian cultures and in the studies of the Negro in the New World. Less frequently mentioned in the various memoranda for study, but prominent in some of the actual studies both in the New World and in Africa, is the occurrence of spontaneous reformulations which often result in the modification of elements from either of the cultures in contact or produce entirely new structures. While the totality of the emergent culture may be regarded in some measure as a syncretism, large areas of the social structure may be essentially new."[1]

---

[1] A good example of this was recently reported in the April 11, 1955, issue of the *Time Magazine,* in which correspondent Keith Wheeler quotes a boss of the Saudi Arabian American Oil Co. who with evident surprise said: "We come to the desert and we bring along radios and washing machines and cars and Lord knows what, and we give a shocking jolt to a culture that was sustained for centuries by dates and camels and faith in Allah. We didn't come here to manufacture a nation of imitation Americans, but it happens whether you like it or not. The trouble is, the imitation is neither American nor Saudi."

A *reaction* in the sense here given to the term cannot be observed on present-day Raroia (but has earlier occurred on several occasions, as pointed out in the historical account in Chapter III), and contra-acculturation movements of the type often met with in Melanesia are conspicuously absent not only on Raroia but also elsewhere in French Oceania. Whether the present situation on Raroia should be labelled as acceptance or syncretism is somewhat difficult to decide, since these terms do not stand for two clearly separate categories but rather indicate differences of degree. *Syncretism* (adoption, modification, reformulation or whatever term one wants to choose) occurs in many instances, and the most striking example, is, of course, the present economic system, which is neither Polynesian nor Western but an entirely new creation. *Acceptance* has in certain cases gone so far as to become complete assimilation. Good examples of this are clothing, tools and implements. Very few European culture elements have been completely rejected.

In order still better to show this *uneven impact* on native culture, which constitutes one of the most interesting and challenging problems for students of acculturation, I have here arranged the various aspects of Raroian culture in a hierarchy, beginning with the most and ending with the least acculturated aspect:

1. *Material culture*	European materials and techniques ars used almost exclusively, and the only noteworthy exceptions are out-rigger canoes and palm-leaf houses.
2. *Religion*	All islanders are practising Christians, but the wide-spread belief in ghosts and the formal-ritual conception of religion are obviously ancient survivals.
3. *Economy*	The use of money and the concentration on producing a surplus are Western traits, but everybody still devotes some time to fishing, turtle catching, egg collecting and other direct subsistence activities.
4. *Political system*	The old hereditary district chiefs have been replaced by a popularly elected chief and council. The highest authority is centralised in Papeete. In fact, however, the Raroians govern themselves according to their ancient customs in most matters of immediate concern.
5. *Language*	The older people still speak almost pure Tuamotuan, but the younger generations use Tahitian to a large extent. Only one person speaks any French at all.

6. *Social structure*	The old kindreds have disappeared and the largest units are now the extended or nuclear families. The households have decreased in size and residence is frequently neo-local. On the other hand there are practically no stratifications or classes, the kinship system is unchanged, the old incest rules are still respected and extensive adoption remains a prominent feature.
7. *Recreation*	Now as formerly dancing and singing are the main recreational activities. The type of dancing and the tunes have, however, been modified by Tahitian and Western influences, and many seasonal celebrations patterned on French models and following the French calendar have been added.
8. *Education*	The old native method of education, characterized by few sanctions, informal learning through participation and early self-reliance, is still the principal one.
9. *General knowledge*	As there are no other books in the native vernacular than the Bible and Hymn book and few Raroians have any formal education, they know next to nothing about the modern world they are living in.

Such an uneven result of the acculturation process does not necessarily lead to a poor integration of the various traits. However, I suspect that there is more often than not a definite connection between differential rates of change and cultural *disorganization,* and at all events on Raroia this may be plainly observed. The adjustments are frequently haphazard, many elements of the old culture have evidently been abandoned before suitable substitutes were found and no new equilibrium has been achieved. Another reason for this disorganization is that our own Western culture is full of conflicts which are sometimes transferred to and continued on Raroia.

The most obvious sign of this cultural disorganization is the existence of numerous *practical* problems, of which the following are the most serious:

Land questions. Much land is uncultivated because of uncertain or disputed titles. Much time is lost in travelling, as the parcels of land are so small and scattered. The necessity of making a trip to Papeete and the cost of legal assistance discourage the islanders from taking any court action.

Health and nutrition. The old healers are dead and have taken their secrets with them. Therefore the islanders do not know how to treat

223

either the ancient diseases or the new ones. About modern hygiene they know of course still less. The diet is poorly balanced with too much imported and canned food.

Lack of co-operation. The old leaders, who were religiously sanctioned and therefore obeyed, have disappeared, and their places have been taken by traders and office seekers, who lack authority. The change-over to a surplus economy has encouraged individualism. The binding force between social and economic activities has disappeared. Many problems which could be solved fairly easily by determined joint action are therefore never attacked.

One-sidedness of the economy. At present the islanders earn consider-able sums, but all their income is derived from mother-of-pearl shell diving or copra preparation, of which only the latter is a regular activity. As there are no other resources on the atoll on which to base a surplus economy, a sudden slump or the disappearance of the demand for copra and shells on the world market would entail a complete col-lapse of the present economic system.

In the first three cases the type of solution which seems most logical is a continued and better guided Europeanization of the islanders through improved school education of future generations. In the fourth case, the one-sidedness of the economy, no such solution seems possible, however, and instead the only alternative points backwards to a return to the old subsistence economy.

This last-mentioned solution was actually tried during the depression in the early 1930s, when all trade virtually ceased. It worked out fairly well, and if the islanders' own statements are to be trusted their health was even improved. The question is, however, whether such a return to the old subsistence economy is still possible, especially as a permanent solution. The main difficulty is of course that the persons who were the carriers of the old culture and the leaders during the native revival in the early 1930s are now almost all dead, and that the present Raroians have no knowledge of ancient techniques. If such a solution were to be tried once more in the case of the complete collapse of the copra trade, it would therefore certainly be necessary, no matter how ridiculous it may sound, to call in a team of anthropologists and teach the poor islanders Polynesian survival techniques.

Whether two such conflicting principles as a more complete Europeanization in some cases and a return to the pre-European patterns in other cases could co-exist is of course extermely difficult to say, and is at any rate a question that lies completely outside the scope of the present study.

Still another result, or rather aspect, of acculturation that must not be overlooked is the *psychological,* i.e. the question of what changes, if any, have taken place in the islanders' personality or character structure. If a community is disorganized and the conflicts are numerous, it seems logical to assume that this should be reflected in the psychology of the people who live there. As many investigations show such is often the case. In their study of a Maori village (1946, p. 333) Ernest and Pearl Beaglehole have, however, ingeniously pointed out that even in a fairly changed and disorganized society the personality type may remain surprisingly homogeneous and stable provided that education is still of the traditional type:[1] "Even though the society in which the Kowhai Maori lives is thus in some gross sociological respects disorganized, the amount and kind of social disorganization are not necessarily incompatible with the development of a fairly coherent and consistent Maori character-structure. This development is possible because the old people with their seniority, authority, prestige, their command of tradition, tribal knowledge, and tapus are still able to present to the younger generations as the customary and right way of life certain crucial patterns of infant care and child-raising whose inevitable impact on the young is the formation of Maori character-structure. Later, as the child grows to maturity, he still finds his code of values and his latent anxieties supported by those patterns of behaviour and feeling relating to tribal traditions and group integration. These are the very aspects of Maori society that have today been least affected by pakeha contact—in which, in other words, there is least social disorganization."

Judging only from my personal impressions, I found all individuals on Raroia remarkably well-balanced and stable, and I have not even hesitated to speak of their "spiritual wholeness" (1953 a, pp. 68—69,

---

[1] Another equally important prerequisite is of course that the personality type was stable and well-balanced already in pre-contact times, which evidently was the case in Polynesia. That the personality type may, however, vary considerably from one culture to another is amply proved by Margaret Mead's studies.

1954 b, p. 9).[1] As can be seen in the above list showing the uneven impact on the various aspects of Raroian culture, education is one of the most conservative elements and practically all believe in the same values, which facts confirm Beaglehole's hypothesis, or at least does not disprove it. It must be added, however, that the great economic prosperity is certainly an important factor contributing to the happy, wellbalanced type of personality.

The discrepancy between the pattern of the culture and the personality of the individuals sharing in it has caused certain experts to doubt whether the term "acculturation" can really be applied at all as long as the transformation is only "external" and not "internal". Redfield's reply during the International Symposium on Anthropology of the Wenner-Gren Foundation in 1952 (Appraisal, p. 128) is to the point: "Dr. Tax and some of his associates have recently enunciated the perfectly outrageous hypothesis that acculturation never occurs, which is very surprising in view of Dr. Beals's review of the literature on the subject. I am all for outrageous hypotheses, and I think this is a good one, although it just is not so if you understand it in the ordinary literal sense of acculturation. Dr. Tax and his associates seem to be saying that the Indians that they are working with listen to radio and wear clothes like ours but, if you talk to them longer, seem to be thinking and feeling just about the same as they did in the past. These investigators say that acculturation there does not occur. What is meant is that something persists and this is, perhaps, more easily understood if you center your interest upon the conception of human personality and in this case look at its typical form."

Let us now turn to the second question: *Which are the processes that have preceded the changes?* As I have already pointed out in the Introduction to the present study, students of acculturation seldom observe the process of change itself, but instead infer it from the results or/and make historical reconstructions. In the case of Raroia I am in the fortunate

---

[1] I regret that I was not competent to undertake a formal study of character structure and sincerely hope that a trained psychologist will one day discover how rewarding field-work in French Oceania could be.

position of having a fair knowledge of the principal culture contacts that have occurred, and I shall here use the account given in Chapter III for a tentative analysis, based on the scheme in the *Outline* of 1938 (Herskovits, pp. 132–134).

One fact which immediately stands out is that owing to the isolation and poverty of the atoll Raroia has not attracted foreigners to the same extent as Tahiti, Hawaii, Samoa and other mountainous islands, and the agents of change have consequently not been representative for our Euroamerican culture but have consisted of *selected groups,* principally traders, missionaries and administrators. All these Euroamerican agents of change have been *men,* with the result that though acculturation had been going on for more than a hundred years when I returned in 1949, my wife, who accompanied me that time, was the first white woman many of the oldest inhabitants of Raroia had ever seen. Some acculturation has also occurred during the visits of Raroians to Tahiti, but it is unlikely that they have had more than superficial contacts with Euroamericans other than those already mentioned, viz. traders, missionaries and administrators, for the simple reason that few others speak the native dialect. More or less acculturated Tahitians have of course often acted as transmitters of Western culture and so to speak *filtered* it by passing it on in a modified form. This has no doubt facilitated the acceptance by the Raroians, but it has certainly also contributed to the already highly *selective* character of the traits offered by the donor group. All these factors could easily explain the differential rates of change noted in my list above, since the greatest transformations are in the fields of material culture, religion, economy and political system, i.e. exactly what we might expect knowing the main agents of change to be missionaries, traders and administrators.

With the exception of the attack against a French trading vessel in 1847 (Chapter III, pp. 89–91) and the enforced introduction of French administration and law in the 1880s (Chapter III, pp. 98–99) the acculturation process has been *peaceful* and very little pressure has on the whole been exercised on the islanders. Raroia is thus a good example of a receiving group that has been offered a *limited* number of cultural traits with the freedom to select *voluntarily.* Why have the islanders chosen as they have done? In their *Outline* of 1938 Redfield–Linton–Herskovits proposed four reasons for a receiving group to adopt foreign traits, and they seem all to have been operative on Raroia. These determinants of change are (Herskovits, 1938, p. 134):

1. Economic advantages
2. Social prestige
3. Congruity of culture-patterns
4. Neccessity to adopt traits functionally related with other ones selected for one of the previous reasons

Of these determinant (1) seems to have been especially powerful as indicated principally by the change over from a subsistence to a surplus economy. A good example of the operation of determinant (4) is the change of settlement pattern correlated with the economic transformation. Another is the division of the island into sectors for copra work as a result of individual ownership and the concentration of the population in a central village. The prestige factor, determinant (2), is far from negligible on Raroia as shown for instance by the list of property holdings (Table XXV, p. 205). It should perhaps be noted here that Linton (1940, p. 474) thinks that prestige and novelty are especially important in the initial phase of acculturation. Determinant (3), changes caused by congruity of culture pattern, has probably played a very small role, and the only case I can think of is that "the Polynesian family and leadership systems ... reminiscent of the Old Testament picture of the early Hebrews, could be aligned more readily with the ethical requirements of missions and governments than with the generally more exotic clan customs and social arrangements of the Melanesians". (Keesing, 1950, p. 21.)

A noteworthy feature that also seems to distinguish the acculturation process on Raroia is its *accumulative* character. The great attraction of European articles has caused the Raroians to change over to a surplus economy. In this way they earn considerable sums of money, which enable them to visit Tahiti and learn more about Western modes of life. This in its turn encourages them to earn still more money, to make new visits to Tahiti, and so on.

Many anthropologists have tried to facilitate the analysis of the acculturation process by means of tables of various types. Malinowski (p. 73) used a special "speciment chart" with the following headings:

A	B	C	D	E
White influences, interests, and intentions	Processes of culture contact and change	Surviving forms of tradition	Reconstructed past	New forces of spontaneous reintegration or reaction

Another possibility would be to group the data in a table adapted from the *Outline* (Herskovits, 1938, p. 134), classifying the traits under the following headings:

Unmodified European	Modified European	Unmodified Native	Modified Native	Disappeared Native

These methodological devices are often helpful, but my experience is that the functional and temporal relationships—which actually are the focus of interest—are too complicated to show in this way. Another device, recently used by Watson in his study of the Cayuá Indians, is therefore a definite improvement. He describes it in the following terms (pp. 128–129): "The configurational analysis dwells, first, on identifying factors of cause or effect, and, second, on establishing relationships among causes and effects. Causes of acculturation mean those changes in the total Cayuá environment initially traceable to the presence or influence of members of an alien, European society and which have produced changes in Cayuá culture. All such causes, then, are specifically defined as limited to changes in the situation as a direct consequence of whites. Effects distinguished herein, of course, are of two kinds, primary or immediate, and secondary or derived, the latter reflecting the more complete adjustment process or ramification of change within the indigenous culture."

Watson's chart is logical rather than temporal, i.e. the sequences are often reconstructed on the basis of his knowledge of the present situation, for the perfectly comprehensible reason that the history of this Indian tribe is but imperfectly known. I have therefore been in a much more fortunate situation when I have here (see Figure XIII) tried to prepare a similar chart of the temporal sequences on Raroia, as the principal phases in Tuamotuan history are recorded. In spite of this, the shortcomings of the chart are apparent. It could rightly be objected for

229

instance that changes due to *internal* causes (independent evolution to use a classical expression) are not shown, that certainly a *combination* of various so called causes and primary effects sometimes results in secondary and (why not?) tertiary effects, or, finally, that a *persistence* of an old custom in one segment of the native culture in conjunction with changes in other segments may bring about new conditions.

The most serious criticism that could be levelled however, is in my opinion that the data are not *quantitative* and that a mathematical analysis of all the intricate correlations—which certainly is the only completely satisfactory approach—therefore cannot be undertaken. At the present stage of the development of anthropological science such a chart may nevertheless have a certain usefulness as a rough exploration of a previously unknown society.

The third and final question which requires an answer is: *Can any universally valid regularities be discovered?* As may be expected in the case of a science as young as anthropology and with only a small number of acculturation studies of an extremely heterogeneous character at our disposal no definite conclusions can be reached. Or in Linton's words (1940, p. 520): "These phenomena are so poorly understood at present and there is such a lack of factual material by which conclusions can be checked that any statements made about them must be considered tentative and valid only in the light of our present very limited information." The so-called regularities or laws that have hitherto been proposed are consequently either such self-evident truths as that duration, closeness and continuity of contact determine the course of the process of acculturation, or they are such empirically unproved statements as that women are more conservative than men or that the persistence of an aboriginal trait is due to the fact that this aspect of the culture has not been exposed to influence.

The only hypotheses that are yet worthwhile taking seriously are some relating to the question of the differential rates of change. Thus Linton (1940, p. 485) has proposed the following seductive explanation:
1. Tangible objects are more easily transferred
2. Patterns of behaviour permeate moderately well
3. Elements which lack concreteness and ready observability meet with the greatest resistance

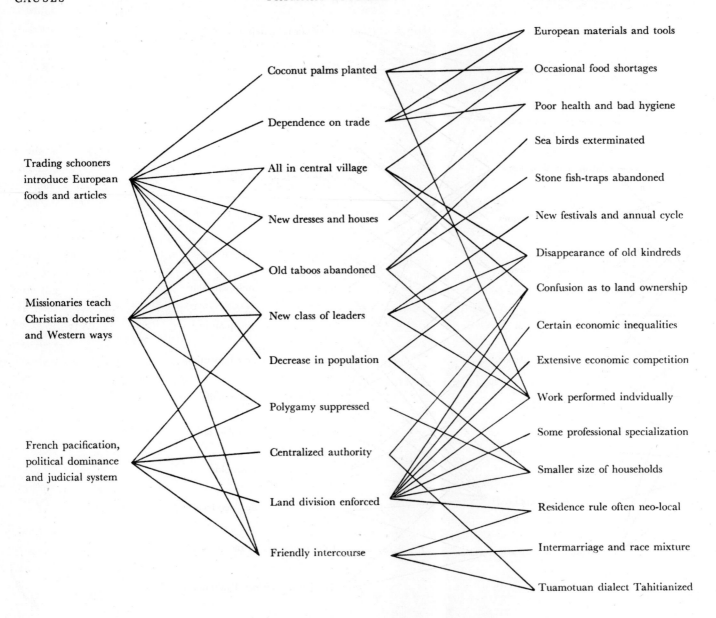

CAUSES   PRIMARY EFFECTS   SECONDARY EFFECTS

Trading schooners introduce European foods and articles

Missionaries teach Christian doctrines and Western ways

French pacification, political dominance and judicial system

Coconut palms planted

Dependence on trade

All in central village

New dresses and houses

Old taboos abandoned

New class of leaders

Decrease in population

Polygamy suppressed

Centralized authority

Land division enforced

Friendly intercourse

European materials and tools

Occasional food shortages

Poor health and bad hygiene

Sea birds exterminated

Stone fish-traps abandoned

New festivals and annual cycle

Disappearance of old kindreds

Confusion as to land ownership

Certain economic inequalities

Extensive economic competition

Work performed individually

Some professional specialization

Smaller size of households

Residence rule often neo-local

Intermarriage and race mixture

Tuamotuan dialect Tahitianized

FIG. XIII. *Configurational analysis of the acculturation process on Raroia.*

If we want to verify this hypothesis we must, however, first regroup all anthropological data in a new way, as suggested by the recent American committee on acculturation: "In point of fact, the conventional categories of cultural description—technology, social organization, religion, etc.—do not readily lend themselves to an analysis of differential change. *All* cultural segments have their concrete aspects." (Seminar, pp. 990—991.) The members of the committee nevertheless agree that "these more explicit behaviors and apparatus are as a rule more readily mastered than symbolic and valuational aspects." (Seminar, p. 991.) In addition the same group of specialists propose the very probable hypothesis that "intangibles also appear to show levels of differential change. Specific and isolated ideas and behaviors are thought to be more vulnerable than those integrated with a more inclusive set of values. The more generalized values are, the more persistent they seem to be." (Seminar, p. 991.)

Keesing uses another criterion, zones of interests or needs, and has made an attempt—the only comprehensive one so far—to verify his hypothesis with the aid of a large number of empirical data from the existing literature. Keesing himself summarizes the attempt (1953 a, p. 83), which is still in manuscript form, thus: "By tabulating loci of persistence and of mobility as shown in a number of acculturation studies, he develops a broad framework of hypotheses in relation to each of these facets of dynamics. First are set out those zones in culture which appear to show a high frequency of persistence, as pertaining to basic survival, security, integrity, value, problem solving, for the group concerned, and in which, if change or interference occurs, the greatest disturbance and tension is likely to be generated. Categories cover essentials of psycho-somatic conditioning, communication, organic maintenance, primary group relations, prestige status maintenance, territorial security, and ideological (including religious) security. By contrast, zones in which mobility or ready change tend to appear with high frequency are nonaffectively charged techniques summarized as "instrumentalities" (e.g., tools, etiquette, military tactics); voluntary elements of taste and self-expression, achieved status systems, and other effective or competitive types of behavior, and more impersonal or mass social structures. It is recognized, of course, that great variability shows as regards group and personal response within these broad tendencies and such variations challenge further propositional analysis."

This seems to be a promising approach to the problem, but many more studies to draw upon are of course needed before we stand on reasonably firm ground.[1] In the meantime a sort of acculturation index would be extremely useful, as Ernest and Pearl Beaglehole (1941, p. 136) have pointed out: "What is needed in this connection is the development of some techniques whereby the student of contemporary primitive cultures could express an index of acculturation that would state concisely and adequately the cultural level of the culture studied. This index would then constitute a simplified way of describing the position of the culture in question on an imaginary line whose polar limits would be aboriginal culture at one end and western European culture at the other end. If it were possible to establish such an index-expression for the various contemporary Polynesian cultures, we would have gone far in our understanding of what is meant by the processes of acculturation and culture change. This index might express theoretically either the number of aboriginal elements surviving in the present-day culture or else the number of new elements transferred from the carriers of the alien culture. This index-expression of the status of contemporary culture together with complete knowledge of the temporal order in which various elements of culture have been transferred from alien to aboriginal culture would then open the way for a more realistic attack upon the dynamics of the processes underlying the diffusion of culture."

If we consider the difficulties of discovering any universal regularities in the differential rates of change, which are easily observable phenomena, we cannot immediately expect to find any regularities in the *time sequences* of the acculturation process, which are of an infinitely more complex character. The members of the latest American committee of acculturation specialists (Seminar, p. 992) summarize the most important attempts hitherto in this field: "Some of these formulations deal with large ethnographic areas, others with single tribes. Some treat total

---

[1] An extremely interesting and fruitful approach to the problem of universal regularities in the processes of change is a recent book by H. G. Barnett: *Innovation, The Basis of Cultural Change,* in which he studies the *psychological mechanism* involved, be the causes of change external (acculturation) or internal *(invention)* in relation to the culture studied.

cultural systems in process of change, others restrict themselves to statements about acculturating groups or individuals. A few take into account the intercultural nature of the process; others treat only one side of the equation, typically the 'native' culture. As matters now stand, comparative study of the phenomenon is difficult, if not impossible, because the approach to the problem is so uneven."

The main reason why it is so difficult to make any comparative studies of the type needed for discovering general sequences is best stated by Broom (pp. 630–631): "The failure by students of acculturation to quantify their data is an impediment to the fullest utilization of the research by others. In part this may be due to the nature of the phenomena which resist numerical statement, or because the investigators disdain anything that looks like nose-counting. Anyone who has watched the recent proliferation of research in acculturation must have noted that, however penetrating and significant each study may be, data from different investigations can rarely be compared. If this is because of methodological difficulties, it is nevertheless a methodological duty to make it possible to bring together facts from diverse sources."

Another point to remember is the difficulty, mentioned above in connection with the configurational analysis (Fig. XIII), in recording all the complex interrelationships. An additional difficulty often overlooked is that we are never concerned with static cultures, but that *both* the donor and the receiving culture continuously change during the period of contact. Finally, the problem is still further complicated by the existence of *individual variations* within one and the same culture. Spoehr (Appraisal, p. 132) has aptly remarked: "Anyone who has been in an outrigger canoe out of sight of land, with a tropical front approaching, knows that it takes a particular personality type to cope with these conditions. We could very possibly reconstruct the personality type that was a necessary and sufficient condition for the migrations into the Pacific, Furthermore, today, under conditions of acculturation, say in the Marshalls or Carolines, you get a very remarkable differentiation in the community between those still willing to take an outrigger canoe five and six hundred miles across the sea, and those who would prefer to remain and become schoolteachers." Such variations in personality type have very likely contributed to the direction the acculturation process has taken in each specific case.

Some reliable conclusions about the acculturation process may no doubt be reached by means of continued comparative historical studies, and even rigorously scientific diffusion studies can help a great deal. But like other anthropological problems this one will probably not be solved until well-planned, *co-ordinated* field studies and controlled experiments are finally used. Keesing envisages for instance (1953 a, pp. 78 —79) "controlled observation and experiment in contemporary settings, with this problem as the direct focus of research attention. A series of carefully planned experiments in presenting a group with new cultural elements, familiar to completely exotic, competing and not competing, simple to complex, and so on through other variable dimensions would yield case materials of great importance."

I am all for experiments, but as everybody knows ethical considerations prevent us from using such methods in the social sciences to the same extent as in the natural sciences. Fortunately there is a good substitute, viz. well-planned comparative studies in societies chosen in such a way that the different variables—environment, aboriginal culture, acculturative forces, demographic set-up and so on—are combined as in a controlled experiment. I have previously pointed out (Danielsson, 1950, pp. 83—84) the great possibilities of undertaking studies of this type in the Amazonas, but prospects seem to be still better in the Pacific region, where conditions probably approximate more closely to the laboratory situation than anywhere else on earth today.

To begin with there are three principal groups, Polynesia, Micronesia and Melanesia, each one with its distinct culture, represented by numerous sub-types. Furthermore, within each of these groups we find at least two ecological types: fertile, mountainous islands and low, arid atolls. Finally, all possible combinations of habitat and native culture are found in every political sphere into which the Pacific is divided and the principal colonial powers have at various times or simultaneously been Spain, England, Germany, France, Japan and America, which obviously represents a great range of cultures and sub-cultures. A great number of varying situations, from a simple meeting between two cultures as on Raroia to the extremely complex cross-cultural relationships in Hawaii are thus found in the Pacific.

It goes without saying that a research program which aims at the chartering of these complex phenomena cannot be carried out in the way so far used in acculturation studies and other anthropological field research, but that team-work in the form of intimate co-operation among various specialists will ultimately be needed. Even so it will probably take a long time before any universal regularities can definitely be established. As Lundberg has put it (p. 65): "The protracted work by which measuring instruments have been invented and perfected in the physical sciences remains to be done in sociology. How long did it take, for example, to develop the modern microscope? Such work must be performed as a condition of progress. In the meantime, the theoretical rationale here presented is demanded both as an hypothesis on which to work and as a justification for devoting ourselves to the slow and undramatic labor upon technology which always has been and always will be the principal condition of scientific progress in all fields."

In addition to this *theoretical* justification for devoting so much time to the minutiae of the daily work an life on Raroia, I have, however, another of a much more limited range. As my previous data have amply demonstrated, the islanders suffer in many instances from the effects of serious conflicts and contradictions in their present hybrid culture, and few completely satisfactory adjustments have been made. I therefore sincerely hope that this study will also, at least to some extent, contribute to a better understandring and the final solution of these practical problems.

References

The following abbreviations are used:

AA   American Anthropologist
ARB   Atoll Research Bulletin
BMB   Bernice P. Bishop Museum Bulletin
BSEO   Bulletin de la Société des Etudes Océaniennes
HS   Hakluyt Society
JPS   The Journal of the Polynesian Society

ANNUAIRE
    1863   Annuaire des Etablissements Français de l'Océanie. Imprimerie du Gou-
            vernement. Papeete.
ANONYMOUS
    1934   Arrestation des sauvages de Fakahina. BSEO 52, pp. 409—415.
APPRAISAL
    1953   An Appraisal of Anthropology Today. Sol Tax and others, Editors. The
            University of Chicago Press. Chicago.
AUDRAN, HERVE
    1917   Moeava, ou le grand Kaito Paumotu. BSEO 2, pp. 53—62.
    1918   Napuka et ses habitants. BSEO 3, pp. 126—136.
    1919   Traditions of and notes on the Paumotu (or Tuamotu) islands. JPS,
            Vol. 28, pp. 232—239.
    1923   Noms d'illustres marins Paumotu des temps passés. BSEO 7, pp. 19—20.
    1930.   Te tamakianga kaka o Moeava. Torea Katolika, May 1930, pp. 561—562.
            Avarua, Rarotonga.

BARNETT, H. G.
    1953   Innovation: The Basis of Cultural Change. McGraw-Hill Book Company.
            New York.
BEAGLEHOLE, ERNEST
    1939   Some Modern Hawaiians. University of Hawaii Research Publication 19.
            Honolulu.
    1940   The Polynesian Maori, JPS, Vol 49, pp. 39—68.
BEAGLEHOLE, ERNEST & PEARL
    1941   Pangai, Village in Tonga. Polynesian Society Memoir 18. Wellington.
    1946   Some Modern Maoris. New Zealand Council for Educational Research.

REFERENCES

BEALS, RALPH
  1953 Acculturation. *In:* Anthropology Today, pp. 621—641. University of Chicago Press. Chicago.
BEECHEY, FREDERICK W.
  1831 Narrative of a Voyage to the Pacific and Beering's Strait. Vols. I—II. London.
BEHRENS, CARL
  1739 Histoire de l'expédition de trois vaisseaux aux terres australes en 1721. Vols. I—II. The Hague.
BELCHER, EDWARD
  1843 Narrative of a Voyage round the World. Vols. I—II. London.
BELLINGSHAUSEN, THADDEUS
  1945 The Voyage of Captain Bellingshausen to the Antarctic Seas 1819—1821. HS XCI. Vols. I—II.
BELTRAN Y ROZPIDE, RICARDO
  1883 Las Islas Tuamotu. Boletín de la Sociedad Geografica de Madrid 15, pp. 23—42.
BODIN, H.
  1932 Les pirogues cousues des Tuamotu. BSEO 42, pp. 1—8.
BOUGAINVILLE, L. A.
  1771 Voyage autour du monde. Paris.
BROOM, LEONARD
  1945 A Measure of Conservatism. AA pp. 630—635.
BROWN, FORREST B. H.
  1931 Flora of Southeastern Polynesia. Vol. I. Monocotyledons. BMB 84.
BUCK, PETER
  1938 Vikings of the Sunrise. Lippincott Co. New York.
  1945 An Introduction to Polynesian Anthropology. BMB 187.
  1953 Explorers of the Pacific. Bishop Museum Special Publication 43. Honolulu.
BURROWS, E. G.
  1933 Native Music of the Tuamotus. BMB 109.
  1938 Western Polynesia, a Study in Cultural Differentiation. Etnologiska Studier 7. Göteborg.
  1940 Culture-Areas in Polynesia. JPS, Vol. 49, pp. 349—363.
  1947 Functional and Psychological Studies in Polynesia. *In:* Specialized Studies in Polynesian Anthropology, pp. 75—85. BMB 193.
BUTTERWORTH, F. EDWARD
  1952 Series of Lectures on the Origin of the Polynesians and the History of the Latter Day Saints' Mission in French Oceania. Mimeographed copy.
BYRON, JOHN
  1773 An Account of a Voyage round the World. Edited by John Hawkesworth. London.

CAILLOT, EUGENE
  1909 Les polynésiens orientaux au contact de la civilisation. Ernest Leroux. Paris.
  1910 Histoire de la Polynésie Orientale. Ernest Leroux. Paris.
  1932 Histoire des religions de l'archipel Paumotu. Ernest Leroux. Paris.
COOK, JAMES
  1773 An Account of a Voyage round the World. Edited by John Hawkesworth. Vols. I—II. London.
  1777 A Voyage towards the South Pole and round the World. Vols. I—II. London.

CORNEY, BOLTON G.
   1913—1919 The Quest and Occupation of Tahiti by Emissaries of Spain in
             1772—1776. HS Second series XXXII, XXXIV, XLIII. Vols. I—III.
CUZENT, GILBERT
   1883—1884 Archipel des Pomotu. Société Academique, Bulletin 9, pp. 49—90. Brest.

DANIELSSON, BENGT
   1950 Some Attraction and Repulsion Patterns among Jibaro Indians. *In:* So-
         ciometry in France and the United States, Edited by Georges Gurvitch,
         pp. 82—105. Beacon House. New York.
   1951 Quelques observations météorologiques faites à Raroia (Tuamotu). BSEO
         94, pp. 192—199, 95, pp. 236—243.
   1952 A Recently Discovered Marae in the Tuamotu Group. JPS, Vol. 61, pp.
         222—229.
   1953a Raroia, Happy Island of the South Seas. Rand McNally. Chicago. British
         edition published by George Allen & Unwin, London, 1952.
   1953b Tuamotuan Kinship Terms. Ethnos, pp. 155—166. Stockholm.
   1953c Dernières recherches scientifiques à Raroia. BSEO 105, pp. 139—141.
   1954a L'état actuel des recherches ethnologiques en E. F. O. Nouvelles Tahi-
         tiennes 2, pp. 30—31. Papeete.
   1954b Raroian Culture. ARB 32.
DARWIN, CHARLES
   1950 The Voyage of the Beagle. Everyman's Library 104. J. M. Dent & Sons.
         London.
DOTY, MAXWELL S.
   1954 Floristic and Ecological Notes on Raroia. ARB 33, pp. 1—41.
DOTY, MAXWELL S. & MORRISON, J. P. E.
   1954 Interrelationships of the Organisms on Raroia Aside from Man. ARB 35.
DUMONT D'URVILLE, JULES S. C.
   1841—1846 Voyage au Pôle Sud et dans l'Océanie sur les corvettes "L'Astrolabe"
             et "La Zélée". Vols. I—X. Paris.
DUPERREY, L. I.
   1826 Voyage autour du monde. Paris.
DU PETIT-THOUARS, ABEL
   1840—1845 Voyage autour du monde sur la frégate "La Vénus". Vols. I—IV. Paris.

ELLIS, WILLIAM
   1853 Polynesian Researches. Vols. I—IV. London.
EMORY, KENNETH P.
   1932 The Tuamotu Survey. *In:* Report of the Director for 1931. BMB 94, pp.
         40—50.
   1934 Tuamotuan Stone Structures. BMB 118.
   1939 The Tuamotuan Creation Charts by Paiore. JPS, Vol. 48, pp. 1—29.
   1940 A Newly Discovered Illustration of Tuamotuan Creation. JPS, Vol. 49,
         pp. 569—578.
   1947 Tuamotuan Religious Structures and Ceremonies. BMB 191.
   n. d. Tuamotuan Material Culture. Manuscript in the Bernice P. Bishop
         Museum, Honolulu.

FIERENS, GERMAIN
   1872 Lettre du 28 juin 1871. Annales de l'association de la propagation de la foi,
         Vol. 44, pp. 124—136. Lyon.
   1879 Lettre du 28 août 1878. Annales des Sacrés-Cœurs, pp. 434—440. Paris.

REFERENCES

FIRTH, RAYMOND
 1929 Primitive Economics of the New Zealand Maori. E. P. Dutton & Co. New
       York.
FITZ-ROY, ROBERT
 1839 Narrative of the Surveying Voyages of HMS "Adventure" and "Beagle".
       London.
FRIEDERICI, G.
 1910 Ein Beitrag zur Kenntnis der Tuamotu-Inseln. Mitteilungen des Vereins
       für Erdkunde zu Leipzig, pp. 97—176. Leipzig.
FORSTER, GEORGE
 1777 A Voyage round the World. Vols. I—II. London.
FORSTER, J. R.
 1778 Observations made during a Voyage round the World. London.

GIBBINGS, ROBERT
 1948 Over the Reefs. J. M. Dent & Sons. London.
GIFFORD, E. W.
 1929 Tongan Society. BMB 61.
GIOVANNELLI, J. L.
 1940 Les cyclones en Océanie Française. BSEO 68, pp. 250—265.
GOODENOUGH, WARD H.
 1955 A Problem in Malayo-Polynesian Social Organization. AA 1, pp. 71—83.
GREEN, JAMES L.
 1878 Letter from Tahiti. The Friend, May issue. Honolulu.

HALE, HORATIO
 1846 Ethnography and Philology. United States Exploring Expedition, Vol. VI.
       Philadelphia.
HAMILTON, GEORGE
 1915 Voyage of HMS "Pandora". Francis Edwards. London.
HANDBOOK
 1953 Handbook for Atoll Research. ARB 17.
HANDY, E. C. S.
 1923 The Native Culture in the Marquesas. BMB 9.
 1932 Houses, Boats, and Fishing in the Society Islands. BMB 90.
HARRY, ROBERT R.
 1952 Ichtyology. In: Field Team Report on Coral Atoll Project at Raroia,
       Tuamotu Archipelago, pp. 21—22. Mimeographed copy. Pacific Science
       Board. Washington D. C.
 1953 Ichthyological Field Data of Raroia Atoll, Tuamotu Archipelago. ARB 18.
HAWTHORN, H. B.
 1944 The Maori: A Study in Acculturation. AA Memoir 64.
HENRY, TEUIRA
 1930 Ancient Tahiti. BMB 48.
HERSKOVITS, MELVILLE J.
 1938 Acculturation. J. J. Augustin. New York.
 1945 The Processes of Cultural Change. In: The Science of Man in the World
       Crisis, Edited by Ralph Linton, pp. 143—170. Columbia University Press.
       New York.
 1948 Man and his Works. Alfred A. Knopf. New York.
 1952 Economic Anthropology. Alfred A. Knopf. New York.

HERVE, ANNE
1948 Magie et sorcellerie chez les indigènes de l'archipel Paumotu. Journal de la Société des Océanistes 4, pp. 49—56. Paris.

HEYERDAHL, THOR
1952 American Indians in the Pacific. George Allen & Unwin. London.

IZIKOWITZ, K. G.
1951 Lamet, Hill Peasants in French Indochina, Etnologiska Studier 17. Göteborg.

JACQUIER, HENRI
1949 Contribution à l'étude de l'alimentation et l'hygiène alimentaire en Océanie Française. BSEO 86, pp. 584—606.

KEESING, FELIX
1945 The South Seas in the Modern World. The John Day Co. New York.
1947 Acculturation in Polynesia. In: Specialized Studies in Polynesian Anthropology. BMB 193, pp. 32—46.
1950 The Pacific Island Peoples in the Postwar World. Oregon State System of Higher Education. Eugene, Oregon.
1953a Culture Change. Stanford University Press. Stanford.
1953b Social Anthropology in Polynesia. Oxford University Press.

KOSKINEN, AARNE A.
1953 Missionary Influence as a Political Factor in the Pacific Islands. Annales Academiae Scientarum Fennicae, Ser. B, Tom. 78, 1. Helsinki.

KOTZEBUE, OTTO VON
1821 A Voyage of Discovery. Vols. I—III. London.
1830 A New Voyage round the World. Vols. I—II. London.

KROEPELIEN, BJARNE
1939 Pierre Félix Ribourt. BSEO 65, pp. 139—140.

KUYKENDALL, RALPH S.
1949 The Hawaiian Kingdom 1778—1854. University of Hawaii Press. Honolulu.

LAVAL, HONORE
1851 Lettre du 16 mai 1849. Annales de la propagation de la foi, Vol. 23, pp. 392—399. Lyon.

LE MAIRE, JACOB
1906 The Australian Navigations of Jacob Le Maire. In: The East and West Indian Mirror. HS Second Series XVIII.

LESSON, RENE PRIMEVERE
1839 Voyage autour du monde. Vols. I—II. Pourrat. Paris.

LINTON, RALPH
1940 Acculturation in Seven American Indian Tribes, Chapters 8—10, pp. 463 —520. D. Appelton Century Co. New York.

LOWIE, ROBERT
1948 Social Organization, Rinehart & Co. New York.

LUCETT, EDWARD
1851 Rovings in the Pacific. Vols. I—II. London.

LUNDBERG, GEORGE A.
1939 Foundations of Sociology. The Macmillan Co. New York.

MALINOWSKI, BRONISLAW
1945 The Dynamics of Culture Change. Yale University Press. New Haven.

REFERENCES

MARSHALL, DONALD S. & SNOW, CHARLES
1954 Polynesian Craniology. Typescript in the author's possession.
MEINICKE, CARL
1870 Der Archipel der Paumotu. Zeitschrift der Gesellschaft für Erdkunde zu Berlin, Vol. V, pp. 340—369, 385—407. Berlin.
MOERENHOUT, J.-A.
1837 Voyages aux îles du Grand Océan. Vols. I—II. Paris.
MONTITON, ALBERT
1855 Lettre du 6 avril 1854. Annales de l'association de la propagation de la foi, Vol. 27, pp. 438—45. Lyon.
1873 Lettre du 4 septembre 1872. Annales de l'association de la propagation de la foi, Vol. 45, pp. 275—295, 371—385. Lyon.
1874 Les Paumotus. Missions Catholiques, Vol. 6, pp. 339, 342—344, 354—356, 366—367, 378—379, 491—492, 498—499, 502—504. Lyon.
MORRELL, BENJAMIN
1832 A Narrative of Four Voyages. J. & J. Harper. New York.
MORRISON, J. P. E.
1954a Ecological Notes on the Mollusks and Other Animals of Raroia. ARB 34, pp. 1—18.
1954b Notes on the Birds of Raroia. ARB 34, pp. 19—26.
MÜHLMANN, WILHELM E.
1934 Die Begriffe 'Ati und Mataeinaa: Ein Beitrag zur politischen Entwicklung und Besiedlungsgeschichte Polynesiens. Anthropos, Vol. XXIX, pp. 739—756. Wien.
MURDOCK, GEORGE P.
1949 Social Structure. The Macmillan Company. New York.

NEWELL, NORMAN D.
1954a Expedition to Raroia, Tuamotus. ARB 31, pp. 1—12.
1954b Physical Characteristics of Raroia. ARB 31, pp. 13—21.
1954c General Map of Raroia. ARB 31.

PAEA
n. d. Traditional History of Raroia. Copy of manuscript in the author's possession.
PICKERING, CHARLES
1848 Races of Man and their Geographical Distribution. United States Exploring Expedition. Vol. IX. Philadelphia.

QUIROS, PEDRO
1904 The Voyages of Pedro Fernandez Quiros. HS Second Series XIV. Vols. I—II.

RANSON, G.
1952a Procès-Verbal de la séance extraordinaire de la Chambre de Commerce des E. F. O. du 20 mai 1952. Mimeographed copy. Papeete.
1952b Procès-Verbal de la 2ème séance extraordinaire de la Chambre de Commerce des E. F. O. du 12 août 1952. Mimeographed copy. Papeete.
REY-LESCURE, PHILIPPE
1939 La tragédie de la goélette "Sarah Ann". BSEO 67, pp. 222—234.
REYNOLDS, J. N.
1835 Voyage of the United States Frigate "Potcmac". New York.
ROBERTSON, GEORGE
1948 The Discovery of Tahiti. HS Second Series XCVIII.

ROGGEVEEN, JACOB
1911 De Reis van Mr. Jacob Roggeveen ter ontdekking van het Zuidland. Uitgegeven door F. E. Baron Mulert. The Hague.
RUSSELL, EDWARD
1837 New Groups of Islands in the Pacific. The Journal of the Royal Geographical Society, Vol. 7, pp. 454—455. London.

SEMINAR
1954 Social Science Research Council Summer Seminar on Acculturation 1953. Acculturation: An Exploratory Formulation. AA 6, pp. 973—1002.
SEURAT, L. G.
1905 Procédés de pêche des anciens Paumotu. L'Anthropologie, Vol. 16, pp. 295—307. Paris.
SHAPIRO, H. L.
1930 The Practice of Incision in the Tuamotus. Man, pp. 140—143. London.
1942 The Anthropometry of Pukapuka. Anthropological Papers of the American Museum of Natural History, Vol. XXXVIII, Part III. New York.
1943 Physical Differentiation in Polynesia. In: Studies in the Anthropology of Oceania and Asia. Peabody Museum. Cambridge, Mass.
SPOEHR, ALEXANDER
1954 Tri-Institutional Pacific Program. In: Bernice P. Bishop Museum Annual Report for 1953. Honolulu.
STEVENSON, ROBERT LOUIS
1901 In the South Seas. Vols. I—II. Tauchnitz Edition. Leipzig.
STIMSON, J. FRANK
1928 A System of Diacritical Marks. JPS, Vol. 37, pp. 318—325.
1933 The Cult of Kiho-tumu. BMB 111.
n. d. Dictionary of the Tuamotuan language. Photostatic copy in the author's possession.

TAYLOR, C. R. H.
1951 A Pacific Bibliography. The Polynesian Society. Wellington.
TEISSIER, RAOUL
1953 Etude démographique sur les Etablissements Français de l'Océanie. BSEO 102, pp. 6—31.
TERLYN, VINCENT DE PAUL
1900 La Mission des Tuamotu. Annales des Sacrés-Cœurs, pp. 188—194. Paris.
TRANSACTIONS
1803—13 Transactions of the London Missionary Society. Vols. I—III. London.
TURNBULL, JOHN
1813 A Voyage round the World. 2nd edition. London.
TYERMAN, DANIEL & BENNET, GEORGE
1831 Journal of Voyages and Travels. Vols. I—II. London.

VALENZIANI, C.
1949 Enquête démographique en Océanie Française. BSEO 87—88, pp. 658—684.
VISHER, STEPHEN SARGENT
1925 Tropical Cyclones of the Pacific. BMB 20.

WAGNER, GUNTER
1936 The Study of Culture Contact and the Determination of Policy. Africa, Vol. IX, pp. 317—331. London.

243

REFERENCES

WALLIS, SAMUEL
    1773 An Account of a Voyage round the World. Edited by John Hawkesworth. London.

WATSON, JAMES B.
    1952 Cayúa Culture Change: A Study in Acculturation and Methodology. AA Memoir 73.

WHEELER, KEITH
    1955 Alchemy in the Desert. Time Magazine, April 11.

WILLIAMSON, ROBERT W.
    1939 Essays in Polynesian Ethnology. Cambridge University Press. Cambridge.

WILKES, CHARLES
    1844 Narrative of the United States Exploring Expedition. Vols. I—V. Philadelphia.

WILLIAMS, H. W.
    1928 The Nights of the Moon. JPS, Vol. 37, pp. 338—356.

WILSON, JAMES
    1799 A Missionary Voyage to the Southern Pacific Ocean. London.

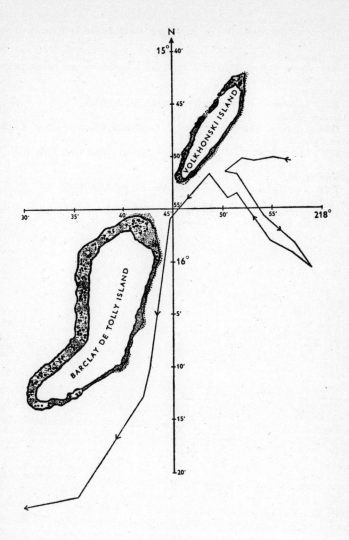

N
15°·40′
·45′
·50′
·55′
30′   35′   40′   45′   50′   55′   **218°**
·16°
·5′
·10′
·15′
·20′

VOLKHONSKI ISLAND

BARCLAY DE TOLLY ISLAND

BELLINGSHAUSEN'S MAP

Sketch map of Raroia and Takume from 1820 with the track
of the Russian ships. (Bellingshausen, I, plate facing page 250.)

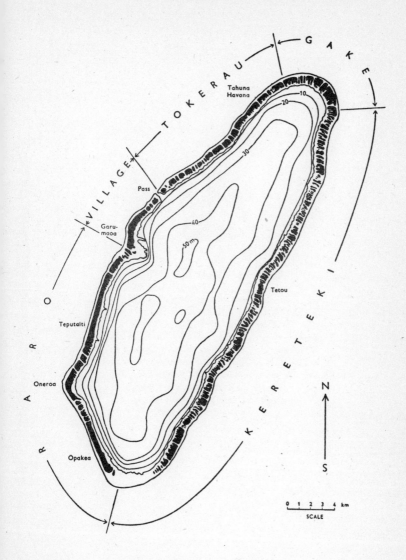

RAROIA ATOLL

From the Pacific Science Board survey in 1952.

GEORGE ALLEN & UNWIN LTD
London: 40 Museum Street, W.C.1

Auckland: 24 Wyndham Street
Sydney, N.S.W.: Bradbury House, 55 York Street
Cape Town: 58-60 Long Street
Bombay: 15 Graham Road, Ballard Estate, Bombay 1
Calcutta: 17 Chittaranjan Avenue, Calcutta 13
New Delhi: 13-14 Ajmere Gate Extension, New Delhi 1
Karachi: Haroon Chambers, South Napier Road, Karachi 2
Toronto: 91 Wellington Street West
Sao Paulo: Avenida 9 de Julho 1138–Ap. 51